Campaigning with King

DON RUSSELL

Campaigning with King

Charles King, Chronicler of the Old Army

Edited and with an introduction by Paul L. Hedren

University of Nebraska Press   Lincoln & London

Library of Congress Cataloging-in-Publication Data
Russell, Don, 1899–
    Campaigning with King: Charles King, chronicler of the old army /
by Don Russell: edited and with an introduction by Paul L. Hedren.
        p.   cm.
    Includes bibliographical references.
    ISBN 0-8032-3877-0 (alk. paper)
    1. King, Charles, 1844–1933.   2. Generals—United States—
Biography.   3. United States. Army—Biography.   4. Indians of
North America—Wars—1866–1895.   5. United States—History,
Military—To 1900.   I. Hedren, Paul L.   II. Title.
E181.K5R87   1991
973.8′092—dc20   90-12335
CIP

Title page:
Captain Charles King,
"America's Kipling,"
as depicted in the frontispiece
to *Warrior Gap* (1897).

CONTENTS

ILLUSTRATIONS

Charles King, "America's Kipling," *title page*

General King in 1926, xiv

Don Russell in the 1970s, xxi

Following page 78

Charles King at age fourteen

King's Milwaukee home

General Rufus King

Cadet Charles King

Lieutenant General Winfield Scott

Men of the First U.S. Artillery, 1867

First Lieutenant Charles King, 1870

Taylor rescuing King at Sunset Pass, Arizona

Fort Laramie's "Old Bedlam"

The "first scalp for Custer"

"The Dandy Fifth"

Captain Charles King, 1879

A King family picnic

Charles King, thespian

Teatime with the Kings

A King bubble gum card

General Charles King, USV, during the Philippine
Insurrection

General Charles King was the author of sixty-two books, made substantial contributions to eleven others, and wrote more than two hundred articles and stories for periodicals. For half a century his name was intimately connected with the history and fiction of the American West. Yet since his death in 1933 he has been virtually unknown despite a considerable revival of interest in the period of the Indian Wars.

Few accounts of Indian campaigning exceed King's *Campaigning with Crook* (1880 and 1890) in vividness, stirring narrative, and accurate, detailed description. The book is good reporting and good literature. In addition to other factual material that deserves a place in western Americana, King wrote fifty-two novels and numerous short stories. Virtually the same plot served for all his fiction. Most of his books were reprinted, often many times and sometimes by several publishers. Yet the works' enduring value lies in the fact that King's stories depict with great veracity life at frontier army posts and on Indian expeditions. King was the first to popularize this unique army world, enthralling readers with American stories just as his contemporary Rudyard Kipling did with tales of British soldiers during the days of empire and as Tom Clancy does a century later with his technomilitary thrillers like *The Hunt for Red October* and *Red Storm Rising*.

If one knows King's life, one can trace to some personal experience nearly every episode in his stories, even those that seem wildly extravagant today. But his was an age of melodrama in life as well as on the printed page—Custer and Buffalo Bill remain controversial figures today precisely because we can scarcely believe anyone like them really existed. King was in the campaign that resulted in Custer's Last Stand. He saw Buffalo Bill fight Yellow Hair. He knew intimately Winfield Scott, Abraham Lincoln, Ulysses S. Grant, Philip H. Sheridan, Nelson Miles, and Arthur MacArthur and his son Douglas. He was the only soldier in American history to wear campaign medals from five American wars—the Civil War, Indian Wars, Spanish-American War, Philippine Insurrection, and World War I—in addition to a Silver Star awarded after an Apache fight in 1874. King was credited with seventy years of active military service. His life was a greater romance than any he created, and he actually lived all his adventures. That is why his story is worth telling.

As remarkable a figure as King was, it is equally remarkable that more than fifty years should pass between his death and the appearance of a detailed biography. Surely Don Russell never anticipated this delay. As a young journalist in the late 1920s, Russell befriended King, and immediately after King's death in 1933 he wrote a book-length biography. But his numerous attempts to have the manuscript published failed, and he soon moved on to more promising projects. By the 1970s few people knew about this unpublished work, though Russell had emerged as the most visible champion of King's career and accomplishments.

In 1984, John M. Carroll, a collector of Custer material, acquired a copy of Russell's biography of King from an antiquarian bookseller. Carroll knew I was interested in Charles King and invited me to inspect the manuscript. In earlier correspondence with me Russell had mentioned this work, but he dismissed it as a failed effort. He seemed genuinely surprised that a copy had surfaced, and he was amused by my suggestion that it had great merit and should be published. Both Carroll and I pursued the idea and Russell soon endorsed it, but he died before any preparations were begun.

The present publication of *Campaigning with King: Charles King, Chronicler of the Old Army* reproduces Russell's manuscript with few alterations. Certain terms that are now dated were changed—for example, it is World War I today, not simply the World War—but for the most part this biography remains much as Russell wrote it. My greatest challenges were the source citations. Russell's intimate knowledge of King's books led to inconsistencies in documentation, and readers must assume that the first mention of a novel is reference enough for further discussion. This I did not alter. Russell's citations followed no modern form, however, and though I did not change the substance, I revamped the notes to conform to current style. All the chapter titles, supplied by Russell, are titles of books by King.

In an attempt to bridge the fifty-year gap in scholarship between the completion of Russell's initial manuscript and this publication, I paid considerable attention to recent work on King.

Much new material is noted in the Introduction. I also added a
bibliographical essay that explores other King material made available in the past several decades. I provided a completely new bibliography of King's books that incorporates an updated list of first editions (no bibliographer has yet undertaken to compile a listing of King's writings appearing in periodicals). And I added the photographs that appear in this book.

Don Russell wrote that much of the information for this biography was gathered shortly after General King's death from members of his family, friends, and associates, many of whom went to considerable trouble to contribute material. Among them were Commander Rufus King, United States Navy, son of the general, and Mrs. Charles J. Simeon and Mrs. Donald R. MacIntyre, General King's daughters. Lucille Rhoades, for many years the general's private secretary, made available papers, correspondence, scrapbooks, and much more.

Others who contributed information to Russell were General Douglas MacArthur, Major General James G. Harbord, Major General Charles D. Rhodes, Brigadier General Samuel E. Tillman, Brigadier General Samuel S. Sumner, Brigadier General Ralph M. Immell, Colonel George M. Russell, editor of the *Cavalry Journal*; Captain Peter F. Meade, recorder of the Order of Indian Wars of the United States; Master Sergeant Alvin Jevne of the Fifth Regiment, United States Cavalry; William H. Briggs of Harper and Brothers; B. Lippincott of J. B. Lippincott and Company; Elizabeth Toohey, Arizona State Library; and Fred C. Best, Frank M. Weinhold, Grant Fitch, William H. Hendrix, and Sarah Ewing King. Russell also acknowledged Alice Katherine Gregory, who gave him a copy of her thesis, "Captain Charles King, The Army's Novelist," presented to Reed College in 1945, an excellent study that includes a notable bibliography.

Russell was particularly grateful to Brigadier General William Carey Brown, who made hundreds of suggestions and read the original manuscript, detecting numerous errors that were subsequently corrected. Like all authors, Russell accepted any remaining faults as his own.

In preparing the manuscript I was fortunate to have the support of Don Russell's family, particularly his wife, Ruth, and his daughters Elaine R. C. Jones and Martha Jane Bissell, who provided important copies of letters and documents that were long ago tucked away in Don's workroom and who gave me much trust.

Much stimulating correspondence and conversation were provided by descendants of the King family. I am particularly grateful to Dugald S. MacIntyre, M.D., Eliot Fitch Bartlett, Ellen Macneale, and Jacqueline W. Smith for their stories, photographs, and encouragement.

Fred R. Egloff, Dan J. Lapinski, and Ellis C. Gravlin of Don Russell's revered Chicago Corral of the Westerners answered letters, collected and copied reference material, and provided the photograph of Russell that appears in the book.

Other photographs of King and his associates were provided by Cassandra M. Volpe and David M. Hays of the University of Colorado; General Norbert C. Smith, Arlene E. Boon, Nina B. Smith, and Ann Duggan of St. John's Military Academy; Edward Beyler of Waukesha, Wisconsin; John Burns of the Fort Laramie National Historic Site; Elizabeth Holmes of the Buffalo Bill Historical Center; Myrna Williamson of the State Historical Society of Wisconsin; Lynnette Wolfe of the Wisconsin Veterans Museums; Judith A. Simonson of the Milwaukee County Historical Society; and Marie Capps of the United States Military Academy. Harvey O. Thompson of Williston, North Dakota, cheerfully provided photographic copying services.

Other assistance was graciously provided by Donald C. Steffens, Mike Harrison, D. R. Doerres, J. Scott Harmon, Paul A. Hutton, Jerome A. Greene, Marvin L. Kaiser, Darlis A. Miller, and Greg W. Hennessy. As I noted earlier, John M. Carroll acquired the original manuscript and encouraged both my involvement and that of the University of Nebraska Press. Paul Fees of the Buffalo Bill Historical Center coaxed me to some early thought on the King and Russell friendship that I presented at a 1985 military history symposium honoring Russell and was a gracious supporter in many other ways. Edward J. Hagan, M.D., translated medical terms into layman's language. Julie M. Franklin guided me to the considerable collection of Charles King's books at the Library of Congress. Lou Hieb, son of Russell's friend David Hieb, generously shared his own bibliographic work on King and helped me understand the subtleties of book editions. Harold L. Miller and Geraldine Strey of the State Historical Society of Wisconsin copied King's diaries and provided other valuable information. Harry H. Anderson of the Milwaukee County Historical Society ferreted out details on Lucille Rhoades and other matters and has been a generous correspondent for many years; the fruits of this association are seen throughout the Introduction and in the Bibliographical Essay. And Robert M. Utley and Thomas Buecker read the edited manuscript for substance and clarity and suggested many corrections and improvements.

My wife, Janeen, and my daughters Ethne and Whitney continue to believe that visiting archives and cemeteries is what one does on vacations.

To one and all, thank you.

Paul L. Hedren

General Charles King in 1926. King, the seventy-year army veteran, is wearing his five army campaign medals, including the Indian Wars medal (second from the left), which is topped with a Silver Star. He shared many copies of this favorite photograph with his friends. (Western Historical Collections, University of Colorado Libraries)

INTRODUCTION

Students of General Charles King, William F. "Buffalo Bill" Cody, and Don Russell instantly recognize the interwoven threads of these three unique westerners. King and Cody formed a friendship on the prairies of nineteenth-century Nebraska that weathered nearly fifty years. They shared exploits, and it is impossible to tell the story of one without paying tribute to the other. Largely because of King, Don Russell discovered Cody and eventually took up the complicated challenge of sorting out the lives and legends of that great scout and showman. But Russell found qualities in King that were equally fascinating. Here was a truly remarkable soldier and writer—a man who still holds several unsurpassed records of military accomplishment. Moreover, here was a man who almost single-handedly fashioned the twentieth century's vision of America's little nineteenth-century Indian-fighting army. An eager journalist, Russell challenged King and quickly learned his story. It was logical that he should be General King's first major biographer, but illogical that it should take more than fifty years for his effort to be published.

The fruits of the Russell-King relationship were manifested in many ways. Members of the Chicago Corral of the Westerners recall how frequently Charles King was the subject of monthly programs—some by Russell and more by his friends—and how Russell offered informal bits of information on King as "Campfire Comment" at those meetings.[1] Others know that it was Don Russell who added an insightful introduction to the widely cited 1964 reprinting of King's most important book, *Campaigning with Crook*; that he compiled the first useful bibliography of Charles King's works; or that he wrote a foreword to an even more substantial and still widely used bibliography of King's books.[2]

For all its later vitality, the Don Russell–Charles King partnership began unremarkably enough. In 1929 Russell was a copyreader for the *Chicago Daily News*. In those days the paper had a magazine supplement called the *Mid-Week Pictorial*, and it had printed a reminiscent article quoting General Crook. Russell, then thirty years old, was already well read in American history. Recall, or perhaps intuition, suggested that the Crook piece was flawed. He protested to his editors but was ignored, a slight he understood better when he learned that the author was related to one of those he had complained to. Although there was nothing to be gained by pressing the issue, Russell sought personal satisfaction by writing to General King, who lived in Milwaukee and had written a book titled *Campaigning with Crook*. Russell had not read *Campaigning*, but he received a prompt and cordial response to his letter. King was amazed that a newspaperman would seek out facts in a such a matter, and he thought the story was a practical joke. After correcting several important details, he closed by asking that he not be drawn into any controversy.[3]

Although Russell did not know it then, King was enmeshed in a dispute surrounding the recent publication of the debunking biography *The Making of Buffalo Bill*, by Richard J. Walsh, and his defense of Cody had garnered considerable national attention. Nor did Russell know that King had battled newspapermen on other occasions. Russell soon invited King to stop by for an interview when he was next in Chicago, and within weeks a meeting occurred. The two discussed the Cody–Yellow Hair fight in 1876 at Warbonnet Creek, Nebraska, where King was not only a witness but also a prominent participant. They explored the Walsh controversy, which King saw as casting doubt on Cody's exploits at Warbonnet, and talked through other matters related to the Great Sioux War of 1876.[4]

In this and other meetings Russell was struck by King's precision in relating events he had witnessed and written about decades earlier—a gift of near-total recall. King's version of the Warbonnet fight delivered orally in 1929, for instance, was nearly word for word as he had written it at Fort Laramie, Wyoming, on July 21, 1876, for the New York *Herald* or as it appeared in *Campaigning with Crook* in 1880. Russell learned to press King's memory. Answers were often immediate, though King would sometimes say: "Give me time to think that through. I will tell you next time." And he always did. Russell was convinced that King did not retire to look matters up. "His mind worked that way."[5]

Russell's initial inquiries focused on Buffalo Bill and the Warbonnet episode, but in correspondence and in their frequent meetings the discussions soon ranged over other personalities and incidents from the general's past. King was eighty-five years old,

and he delighted in Russell's curiosity and patience. After one
visit he dashed off a letter thanking Russell for listening to such
"interminable yarns." He was sure Russell had "wished [him] to
the devil" hours before his departure. "Well," King concluded, "I
enjoyed it mightily and shall be glad when once again I can back
you into a corner and 'continue the march.'"6

These letters and visits opened the door not only to King's rich
past but also to an astonishingly busy present. Throughout his life
King mastered the complex demands of multiple tasks, and even
as an octogenarian he participated actively in the Wisconsin National
Guard, St. John's Military Academy, and the business of
history.

Perhaps no duty brought King greater satisfaction than his
service with the Wisconsin National Guard. This association had
been nearly continuous since 1882, and into 1931 it was not merely
condoned in deference to a favorite son but officially ordered by
the United States War Department. Washington had a provision
that allowed officers on the retired list to be recalled to service
with an organized militia. In one capacity or another King was
fully occupied as a commander, an instructor, or an inspector of
the national guard until July 20, 1931, and he had even attended
tha guard's rigorous summer training encampment at Camp
Douglas, Wisconsin, that year. In their armories and at camp
guardsmen remembered King as "Old Eagle Eye" for the way he
found the slightest defect in appearance or equipment. Had he not
been cut down by a nearly fatal heatstroke at the 1931 encampment,
this affiliation might have continued. Governor Philip F. La
Follette presided at King's official retirement ceremony that year,
the last of four or five retirements in the general's life. La Follette
honored King with a citation recognizing seventy years of distinguished
service to his country, participation in five American
wars, and contribution as symbol and inspiration to the state of
Wisconsin. The governor concluded the ceremonies by bestowing
on King the title "Grand Old Man of the Wisconsin National
Guard."7

Because of the scattered breaks in military service that dotted
King's career, recognition of his seventy years of cumulative duty
took a year longer to come from the War Department. But on June
30, 1932, Washington too credited him with seven decades of
active service. Like his record for participating in five wars, this
remains an accomplishment unequaled in the annals of American

military history. The news from Washington "made me quite happy," he wrote Russell.[8]

King's affiliation with St. John's Military Academy at Delafield, Wisconsin, was an extension of his general service to the United States, with a slightly different twist. This Episcopalian school, established in 1884 by Sidney T. Smythe, recruited King in 1885 to instruct students in military science, a commitment King fulfilled until his death. In 1928 King described his St. John's routine to longtime friend, General William Carey Brown.

> With a northerly gale sweeping our campus & sending the "merc" down below freezing I was up & tubbing at 6.30. Out to Del[afield] by a swift Interurban, tramping up the hill to our rough stone barracks, putting the six companies in overcoats through an hour long close order drill—dining with our 417 lads of good soldier caliber—then holding rehearsal of guard mt with [a] fine young adjutant & serg major who had never yet seen a guard mount except from the ranks.[9]

King's Milwaukee-to-Delafield commute was a once- or twice-weekly duty, and like any teacher his only break in routine came in summer when school adjourned. In 1931 he reminded Brown that he "always [had] to be at school for Sunday dress parade & review" at 7:00 P.M. His boundless energy even at age eighty-six astonished friends and associates. A Milwaukee newspaperman remembered King's relentless drive. "A never to be forgotten picture," he wrote, "is one of the general in his olive drab overcoat, trudging off alone through the snow, bound for St. John's."[10]

King's passion for military affairs was manifested off duty as well. He had built a literary career, of course, upon his love of soldiering, and he was widely known as an authority on army history, tactics, and campaigns. It was inevitable that as a new generation of historians and aficionados turned their attention to these matters and particularly to Indian-white relations in the West, they would find King. Soon enough individuals like Walter Mason Camp, Grace Raymond Hebard, Earl A. Brininstool, and other early twentieth-century historians corresponded with him just as Don Russell did. And as more and more of his elderly comrades passed on, King's self-imposed duty to history grew. In a letter to Hebard, for instance, he described how "out at St. John's and here in town my desks [are] covered deep with pamphlets, magazines, professional papers and the like," and to Russell he described how he was "never so far behind in . . . correspondence."[11]

Beyond a mass of manuscripts and letters, King's interest in the Indian Wars found expression in other ways as well. Russell elaborates on the general's partnership with William Carey Brown and tells of their jointly produced map showing topography, routes, and battlefields of the Great Sioux War. In the mid-1920s events of this war passed their half-century anniversaries. In 1926 King had joined the National Custer Memorial Association, founded to plan the semicentennial of the Battle of the Little Bighorn. Regrettably, the emotional strain following the death of his son Rufus's wife, along with other health problems, prevented his active participation in this highly visible event.[12]

King was also drawn into a movement in the 1920s to locate and memorialize western historical sites, particularly Indian Wars battlefields. These efforts were coordinated by individuals like Walter Camp, Robert S. Ellison, and James B. Griffith, who were successful in finding many remote sites. The one that defied searchers longest was the small Warbonnet battlefield in northwestern Nebraska. In their quest, Ellison and Griffith of Wyoming commonly enlisted surviving veterans to provide pertinent details. Soon enough King was invited to travel west to look for Warbonnet. For King, jostling around in an open car and swallowing the dust of "that ghastly desert" when temperatures often exceeded one hundred degrees Fahrenheit was punishing. Yet Warbonnet was so important to his own story and to those of Cody and others that he could hardly shirk the obligation. It took several summer visits and a particularly intensive effort in 1929 and 1930 to locate the spot where Cody had so deftly taken the "first scalp for Custer," but its successful discovery late in 1930 brought peace of mind for General King.[13]

So visible had the King-Cody-Warbonnet association become that a third project arose in the late 1920s, spurred by the Denver artist Robert Lindneux. Lindneux was equally fascinated by the "first scalp" episode. He was well connected to Cody interests and family and had begun painting a monumental canvas of the fight. Like so many others before him, Lindneux sought out King for details. Initially King welcomed the artist's questions. He wrote down specific details and even helped him collect artifacts correct for the era. At first King seem genuinely pleased that Lindneux had the "spirit of the thing," but he quickly soured on the project.[14]

Above all, we must remember that Charles King was obsessed by details, particularly military details. He was a martinet on the drill field, a compulsive daily diarist, and an author who could fabricate a novel rich with the subtle shades and textures of army life. His successes as a soldier and as a writer were based on this thorough command of detail. In his own way, of course, Lindneux was also fashioning a story, but his version of the Cody, Yellow Hair, and Fifth Cavalry episode was substantially different from what King so precisely recalled. Perhaps King would not have cared so had Lindneux not repeatedly credited him as the "authority for every detail portrayed." Appalled by Lindneux's imprecision, King protested publicly. He boycotted the unveiling ceremonies held in Cody, Wyoming, at sunrise on July 17, 1928. But in a calmer moment King concluded that it was best to be quiet about the matter. "This can do Bill no harm," he remarked to General Brown. "We were good friends & I will keep quiet so long as I can." Privately, he never hesitated to criticize Lindneux or the painting.[15]

Not all of King's history-related activities were as stressful as those related to the Warbonnet fight. In 1930 he reported to Russell, for instance, that he would soon be en route to Washington for the annual meeting of the Order of Indian Wars. King was an active member of many historical and fraternal organizations, but the OIW continued to bring him great satisfaction. The order was chartered in 1896 so officers could perpetuate their memories of service against Indians. Over the years King, an original member, served both as the order's senior vice commander and as historian. At the 1921 annual banquet King gave the featured address, speaking on the campaign of 1876. This eloquent reminiscence was warmly received, and the printed version is still often quoted by military historians. The 1930 dinner was again a "Sioux Campaign Night," and both King and General Edward S. Godfrey presented remarks. These dinners and presentations at Washington's Army and Navy Club "crowd the big room," he told Russell.[16]

Except for the continuous flow of correspondence, by the late 1920s King had all but given up his literary labors. His last book, *The True Ulysses S. Grant*, appeared in 1914. He did write fre-

Don Russell in the 1970s. By then Russell was widely known
and appreciated as an authority on Bill Cody and Charles King.
(Ellis C. Gravlin)

quent obituaries of army comrades for the West Point Association
of Graduates' *Annual Report*. And fortunately for Russell and
later biographers, one of his most important literary accomplishments, unheralded as it is, appeared in the 1922 issues of the
Wisconsin Magazine of History as a four-part autobiographical
series titled "Memories of a Busy Life." Despite its rambling
nature, "Memories" is a useful memoir detailing boyhood exploits, salient aspects of King's military career, particularly his
time in the Philippine Islands, and remembrances of famous civil
and military figures. Regrettably, he left this telling of his per-

sonal history unfinished. In 1929 King mentioned to Russell that he planned to write two and possibly even four more chapters should he be spared the time. The additional discourses never appeared.[17]

When King's ability or enthusiasm for disciplining his writing time was all but gone, journalist-historian Don Russell appeared as an eager suitor. They first collaborated in 1929 to introduce and edit the story "Stopping an Apache Battle" by King's old friend George O. Eaton. It was Eaton who helped rescue King from Apaches in 1874, in the same clash where King suffered a disastrous arm wound. Russell polished up Eaton's rambling narrative, and King's foreword provided some perspective, but Eaton died in 1930 before seeing his story published.[18]

Don Russell's curiosity about Buffalo Bill Cody's exploits at Warbonnet Creek was central to the early friendship between King and Russell, and their next collaboration dealt with that subject. "My Friend Buffalo Bill," a story "told" by King to Russell, was an elaboration on details of the 1876 Sioux War that first appeared in *Campaigning with Crook*. The updated story appeared in a 1932 issue of the *Cavalry Journal* and was immediately reprinted by the newspaper *Winners of the West*. Russell was a regular contributor to *Winners*, the newssheet for the National Indian Wars Veterans organization. In 1986 he was the group's last surviving member.[19]

Russell later enjoyed other literary successes spawned during General King's final years. King was so prominently known in America that his acquaintance brought introductions to others in his military circle. "Knowing General King in those days was a card of admittance to the military fraternity," Russell later acknowledged.[20] Soon he was corresponding with William Carey Brown, Charles D. Rhodes, Samuel S. Sumner, George M. Russell, and other figures who had sparkled in King's life and who possessed illustrious records of their own. All added vital details when Don Russell formally commenced compiling Charles King's biography.

Of several recurring plots in General King's life, perhaps the least known is the story of his health. Russell's biography of King gives considerable attention to the fight at Sunset Pass in 1874, where King was wounded in the right arm, just below the shoulder. His doctors predicted—rightly—that his arm would never completely heal. As late as 1930 King reminisced to Brown about how he had gone through the Great Sioux War of 1876 and the

subsequent Nez Perce campaign of 1877 with this wound open and
suppurating, and how one long sliver of bone had projected so far
as to catch in the sleeve of his undershirt. Though this particular
irritant was firmly planted, he picked at it with his teeth and
finally removed it. Of this scrap of bone he told Brown, "I keep it
yet—one of two or three specimens."[21]

The wound occasionally incapacitated King, especially in his
earlier years. It contributed directly to his being relieved from
duty as regimental adjutant of the Fifth U.S. Cavalry in 1878, and
it was central to his retirement from the regular army in 1879.
Ten, even twenty years later, in the heyday of his writing career,
the wound continued to be a nemesis. King was capable of long
hours of desk work laboring over stories, but his writing could be
cut short instantly when a neuralgia that could set his "teeth and
nerves on edge," ran through his "shriveled and shortened old
arm." Eventually he took up the much publicized use of the
phonograph or Ediphone. Yet even this assistance is exaggerated,
because he continued to laboriously and often painfully outline
stories with pen or pencil, and his last major work, *The True
Ulysses S. Grant*, was written entirely by hand.[22]

Other health problems in 1899 led to King's early departure
from the Pacific during the Philippine Insurrection. He was a
vigorous fifty-five-year-old when he sailed from San Francisco,
yet quite early in the Islands he was prostrated by heat and
exposure coupled with irregular hours for food and sleep. He was
also plagued by what he called an "infernal eczema," and the
combination cut short his overseas tour, the doctors declaring that
he must go home "by the first steamer" or in "a fortnight more . . .
[he'd] go home in an icebox."[23]

By the time Don Russell encountered King, the Apache wound
and the Philippine trials were relics of a lingering past. When
Russell asked to see the scar on his arm, King rolled up his right
shirt sleeve to show a "long, irregular, discolored marking." On
health matters King called himself a "monotone of misery," and in
one letter he described his body as "one smear of crimson . . .
stretched over bones that almost talk their distress." In his last
years King was twice struck by automobiles and subsequently
bedridden with broken bones. He survived the near fatal heatstroke at the 1931 national guard camp, and he suffered from
deafness. Yet he could rise from these reversals and carry on at a
pace astonishing for his age and circumstances.[24]

As King convalesced late in 1932 from his most recent ailment, a bladder infection, his doctor and son-in-law, Donald R. MacIntyre, promised at least two more healthy years. But on March 15, 1933, King tripped on a rug in his Hotel Carlton apartment and broke his left arm. At 2:20 P.M. on Friday, March 17, he died of cardiac arrest attributed to shock from the fall.[25] His funeral arrangements were lavish with military tradition. Don Russell could not attend, but a journalist friend who did sent clippings of Milwaukee newspaper coverage along with several poignant comments, one of which read: "Yesterday I went over and gazed at the old warrior. They buried him in the snow today—troops & masons."[26]

Russell had obviously pondered the task of writing a biography of Charles King before the old veteran died, and his continuing correspondence had probed widely into matters of career and accomplishments. Russell was quick to collect the names and addresses of family members and associates who gathered in Milwaukee for the funeral, and he soon exchanged letters with them. More important, he opened correspondence with King's longtime personal secretary, Lucille Rhoades, and his only son, Commander Rufus King, United States Navy. Both pledged to assist with a biography, as did other members of the family.

Of them all, Lucille Rhoades contributed most significantly, particularly since she had access to King's office, his apartment at the Hotel Carlton, and several storage vaults. From these repositories she lent original correspondence, books, pamphlets, and the scrapbooks that she and King had so faithfully maintained. These scrapbooks in particular held a wealth of information on King's public activities, and they are cited throughout the biography.[27]

Russell also read virtually all of Charles King's books, as well as his memoirs and many short stories. As others have since discovered, Russell knew that King's personal history was woven throughout these tales, and with study it was possible to separate fact from fiction. In addition to their autobiographical nature, King's fictional characters often were closely modeled on companions from the frontier. He was well known for this quality, and during the prime of his writing career it became a game for friends, particularly those from the old Fifth Cavalry, to unmask his characters.[28]

Russell also successfully sought out surviving army comrades,
and his acknowledgments read like a *Who's Who* of the Old Army
and the new one. Although names like Douglas MacArthur and
General Pershing's chief-of-staff, James G. Harbord, are prominent, it was General William Carey Brown of Denver who opened
innumerable doors and provided a wealth of background information from his lifelong friendship with King. In subsequent years
Russell and Brown had a "vast correspondence," and no sooner
was the biography of King finished and sent off to reviewers than
Russell commenced another Old Army biography, of Brown's
former commander, General Reuben F. Bernard.[29]

Within several months of General King's death, initial install-
ments of the biography were being compiled. A draft of the first
chapter was sent to Rufus King, who was on sea duty and had
been unable to attend his father's funeral. Rufus's response was
encouraging. Russell worked in haste, and by the end of 1933 the
biography was complete.[30]

But then came a discouraging series of rejections, or "reversals" as Rufus King chose to call them. In the midst of writing
Russell had asked the J. B. Lippincott Company of Philadelphia
whether they would consider his book. Lippincott was King's
foremost publisher, and in 1933 *The Colonel's Daughter* and *The
True Ulysses S. Grant* were still in print. Their reply was dis-
heartening: they could not "handle the publication of a life of
General Charles King," they wrote. "If something were to happen that would again focus attention on General King, it would be
a different matter, but at present we are hesitant in undertaking
his biography." Russell found King's second leading publisher,
Harper and Brothers of New York City, initially more encouraging. Although they would not commit themselves to a book without first seeing the manuscript, some members of the firm remembered working with King. They still had *Cadet Days* in print and
thought a biography had some prospect. But soon enough Harper,
too, sent a rejection. Indian fighters, it seems, were passé.[31]

Despite those setbacks, Russell remained optimistic that he
would find a publisher. Brown recommended the D. Appleton-
Century Company, which had recently published General Hugh
Scott's *Some Memories of a Soldier*, and he also suggested that
Russell consider publishing by subscription. Rufus King implored
a personal friend at Scribner's in New York City to read the
manuscript. Scribner's found the study well written but feared

that too many of King's contemporaries and members of his admiring public had passed on, so they too declined. Rufus had not told his friend that Harper and Brothers had rejected the proposal, and Scribner's concluded by suggesting that Russell try Harper, "who had published so many of [King's] books."[32]

Dismayed by these rejections, Russell temporarily gave up on the biography and turned his scholarly attention to other projects. Two of his strongest supporters, Brown and Rhoades, both died in 1939, and they were among the last who had intimate knowledge of King's early career. Russell resurrected the biography in the mid-1950s and submitted it to yet another publisher, but it was not accepted. Nor was the manuscript even returned. It is this very copy, in fact, that the collector John M. Carroll acquired in 1984 and offered to the University of Nebraska Press.

Russell, meanwhile, carried his interest in western history into other arenas. As a newspaperman, he had discovered that "a couple of pages of typewritten copy could be traded for a five-dollar book," and he was soon writing book reviews for several papers. In 1937 he started the book review section of the *Journal of the American Military History Foundation*, and in 1946 he became editor of the Chicago *Westerners Brand Book*, a task he cherished until his death. In 1973 he estimated that his book reviews alone exceeded three thousand, and by the time he died it was probably closer to four thousand.[33]

Although Russell early on established his preeminence as an authority on King and Cody, his scholarly interests ranged widely into other western American and Civil War subjects. Russell's bibliography, in fact, includes more works on Custer than any other category, and his books *Custer's Last; or, The Battle of the Little Big Horn in Picturesque Perspective* and *Custer's List: A Checklist of Pictures* are regarded as vital contributions to that genre. His articles explored topics related to Indians, cowboys, and general military subjects, and as a professional writer for encyclopedias he estimated that he had written as many articles for reference books as he had book reviews. No doubt with tongue in cheek, he also observed that his "editorial duties made [him] one of a select few who [had] read a fourteen-volume encyclopedia entirely through." In spite of these broad interests, however, as the years wore on it was General King and King's world that seem to bring Russell the greatest satisfaction.[34]

Don Russell died on February 17, 1986. He fully endorsed the current publishing venture and was genuinely gratified that merit

had again been found in what he called his "long lost, strayed, and
stolen mss. on Gen. King." At the time it was written, he remarked, "interest in the West was at a low point, and in King even
lower."[35]

Although Russell did not live to see his biography of Charles
King finally appear in print, on earlier occasions he did excerpt
portions of the manuscript. In 1937, for instance, he revised and
enlarged upon the King-Cody-Warbonnet episode in an essay titled "The Duel on the War Bonnet." This incident was central to
his initial relationship with King. The two wrote a version of the
story in 1932 and for the 1937 revision perspectives were altered
slightly, but chapter 8 of the present biography clearly formed the
basis for the article. Russell shifted perspectives again as he
retold the Warbonnet tale in his masterly 1960 biography of
William F. Cody. Of these several versions the last is superior, but
by 1960 he had a much firmer understanding of Cody's person-
ality, and the additional years of research had yielded other important details.[36]

In a 1952 presentation to the Chicago Corral of the Westerners,
Russell condensed King's history into a few introductory remarks, then focused on the general's literary accomplishments.
The biographical summary was the sort that could be gotten from
any of the official dictionaries bearing highlights of King's service,
but Russell's analysis of King's writing drew heavily on the 1930s
biography and became the first public account of this aspect of the
general's life. For publication in the *Westerners Brand Book*,
Russell's presentation was coupled with a detailed list of General
King's books and other major publications. Although a brief bibliography appeared in the unpublished biography, this enlargement
in the *Brand Book* was the first book list available to collectors
and historians.[37]

By the mid-1950s Russell's enthusiastic admiration of General
King was well established. As he again attempted to publish the
biography, there appeared in the *Westerners New York Posse
Brand Book* a sharp attack on King, leveled by Mari Sandoz. In
this careless diatribe Sandoz suggested that King had distorted
facts. Moreover, she regretted that his inadequacies were largely
forgotten and that he was freely quoted as an authentic source. To
support her argument, Sandoz cited an incident she claimed had
occurred at Fort Laramie in the 1860s. She succeeded in arousing

the ire of Don Russell, who was by then very well connected in western history circles. One of his frequent correspondents was another King enthusiast, David L. Hieb, the National Park Service's superintendent at the Fort Laramie National Monument. A capable historian, Hieb quickly researched Sandoz's allegations and proved them groundless, and he shared these findings with Russell. Until now this episode remained entirely dismissible, and it might have gone no further had not an escalation occurred.[38]

Art Woodward, another western historian with a considerable reputation, published his own essay on King in a subsequent issue of the same *New York Posse Brand Book*. Woodward defended King's writings and offered several well-researched examples that illuminated his authority as a portrayer of the Indian-fighting army. But for unexplained reasons, the editors of the *Brand Book* added a postscript that is worth reprinting in full.

[We agree that Captain King's preservation of Old Army detail and atmosphere outweighs his sins as a fictioneer. Nevertheless, we feel that the point Mari Sandoz made is an important one. Falsification of history in supposedly factual accounts such as *Campaigning with Crook* are inexcusable. They become particularly irritating when quoted over and over as in the case of the obvious fiction of the Yellow Hand fight. Why biographers insist on the truth of this incident is a mystery. It reduces rather than enhances the stature of Buffalo Bill.

We hope that someday, someone will have the interest to run this bit of tomfoolery into the grave where it belongs. E. C.][39]

Russell was furious when he read this. He quickly composed a rebuttal that he first shared with Hieb. He hated to get involved in the "Yellow Hair mess," as he called it, and he commented sarcastically that this "Hudson River School of Western Americana certainly knows it all!" Russell asked Hieb whether it would serve any purpose to send in his piece. Hieb too had "blown a fuse," and he urged Russell to take on the "Broadway Posse." Quickly enough his pointed defense was en route to New York. Whether Russell comprehended the parallel between his own defense of King's reputation and King's protection of the memory of his friend Buffalo Bill in 1928 is not known, but it is striking indeed.[40]

The New York Posse published Russell's essay in 1957. It corrected Sandoz point by point; it praised Woodward for his careful elucidation of King's historical accuracy; and it refuted the accusation by Edmund Collier (the "E. C." of the Woodward postscript) of falsified history. Collier apologized.[41]

Don Russell went on to enjoy the enormous success of his book *The Lives and Legends of Buffalo Bill*, which appeared in 1960. He had recognized General Charles King first among his acknowledgments. In the next twenty years he had two additional opportunities to expound on King. The University of Oklahoma Press, publishers of *Lives and Legends*, arranged for Russell to write the introduction to a new edition of *Campaigning with Crook*. Russell easily assembled an outline of King's life, but he chose to focus on the general's popularization of the Indian-fighting army, a contribution ever more important as the years wore on. This edition remains in print and continues to introduce readers to Charles King and the Old Army.[42]

And in 1980 Russell wrote what he called "A Very Personal Introduction" to yet another version of the Warbonnet saga of 1876. Russell was eighty-one years old, yet he crafted a fine account of his meeting King and working with him in the late 1920s and early 1930s. He concluded with the observation that in 1980 the time had come to "pass on his torch."[43]

A passing has indeed occurred. Yet as historians continue to analyze Charles King's seventy years of army life and further refine their interpretation and understanding of his productive literary career, no one can ever again have a personal friendship with so remarkable a figure from the Old West. Nor can there ever again be the first-person acquaintance with so many others inextricably linked to King's life. Don Russell's *Campaigning with King: Charles King, Chronicler of the Old Army* is an eminently reliable and readable life of General Charles King, as a skilled interviewer and friend tells it.

From School to Battle-field

"The inhabitants of the Southern States are chiefly en-
gaged in agriculture; many of them have large plantations with
numerous slaves." A small youth, so small that his twenty-six
contemporaries in the schoolroom called him "Shorty," conned
this passage from his geography—"adapted to the capacity of
youth"—then glanced at the bottom of the page to see the phrasing of the question he probably would be asked covering this
sentence: "How are the inhabitants chiefly employed?"[1]

"The inhabitants of the Southern States. . . ." Again he went
through it as he conscientiously looked at the large map of the
United States that was unrolled on the wall—conscientiously
because he intended to look at the southern states. But as usual,
he soon found himself wandering upward from Texas through
Kansas Territory to the vast reaches of the Territory of Nebraska, an area spotted only with a few vague-looking rivers and
hills, a fascinating, mysterious region, "the most extensive division of the United States, being a third larger than the state of
Texas" and in the same geography book exemplified by an illustration of armed traders dealing with Indians. With an effort
he returned to his book: "The wealthy classes are generally well
educated, possess cultivated minds and refined manners, and are
noted for their hospitality. Education is not so general among the
poorer."

But while the twenty-six other boys concentrated, more or less,
on the characteristics of the southern states or gazing vacantly at
the deeply carved benches, bare walls, unchalked blackboard,
map of the United States, or furtively, the near-dozing figure of
their instructor at his desk, the twenty-seventh boy, at the back of
the room, was looking out over the three- and four-story buildings
that formed the skyline of metropolitan New York in the late
1850s to the tall fire tower that, like a minaret, overlooked the
mighty business structures of that day.

A blue-coated watchman in this tower, spyglass to his eye, searched the area of the city assigned to him for signs of even the smallest blaze, prepared to clang the bell that hung beside him. Twenty-four hours a day these watchers were on guard in the days before telephones and alarm systems.[2]

And now, as the twenty-seventh boy watched, there were signs of excitement in the tower. As the bell's clapper was raised, the twenty-seventh boy shouted "Fire!" The simultaneous sounds of the first stroke of the bell and the boy's shout galvanized twenty-six dozing youths. There was a rush for the door as the instructor roused himself, stood up, and opened his mouth. But before a word could come forth, all were out into the street.

To the corner they raced, and none too quickly, for already a dozen green-shirted figures pranced into view, dragging behind them a brightly shining contraption on wheels, its most noticeable feature a pair of long, rounded, well-worn wooden rails—a hand-pump fire engine. Even as this vehicle approached the corner, there whirled around it a similar procession, a group of red-shirted figures whose lines led to a similar contraption in red. "Make way! Make way!" sounded a double dozen stentorian shouts, but no one made way, and in a few seconds the two vehicles threatened to collide. Their doughty guardians prevented this. With fists, trumpets, nozzles, and other improvised weapons, Green Shirts attempted to make their way. With fists, trumpets, and a few convenient paving bricks Red Shirts attempted to make theirs. A few blocks away the fire was burning briskly, but here the honor of reaching it first was at stake.

The boys from Professor Charles Anthon's classes, preparatory for Columbia College, were advocates of the Green Shirts. A troop of boys from another district favored the Red Shirts. A junior battle soon added to the confusion, and its participants temporarily lost sight of their champions. At this point, in some mysterious manner the Green Shirts found themselves swept back to their own engine. There was an unexplicable lull in the fight and the Green Shirts, picking up their lines, galloped on. The Red Shirts, awakening to the desertion of the field with a roar of rage, dashed for their own lines and scampered in the wake of their rivals. "Shorty," squirming out from the mass of flailing arms and legs, found both groups of champions gone. "The Engines!" he shouted. The fighting mass disintegrated, and the youthful mob forgot the quarrel in renewing the race to the fire.

It was indeed a fire worth seeing. An entire one-story building was in flames. During the fight the blaze had gained considerable headway. Americus 6 and Manhattan 8 had already arrived with the only hand-drawn steam engines in the city, and the surrounding streets were clogged by a considerable proportion of the city's fifty engine companies, sixty hose companies, each with a high-wheeled, gaily decorated hose cart bearing a reel, and nineteen hook-and-ladder companies. In the excitement an alarm had been sent out for one of the two "exempt companies," which soon arrived with the first horse-drawn fire engine New York had ever known. With such an array of apparatus, the fire was quickly smothered. There was some disappointment in that, but it had been a brilliant display and a show well worth its cost.

By the time the last hose had been reeled up and the last hand-drawn truck escorted back to its station, it was somewhat late in the day to return to Professor Anthon's school. There would be a bill to pay on the morrow, no doubt, and perhaps "Shorty" worried about that a little as he made his way toward the home of his grandfather. Dr. Charles King, president of Columbia College, had no great sympathy for neglect of studies by his namesake.[3]

Certainly Dr. King was not an austere man. Despite being the author of *An Outline of a Course of English Reading, Based on That Prepared for the Mercantile Library Association of the City of New-York, by the Late Chancellor Kent, with Additions*, of *History of the New York Chamber of Commerce*, and of *A Memoir of the Construction, Cost and Capacity of the Croten Aqueduct*, among other works, the college president was so notable for the perfection of his social manners that he was dubbed "Charles the Pink," so Philip Hone records. But young Charles had no inclination just now to answer his grandfather's questions, however politely worded, so he scurried up the back stairs to his own room, where he immersed himself in Captain Mayne Reid's *The Scalp Hunters* until dinnertime.

"Milwaukee!" The bawled geographic hail interrupted the chase of the Indians. It was one of the boy's young cousins calling. The name of his hometown was a necessary designation, since "Charles King" was hardly a distinction in that house where, besides the grandfather Charles King there also resided Charles Ray King, later to become editor of *The Life and Correspondence of Rufus King*; he was the son of Great-Uncle John Alsop King, former governor of New York and a founder of the Republican party.[4]

"Milwaukee" went down to dinner without waiting to be called again. He was very quiet during the meal and slipped off to his room as soon as he could conveniently edge away. It was a boy's room, much like any boy's room today, saved from complete disorder by weekly flourishes of the housekeeper's broom. On the walls were bright-colored prints of "Columbia Engine No. 14" and "Ringgold Hose No. 7," the latter a beautiful four-wheeler with chocolate-colored running gear and plate glass decorated reel—proof that the afternoon's movements represented more than temporary enthusiasm. Among books, author Mayne Reid was the favorite, with *Tom Brown's School Days* and *The History of Sanford and Merton* somewhat less favored. Even farther down the list, the *Illustrated School History of the United States*, by George P. Quackenbos, was only for home study. In one corner were a cricket bat and a baseball, the latter hand made by a cobbler who had found catering to this new sport more profitable than repairing shoes.

But it was the work of Dr. Quackenbos that the virtuous Charles took from the shelves this evening. It might be well to know something about history the next day, he calculated, with the geography of the southern states gone up in smoke.

Dr. Quackenbos had his merits. At least the book mentioned Charles's great-grandfather, which was more than any of the other boys could boast. "At New York, $500,000 was needed to put the city in a state of defense," said Quackenbos, discussing the second war with Great Britain.

> The money could not be procured on the public credit; and Gov. Tompkins was called upon by Senator King to raise it on his personal responsibility. The governor hesitated on the ground it might ruin him. "Then," said Mr. King, "ruin yourself, if it becomes necessary, to save the country, and I pledge my honor that I will support you in what ever you do." Through the efforts of these two patriotic men the necessary sum was obtained and the city was made ready to receive the enemy.

There was much more than this that might have been said about Great-Grandfather Rufus King, who had not been a marked advocate of the unfortunate War of 1812. True, his name did appear in the back of the book as a signer of the Constitution of the United States, but there was no mention of his more significant authorship of that phrase in the Ordinance of 1787 declaring that "neither slavery nor involuntary servitude" should be permitted in the Northwest Territory.[5]

Even now, while Uncle John was dabbling in the affairs of the newly formed Republican party, Charles's own father, a second Rufus, was advocating the nomination of his old friend, William H. Seward, for the presidency on the ticket of the same party.[6]

Yet it was not what various members of the King family had done in American history, but what one young member could get out of American history that would concern him on the morrow. He turned to his book and studied on until a commotion at the front door drew him downstairs. A servant had announced to Grandfather King the arrival of General Winfield Scott.

"Show him in immediately, of course." Young Charles's school affairs could be postponed. And Charles himself forgot them as an immensely tall, immensely large, and immensely dignified figure appeared. It was, in fact, Winfield Scott, commander in chief of the army, the first since Washington to wear the three stars of a lieutenant general. It was commission "by brevet," a fact Scott liked to forget. Charles had seen him before at age five, when Rufus King, Charles's father, had visited West Point as a member of the Board of Visitors to the United States Military Academy. The little boy had thought General Scott, in all the "fuss and feathers" of his full-dress uniform, quite the finest figure of a man he had ever seen, though his admiration had been tempered by almost equal adoration for the splendor of the drum major and the glory of the cadet adjutant.

But now he could more fully appreciate the importance of Winfield Scott. And as he sat there, silent and open mouthed, who can say his admiration was misplaced? Dr. Quackenbos, however flowery the language of schoolbook history in that period, had not erred greatly in referring to the American general as "one of the great captains of the age." His Mexican campaign had been brilliant; he had won a series of victories with a force inferior in number and not nearly so superior in training as is generally believed. And his career in the War of 1812 had been one of the few bright spots in that generally dismal conflict.[7]

Young Charles, of course, was presented to the general, but he sat quietly as the evening discussion ranged from army politics to national affairs. Scott well knew the King family history, and for a moment he focused on young Charles to ask whether he intended to follow in his father's footsteps and attend West Point.

"Just now he seems more interested in following fire engines about the streets, to the neglect of his studies," the elder King interjected.

The general chuckled. "We shall have to attach him to Dr. Myer's signal department and let him trundle reels of telegraph wires across the battlefields."

Promptly at 10:00 the general rose to leave. Young Charles was asked to escort the distinguished guest home, an assignment he accepted with alacrity. The very small boy and the tall general—Scott was six feet four—made a strange contrast. One could hardly say they became companionable, but the general adopted the custom of making solemn and ceremonious visits to Dr. King, his friend of many years' standing, every Thursday evening. Charles continued his duty as aide, a precaution Dr. King probably thought necessary because infirmities were creeping up on the old warrior.

After the first evening with the general, becoming a fireman ceased to interest Charles King. From that date on he was committed to a military career, and unlike many boyhood ambitions, this one was destined to be attained.

It was not a new idea. In the first place, his family had a military tradition, which counted for much in those days. Charles King could trace his ancestry to Captain Richard King, who was commissary at the siege of Louisbourg in the old French war. Even the famous Rufus King had been in military service, as major and aide-de-camp to Brigadier General John Glover in Sullivan's Rhode Island expedition. Grandfather Charles King had been a captain of militia in the War of 1812. His brothers, young Charles's great-uncles, both had commissions in the same war—John Alsop King, the politician, as lieutenant of New York cavalry, and James Gore King, the banker, as assistant adjutant general of the state.[8] Charles's father, the second Rufus, graduated from West Point in 1833 to become brevet second lieutenant of engineers and assistant to Captain Robert E. Lee in the construction of Fortress Monroe. Rufus King resigned from the army on his marriage to Ellen Eliot in 1836, but since then he had been adjutant general of New York and colonel and major general of the militia of Wisconsin.

For that matter, Charles himself was a militia veteran even at this time. At age twelve he had become "marker" for his father's regiment, the First Wisconsin State Militia. His retentive mem-

ory had carried him through the intricacies of the three volumes of
Scott's *Infantry Tactics* and the two volumes of William J. Hardee's *Rifle and Light Infantry Tactics*, which provided for almost
every contingency, from getting around a tree to crossing a bridge
two feet wide while advancing in line of battle. But for almost
every movement, even a simple turn, a "marker" had to be placed
to indicate the point of rest or pivot. Little Charles, in a resplen-
dent uniform, had been a conspicuous and intelligent marker. He
could still recite by rote endless complicated maneuvers.

Not much less arduous had been his duties as drummer for the
Milwaukee Light Guard, Company A of the First Wisconsin, for
there had been a complicated code of drum and fife signals to
memorize. All of this had been in line with the King tradition of
military service as a duty owed the state, and to be paid for, but
not as a profession. Such was Grandfather King's view when
young Charles suggested West Point.

"Your father tried that, and what did it get him?" he pointed
out. "A few years of starving on a second lieutenant's pay, and
then he wanted to get married. So your Uncle James gave him a
position surveying the New York and Erie Railroad." That was
not a very effective argument, however, for Charles knew enough
about his father's affairs to realize that the position on the railroad
of which Uncle James was president had not been very profitable
either. Charles wondered if his father was really glad he had left
the army. Rufus King had tried a variety of occupations before
settling down in Milwaukee. After the death of his first wife in
1838 he had gone to Albany and edited the *Daily Advertiser* there.
Subsequently he was associated with Thurlow Weed on the *Evening Journal*. In Albany Rufus married Susan Eliot, younger
sister of his first wife, and there Charles was born on October 12,
1844.

Then Rufus King went back to surveying, this time undertaking the important, though temporary, task of locating the boundary between Ohio and Michigan—important because that boundary had been disputed so bitterly as to provoke the "Toledo War,"
in which both states called out militia and threatened hostilities
over the strip of land that included the city of Toledo. The West
looked attractive to Rufus King, so he packed his belongings and
brought his wife and year-old son to Milwaukee, a town then
described as "small and cheaply built" but hopeful about its future.

Rufus King prospered, despite a setback when the *Milwaukee Sentinel and Gazette*, of which he was owner and part editor, was wrecked in the Panic of 1857. The newspaper was reorganized, however, as the *Milwaukee Sentinel*, and Rufus King stayed on as editor. Following in his father's footsteps would have given Charles several occupations to choose from—even the fire department. Rufus King was foreman of Engine Company No. 1, besides being a member of the Wisconsin constitutional convention, regent of the University of Wisconsin, superintendent of Milwaukee schools, major general of the state militia, colonel of its First Regiment, and captain of its Milwaukee company.

But despite the military tradition in the King family, Rufus King did not look favorably on Charles's sudden ambition to enter West Point. Of course it was taken for granted that he could secure a West Point appointment if that was decided. The family still had enough political influence for that, though it was long past the days when James Gore King had represented New York and John Alsop King, New Jersey in the same Congress. Nor were any of the present generation such apt politicians as the first Rufus King, "the last of the Federalists," who had signed the Constitution of the United States as a delegate from Massachusetts and then had married Mary Alsop, daughter of a New York merchant. Moving to New York in time to be elected one of the first two senators from that state, he had been nominated for the presidency, but that was in the years when the Federalist party was dying. He was its last candidate.

Then had come the lean years of Jacksonian democracy, which Charles King the elder had opposed as editor of the *New York American*.[9] Now the Kings were turning to the new Republican party, which probably would nominate Seward for the presidency and very likely would elect him. The Milwaukee editor had been Governor Seward's adjutant general in New York during the troubled times of the Anti-Rent Riots, celebrated in the novels of James Fenimore Cooper.

Young Charles was sent to New York to prepare for Columbia College and the practice of law, where these political connections might bring him something more important than a mere appointment to West Point. Shipping Charles to New York was rather unexpected. He had grown up in Milwaukee with a band of "young ruffians" known as the King's Corner Crowd. The King residence was at the northeast corner of Mason and Van Buren streets, and

that the boys congregated on that corner seems to imply that
Charles was more or less their leader—a trait first apparent at age five when he ran away from home and took two boys with him so he would not get lost. In such games as hunt the wolf, crack the whip, pompom pullaway, and follow the leader he played a prominent part, as he did on a camping trip to Lake Pewaukee when the boys "borrowed a man's boat to row across in, when we were so hurried we hadn't time to tell him about it on one side, and forgot about fetching it back when we got to the other. And you'd never believe what a row the man raised about a little thing like that."

They might have got away with that had they not sassed Charles's Sunday school teacher. Indignantly she went to Mrs. King with the warning, "If you don't get your boy away from this godless, graceless gang and send him where he can be among gentlemen, you will rue it to your dying day." So Charles was packed off to Professor Anthon's school. Other boys in his gang grew up to become Lieutenant General Arthur MacArthur, father of General Douglas MacArthur; Rear Admiral James G. Cogswell; George Peckham, eminent scientist; and other legal and business luminaries.

Charles's talents were not unappreciated in his new environment, however. Mr. Meeker, the algebra teacher, required that each boy, as soon as he completed his problem, deposit his slate facedown on a corner of the master's desk. A higher grade was given to the boy finishing first, and the others received additional points in diminishing order. Charles was fascinated by the more interesting problem of what would happen should each boy deposit his slate on top of the preceding one but about half an inch to the right. He mentioned this perplexing point to his classmates, and a delightfully noisy solution was worked out.

Mr. Meeker then required that the slates be put directly in front of him. Now Charles became puzzled by the idea of grading the work by order of completion. What would happen if all twenty-seven boys finished at the same time? In some psychic manner this also was arranged, and the result was even more delightfully noisy as each boy vociferously claimed the right to deposit his slate first.

In some inexplicable manner, in spite of these boyish diversions Charles attained sufficient preparation to enter Columbia College in the fall of 1860. Fire departments were forgotten now, and so too, regretfully, was West Point.

A Knight of Columbia

In the spring of 1861 Charles King was excited to learn that his father had been appointed minister resident to the Papal State. The appointment had come about in somewhat curious fashion. Rufus King had asked his old friend Seward, now secretary of state under President Abraham Lincoln, for appointment as postmaster at Milwaukee. He was told the appointment had already been made.

"And on the recommendation of one of our most valued Republican friends in Milwaukee," Seward had added.

"Who is that?"

"Rufus King."

Then King remembered he had signed a petition for the new postmaster more than a year before. He was promised nothing else, so he was quite unprepared when asked if he would take the post at Rome, capital of the temporal possessions of the pope. He decided to accept.

When Rufus King arrived in New York, prepared to sail for Italy, his son clamored to be taken along and complete his education there, but he was flatly refused.

"You must compete your education at Columbia," he was told.

"But I don't like Columbia, and I will never make a lawyer. If I must go to school, let it be West Point."

"We've been through all that. It's settled."

But things were not as settled as Rufus King thought when he had his baggage taken aboard ship the afternoon of April 11. It was not settled that his son would complete his education at Columbia. It was not even settled that Rufus King was going to Rome. The events of that night were to unsettle many lives besides those of Rufus and Charles King. The next day Rufus King moved his baggage back to shore. He was not going to Rome, he was going to Washington. Fort Sumter had been fired on!

10   Rufus King, as a West Point graduate, naturally offered his

services to the government. He was the twenty-fourth volunteer
on the first list of brigadier generals commissioned by President
Lincoln on May 17, 1861. There were notable names on that list.
First were the regulars, David Hunter, Samuel P. Heintzelman,
Erasmus D. Keyes, Andrew Porter, Fitz John Porter, William B.
Franklin, Don C. Buell, Thomas W. Sherman, Nathaniel Lyon,
and John Pope. Then former regulars, William T. Sherman, Philip
Kearny, Joseph Hooker, Joseph J. Reynolds, Darius N. Couch,
King, and Ulysses Grant. Grant stood nineteenth on this list of
thirty-seven names, though some biographers would have it that
he came to prominence by accident. Somewhat to the rear were
political names such as Jacob D. Cox, Stephen A. Hurlbut, Robert
C. Schenck, Benjamin M. Prentiss, and John A. McClernand.
Higher rank had already been given George B. McClellan, John C.
Frémont, Henry W. Halleck, Irvin McDowell, William S. Rose-
crans, Nathaniel P. Banks, and Benjamin F. Butler. But a few
generals who won marked fame in the war were commissioned
later, George H. Thomas, Philip H. Sheridan, Ambrose E. Burn-
side, and George G. Meade being among the most notable.[1]

Brigadier General Rufus King, United State Volunteers, returned home; there he became also brigadier general of Wisconsin
Volunteers and hoped to command an all-Wisconsin brigade. After organizing recruiting in his home state, he returned to Washington just after the first battle of Bull Run.

Meanwhile, changes had come less rapidly for Charles King, and
he was still at Columbia. Somehow or other he read Latin while
troops marched down Broadway. He saw his old friends of the fire
departments leave as the regiment of "Fire Zouaves" under their
gallant colonel Elmer E. Ellsworth, first Union officer to be killed
in the war. He saw the Massachusetts Sixth go through, under
Ben Butler, on their way to Baltimore, where a riotous mob tried
to stop them from going on to the capital. Many other famous
regiments marched through New York City, but Charles's battles
were with trigonometry.

Then at last came commencement, with some of the graduates
wearing blue uniforms under their academic gowns. Otherwise it
was as dull an affair as the customary Greek salutatory, the Latin
ode, the English poem, the valedictory, and the rest of the usual
program could make it, except that the oratory this year was
patriotic. When this was over there was nothing else to do until
fall, and much could happen before then.[2]

The first event was that General King allowed Charles to join his staff at Washington. The army of Civil War days was not the assemblage of specialists prominent in modern armies, and a number of duties were performed by civilians and "volunteers" that later would have been assigned to regularly enlisted soldiers. Young Charles was made a mounted orderly, though not a soldier, and that his service was authorized military duty was recognized eventually by a Civil War service medal.

Life was pleasant on the heights of Kalorama above Washington, where King's brigade was encamped. His was the only entirely western brigade in the Army of the Potomac. It included veterans of Bull Run, the Sixth Wisconsin, the Seventh Wisconsin, the Nineteenth Indiana, and a regular army battery, Company B of the Fourth U.S. Artillery, commanded by Captain John Gibbon, an officer young Charles was to know in much different circumstances many years later.

Here there were frequent visits from Secretary Seward, who renewed his old friendship with Rufus King, and even a visit from President Lincoln, whom the former Milwaukee editor had known when the tall Illinoisan was so little regarded that no audience came to hear his scheduled address in Milwaukee.[3] Perhaps General George McClellan did not favor these too-frequent visits to one of his subordinates from the president of the United States and the secretary of state. He ordered King's brigade to move across Chain Bridge into Virginia, a somewhat embarrassing order since it required General King to support his junior, Brigadier General William F. "Baldy" Smith. It was a bit embarrassing to Baldy Smith too, for it seems he suggested that three regiments of King's brigade be left across the Potomac but that General King take his headquarters and one regiment back to the north bank.

Into this delicate situation young Charlie King blundered with youthful enthusiasm. Fatigue parties from the Sixth Wisconsin had been sent a mile or so up the river to cut down trees and clear ground for some earthworks. Baldy Smith had a battery on the heights near his headquarters on the opposite shore. One afternoon he demonstrated to some visitors how accurately his artillerymen could burst their shells in the woods across the river, the very spot where the fatigue parties were working.

"Presently down came an officer full gallop to say that the shells were flying through the woods and had driven the Sixth to cover." As Charles told the story,

He handed a big fragment of shell to our general and our general turned to me, the only person present whose horse was saddled, and bade me gallop across to General Smith's headquarters, show him the shell and tell him the battery had driven our working parties out of the woods.

Big with importance, I put spurs to my horse and darted away full tilt. The bridge sentries halted me and added to the mischief, for all this time Mott's guns were banging, and I thought every shot meant murder to our men. Ten minutes later and the dignified and martial group at Smith's headquarters were properly shocked and scandalized when a small boy orderly, on a big reeking horse, came spurring into their midst, and, with a spatter of mud, saluted the general and said, "That battery, sir, is firing right into the woods where the Sixth Wisconsin are working."

The General slowly turned, looked me blandly and benevolently over, and remarked, "Ah! and has anyone been hurt?"

"No sir," I answered, consumed with wrath over the fact that my message had had no other effect, "but lots of 'em might have been if they hadn't cleared out and hid in a ravine," and I held up a fragment of shell. The general coolly, critically surveyed it, then as calmly remarked, "Ah, well, ride back and tell the General I'm very glad to hear no one has been hurt," and then to my unspeakable indignation bade the battery fire away. Just fancy how mad our Wisconsin fellows were when that message was delivered! Yet the General probably intended only to rebuke my impetuosity; at least that was the way our General looked at it, but then I always thought him far more tenacious of other people's rights than of his own.[4]

A more pleasant experience was Charlie King's meeting with Brigadier General Winfield Scott Hancock, one of several famous namesakes of General Scott. Hancock was once known as a great corps commander in the Civil War and, in the course of time, was nominated for the presidency against a general of less military fame, James A. Garfield.

"It was a stormy afternoon in late September of 1861," Charles afterward recalled. "It was on the banks of the Potomac just opposite Chain Bridge. The Sibley tents of the Sixth Maine Infantry were still standing on the broad plateau which lay between the overhanging bluff that skirted the river road from Washington, and what was called the Georgetown Pike, perhaps five hundred yards to the north." The Sixth Maine was in bivouac with the rest of Baldy Smith's brigade beyond the wooded heights on the south bank of the river. The Sixth Wisconsin had pitched their tents on the north side of that pike; their sentry line on their eastward flank was only forty or fifty paces from the headquarters tents of General King, his staff, and the telegraph station. The sentries, with rifles at "secure" and coat collars about their ears, paced dismally in the rain. General King and most members of his staff were away in Washington or on duty about camp, leaving two or three orderlies in charge of headquarters, when a long column of infantry was seen coming up the pike. Two mounted officers spurred ahead to the general's "marquee."

"Is General King here?" asked the foremost rider, the tallest, handsomest man the Wisconsin boy had yet seen at the front.

"No, sir, gone to Washington," promptly answered the smallest and least conspicuous of the group.

"Any of his staff here?"

"Yes, sir, I am," was the answer, in all the valorous importance of sixteen years and five foot four. And the big general was too much of a gentleman to laugh.

"Well," he said, "I was told I could find a mounted guide here to lead me by the shortest route to General Smith's command."

"I can take you, sir. I go there every day," said the youngster. . . .

Five minutes later the small orderly, on a big mettlesome bay, was riding side by side with the tall general down the ramp the Engineers had carved out of the side of the bluff, and past the saluting guards of the Third Vermont, into the long, dim, tunnel-like vista of the old Howe truss bridge that bore away to the southern shore. . . .

"Isn't that a pretty big horse for a lad of your size? How old are you?"

"Seventeen next month, sir."

"Indeed! You look much younger. Who taught you to ride?"

"My father, sir, if anybody. He's a West Pointer, too," I ventured.

"Oh, you are General King's son. You ought to be going to the Point one of these days."

"That's been my hope and ambition these last three years, General, and I wish you would tell him that you agree with me."

He threw back his head and laughed a hearty, ringing laugh. "Indeed I will, and if all goes well, possibly I can help you one of these days—My name's Hancock."[5]

Afterward Charles was very proud of having guided General Hancock on his first crossing of the Potomac at the head of his brigade. Nor did General Hancock forget his promise to mention West Point to Charles's father. At last Rufus King consented, and an appointment was sought of President Lincoln and promised by Secretary Seward. But in March 1862, when the names were to be announced, there came a great disappointment. William H. Upham of the Second Wisconsin had been shot through the lungs and left for dead on the field of Bull Run when his regiment fell back with the rest of the defeated army, and he was mourned for dead at his Racine home. After a time at Libby Prison he recovered from his desperate wound and was sent back to Washington and exchanged. With Wisconsin's Senator James R. Doolittle to champion his cause, he begged the president to send him to West Point. He would be twenty-one in August; he must enter in June or not at all.[6]

Charles graciously stepped aside, and President Lincoln was so impressed with the letter in which the boy said he would not stand in the way of a wounded hero of the first big battle of the war that he promised the next appointment to the son of General King. The chance came in May when one of the ten candidates was found to be too young. The note to General King at Fredericksburg, scrawled by Secretary Seward on War Department stationery, said, "Give General Totten the right name of your son for appointment as Cadet. Is it Charles King." So Upham and King entered the Military Academy together. Many years later Upham, as governor of Wisconsin, was to have King as his adjutant general.[7]

"President Lincoln's only visit to West Point was paid one beautiful day in June, before his appointees were in uniform," Charles recalled many years later. "He strode over to the barracks and sent for his ten boys. Tall, angular, and ungainly, as said some spectators, with a silk hat of exaggerated height, nevertheless, when he put his great hand on my head, and looked kindly down into my flushed and boyish face, saying, 'Well, son, you have got your wish at last,' I could well nigh have worshipped him."[8]

By entering West Point Charles missed the campaign that gave his father's brigade its proud nickname the "Iron Brigade." Yet General Rufus King's fight at Gainesville, opening the battle known as Second Bull Run or Second Manassas, was later one of Charles King's frequent literary subjects.[9]

After being detached from the forces of Baldy Smith, King's brigade was sent across the Long Bridge to occupy Arlington, where the general made his headquarters in the home of his former commanding officer, Robert E. Lee. The organizing of the Army of the Potomac under McClellan gave Rufus King promotion as major general and command of a division of the First Corps under Major General Irvin McDowell. As McClellan moved to the Peninsula, McDowell's corps was held to cover the defenses of Washington. When Major General John Pope was called to command the new Army of Virginia, King's divison was at Fredericksburg, and so much was it rushed back and forth during the assembling of Pope's forces that it became known as the "Pendulum Division."[10]

Then General Thomas J. "Stonewall" Jackson performed the famous flanking movement that disrupted Pope's campaign and gave the "Iron Brigade," now the Third Brigade of King's division, its name in tribute to its firm stand against the South's "Stonewall Brigade." The division had been ordered to march to Centerville by the Warrenton Pike. It had gone only a short distance when the Third Brigade, commanded by Brigadier General John Gibbon, who formerly had commanded its battery, ran into the fire of Confederate guns. As more enemy forces came up, the Iron Brigade charged and held its own against a considerable portion of Jackson's corps. "The Black Hats"—the Second Wisconsin, veterans of First Bull Run, wore the quaint, stiff Kossuth hat, looped up on one side and garnished with cord and brasses and feathers—the headgear of the regulars at that time—met the Stonewall Brigade itself. Colonel "Sol" Meredith's Nineteenth Indiana clashed with General William B. Taliaferro's brigade, while the Seventh Wisconsin was ordered by its lieutenant colonel, Charles A. Hamilton, to "change front forward on tenth company," a difficult parade-ground maneuver, executed perfectly in the face of the enemy attack.

Jackson had blundered and betrayed his position, but General King did not realize the fact. That night he called a conference of his brigade commanders and learned that an entire corps was on

his front, with another—that of General James Longstreet—
close by. Having received no orders and no assurance of support, *A Knight*
King ordered a retreat from his perilous position. Pope, hearing *of*
the sound of battle at Gainesville, knew what was happening and *Columbia*
made dispositions to meet it. According to his account, he sent
King messages, both directly and through General McDowell, to
hold his ground, but none of the messengers reached the division
commander. According to Charles King, Pope later admitted he
had sent no message directly to Rufus King.[11] In any event, a
chance to defeat Lee's army was lost and was immediately followed by the disastrous second battle of Bull Run.

Rufus King, however, had no part in the larger battle. He
became ill and was forced to give up his command.[12] He continued,
however, in the military service, performing duties around Washington, including sitting on the court-martial of Major General
Fitz John Porter.[13] In 1863 Secretary Seward again offered Rufus
King the post at Rome. During King's four years at the Vatican,
the only event of considerable interest was the capture of John H.
Surratt, indicted for participating in the conspiracy to assassinate
Lincoln. Surratt was returned from Rome to the United States for
trial, but the jury disagreed in his case, and eventually he was
released.

King's ministry ended in a curious fashion. In 1867 Congress
failed to appropriate funds for the American legation on "the
alleged but erroneous grounds that the Pope refuses to permit
Protestant worship within the walls of Rome." [14] King protested
that this charge was untrue, but Congress again failed to make an
appropriation at its succeeding session, so King resigned on January 1, 1868. He served as deputy collector of customs at the port of
New York for a time, and he died in Milwaukee on October 13,
1876.

The Iron Brigade added to the laurels won under King's command in the subsequent campaigns of the Army of the Potomac.
At Antietam it again met the Stonewall Brigade in a stand-off
fight that almost duplicated their previous encounter at Gainesville.[15] The brigade's diminutive courier, however, departed in
the summer of 1862, bound for the United States Military Academy and laurels of his own.

Cadet Days

Those who have read many of General King's novels have probably noticed a recurrent plot structure that seems, by modern standards, artificial and melodramatic. The hero is accused of some crime or misdemeanor based on circumstantial evidence. The villain, the real criminal, has planted certain documents that intensify suspicion against the hero. Though it may not be sufficient to convict him in a court of law, the hero is ostracized and suffers the tortures of isolation. Everything he does is tragically misunderstood. At length the villain is striken with some malady—brain fever, perhaps, brought on by worry over his guilt. He admits his crime in delirium, or perhaps he repents and confesses. The hero is vindicated. King's book *The Deserter* is a story of this kind, and there are many others. Modern readers are apt to say that such things do not happen. They seem the stuff that made up those roaring stage melodramas and the romantic, impossible novels of that period.

But such a thing did happen to Cadet Orsemus B. Boyd in 1865. To understand how this came about, it is necessary to know something of cadet life at West Point during the Civil War. According to *A West Point Parallel*, a story King wrote as a pendant to a Prussian cadet story, *Noble Blood*, by Ernst von Wildenbruch, the famed discipline of the academy during the war "was far from being what is is today." And though King perhaps exaggerates this situation, it is evident that in wartime many fine officers ordinarily available as instructors at the academy were performing more important duties elsewhere. King remarks that staff appointments were often given to disabled men: "Many of the officers on the academic staff limped painfully, used canes or crutches or both," and "there were days when even that person so constantly in evidence now, the officer in charge, was only seen at parade, and not always there."[1] There was at least one day when the presence of the officer in charge at parade would have prevented tragedy.

So few officers were assigned to the academy during wartime that occasionally senior cadets served as instructors. Unaccustomed duties and responsibilities were given to the cadet adjutant and first captain, and they sometimes assumed unusual authority.

King entered West Point in 1862, and during that summer minor thefts of money and valuables occurred in cadet camp. The culprit was caught, taken out by a mob headed by the cadet adjutant, and tarred and feathered. The cadet adjutant was reduced to the ranks as a result of this incident.

In the winter of 1865–66 King was cadet adjutant and faced the same problem. Again money and valuables were disappearing from the cadets' rooms. "In my time we never would have rested until we had discovered the culprit and given him a coat of tar and feathers," the commandant of the academy told the cadet officers.[2] Considering this invitation, the moderation of Cadet Adjutant King when the matter came to a test is remarkable.

A number of cadets determined to discover the thief. Though their detective work was somewhat amateurish, it seemed to have results. They left a number of marked bills in conspicuous places. Though they promptly disappeared without aiding the case much, the cadets tried again. Someone suggested that Cadet Boyd had spent a great deal of money and so his room was searched, but with no results. A second search a few days later was more successful. A marked ten-dollar bill was discovered between the leaves of his dictionary, and other bills were also found in his room.

The cadet sentinel and cadet officer of the guard were called in as witnesses; the cadet adjutant, the four cadet captains, and other class leaders were called in for consultation, and there was much further searching of Boyd's room.[3] At length a delegation was sent to confront Boyd with the evidence. With this delegation was a member of the third class, John Joseph Casey.[4]

Curiously, Cadet Adjutant King was not on speaking terms with either Boyd or Casey, the two principal actors in the tragedy. King does not explain his trouble with Casey except to say that it was a "lasting difference" and that "from the summer of 1865 I had refused to speak to him."[5] But about Boyd he tells a more detailed story. Boyd had enlisted in the Eighty-ninth New York Volunteer Infantry on September 1, 1861, and served with credit in the Civil War, being mentioned for gallantry at Roanoke Island. He was appointed to the Military Academy July 1, 1863, just a year later than King. "In those days the newcomers were always required to make up the tents and bedding of the upper classmen, to see that the water buckets were filled, the rifles and brasses polished," King explains, but "having been at the front myself I could not exact such service of such men," although Boyd happened to be in the next tent during summer camp. Among cadets entering in September appeared an old of friend of King's, Sergeant Major Charles Powell of the Fifth Wisconsin. According to King, Boyd presumed to demand that Powell, as a "Sep plebe," "stand attention and salute his betters" of the June group, and King, who was present, ordered Boyd to go about his business. For this Boyd had never forgiven King.[6]

King paints a rather unpleasant picture of Boyd otherwise, describing him as "a burly fellow, strong and heavily built," with bullying ways that caused many of his classmates to "cut him dead." There is a story about a fight, of which we have two versions written long afterward, one by King, the other by Mrs. Boyd, and it is somewhat difficult to steer a middle course between the two extremes presented. It seems that Boyd had picked a fight with another cadet, or the other cadet had picked a fight with Boyd, and both accounts agree that Boyd was the winner—about all they do agree on. King says Boyd continued to hammer his opponent unmercifully until dragged off and beaten by a man of his own weight. Mrs. Boyd says it was not until the fight was over it was called unfair because Boyd was the bigger man and that he was then challenged by an opponent larger than himself but refused to fight again. Both agree again that as a result of this fight Boyd became so unpopular he could find no man to room with him in barracks. It is easy to see that, having no friends to defend him, the worst would be believed.

One can imagine the scene. The angry cadets, concerned about the honor of the corps, upset over their own losses of money, perhaps pleased that the thefts apparently had been proved against the least popular of their number, are still trying to make their accusations judicially. Boyd, friendless, knows nothing he can say will be believed. He tries to make his denials so forceful that they will be accepted but is so frightened that he does not know what to say. Confused by the questions shot at him by his accusers, he becomes tangled in his statements, and they believe

the worst. Then Casey, his neighbor across the hall, identifies a
letter believed mailed a year before and now found in Boyd's room. Also, there is mention of the finding of a dirk—probably of no importance to the case except that it appears at times in General King's stories.

Boyd at first swears he knows nothing about any money hidden in his room. Later he swears that he knows of none except for five dollars hidden in a book. This is one discoverable contradiction, but since no one can identify the five dollars, it is given back to Boyd. He begs to be allowed to leave West Point, but his accusers are insistent that he not be allowed to leave in the uniform he is believed to have disgraced.

Further council is taken, and now Cadet Adjutant King insists upon one thing that is much to his credit, and he carries it through. He demands that the affair be handled in an orderly manner; that there be no mobbing or tarring and feathering. Others, recalling the unpopularity of Boyd among members of the second class and the dishonor they feel attaches to them because of his alleged discovery as the long-sought thief, agree that mob action might seriously injure the victim.

So at evening parade the cadet adjutant warns the corps of cadets, "In the event of anything of an unusual nature taking place at this formation, any man who attempts to leave his place in the ranks will at once be placed in arrest by any one of the cadet officers." At this the cadet captains and lieutenants step to the front and face their men. Then Boyd appears at the door of the "first division." His cadet uniform stripped off and replaced by a flannel suit, with a broad placard stating THIEF on his back. He is escorted by three accusers. The drums and fifes strike up "The Rogue's March," and the unfortunate Boyd is led across the front of the battalion from right to left and around its rear to the center, where he is released. He flees in terror, while Adjutant King holds the battalion in ranks and reads a long report of deliquencies. Not until he is sure Boyd is safe from pursuit does he order "Dismiss your companies." Then "with something almost like a scream, the whole Second Class and many of the Third sped madly in pursuit, but were brought up standing by the sight of the Superintendent, General Cullum, coming up the road."

Meanwhile Adjutant King had reported the action to the commandant. "He, looking dazed for a moment, said: 'You have taken a grave responsibility on your shoulders,' and then, perhaps recalled what he had said as to what the corps would have done in his day, for not another word did he utter, but, taking his cap, went forth in search of the Superintendent." Probably the commandant was profoundly thankful that these young fellows had had better sense than to take his advice about tarring and feathering.[7]

But the superintendent, Brevet Major General George Washington Cullum, later author of *Cullum's Register* of graduates of the Military Academy, had encountered Boyd in full flight and halted him, amazed to see a cadet in civilian clothing and supposing him to be stealing off for some amusement.

"What do you mean, sir?" the general demanded. "Return at once to your quarters!"

"I'm afraid to, sir. They'll kill me," or something to that effect, was Boyd's reply, and the general, seeing something serious was in hand, took Boyd to the superintendent's office, where the whole story was told. The boy remained in Cullum's quarters until his father could be summoned.[8]

A court of inquiry heard all the evidence and decided it was inconclusive. It was brought out that Boyd's father had liberally supplied the cadet with money, about three hundred dollars, quite enough to cause comment, that there was no reason for him to steal, and that there was nothing to connect Boyd directly with the marked money found in his room. The court recommended that the ringleaders in Cadet Boyd's humiliation be brought to trial.[9]

At the trial King pleaded guilty to the charge and expressed his sorrow and mortification at having administered this degrading punishment to a man declared innocent. As cadet adjutant he took all the blame, but the three cadets who had led Boyd down the front of the battalion were also found guilty. These three are identified as Frank Soule, a Mississippian of the class of 1866 and cadet captain, who resigned as a second lieutenant of ordnance in 1870 and died in 1919; Edward Maxwell Wright of the class of 1866, a native of New Jersey, who died a captain of ordnance in 1880; and Arthur Cranston of the class of 1867, born in Massachusetts, who enlisted as a private in the Seventh Ohio on April 25, 1861, won a commission as second lieutenant in the Fifty-fifth Ohio, and was killed in action against Modoc Indians at the Lava Beds on April 26, 1873, when a first lieutenant of the Fourth U.S. Artillery.[10]

The court, however, seems to have been much moved by King's

pleas and recommended mercy, in great measure because of
King's previous record. But Secretary of War Edwin M. Stanton, according to King, "was said to have been exasperated because the court, the superintendent, and the commandant had actually pleaded mercy for us." The great war secretary relented, however, and ordered that the sentence of dismissal from the service be remitted in King's case and suspended until further orders in the three other cases, but that Cadet King be deprived of his position of adjutant.[11]

By this time, King tells us, he had formed the absurdly melodramatic theory that "some desperate criminal in the corps had hidden that marked money in the dictionary in order to throw suspicion from himself and fix the crime on the man whom the corps would be most ready to believe guilty of anything." Boyd's classmates had no such romantic ideas. To them the verdict was the Scotch one of "not proved," and they refused to have anything more to do with him. To the day of his graduation Boyd lived "in a lonely desert of solitude" generally ostracized by his companions, "a life which was a living hell." He would resent no insult, yet solitude, self-examination, and study made him a changed man, according to King.

It seems probable that King told Boyd he believed in his innocence. We have the report of one, unnamed, "whose report when a cadet was more severe than any other" against Boyd, and this unknown writer, who might possibly be King himself, said that

I gave at an early day, my apologies to the injured man, and assured him of my belief in his innocence. Although the prima facie evidence against him at that time seemed irrefutable, there was something in the conduct, bearing and moral courage of the poor fellow, which seemed to be utterly impossible to a guilty man. He received my words quietly, yet, I thought, in a gratified spirit, and pleasantly replied that he felt sure I had acted my part in the sad affair with a view only to vindicate the honor of the Corps of Cadets and the good name of West Point, and that he had nothing to complain of or hold against me.[12]

Happily, the story has a heroine. A girl attending a finishing school in New York met Boyd in 1866 at West Point. She knew about the charges against him, was immediately convinced that he was innocent, and told him so. Perhaps nothing more was needed to make this a romance. Three months after his graduation from West Point in 1867, they were married. Realizing the unpopularity that would follow him, Boyd chose the cavalry service, which meant hardship on the frontier, and Fannie A. Boyd loyally accompanied him there, as she tells in her book *Cavalry Life in Tent and Field*, published in 1894.

Boyd was assigned to the Eighth U.S. Cavalry, and at first the scandal did follow him. A few West Pointers would not speak to him. One result, as Mrs. Boyd points out, was that he was extremely sensitive about asking favors. On one occasion he was ordered to change station in California on one day's notice, and he did it rather than point out to a superior the injustice of the order, which was probably an oversight. But many years of exemplary behavior built up for him the reputation of a model duty officer, scrupulously honest. For these reasons this man, once branded as a thief, often was chosen to handle large sums of government money. For example, Major General John Pope directed Boyd to take charge of the building of Fort Bayard, New Mexico, where he had charge of the expenditure of all quartermaster funds during construction. Boyd won many friends while serving in Indian campaigns in Arizona, New Mexico, and Texas. He was promoted first lieutenant in 1868 and captain in 1882.

Shortly after Boyd's graduation, the sentimental and melodramatic theory of the case held by Charles King was proved true. Quite in the manner of the later King novels, Cadet Casey, principal witness against Boyd, was striken with dementia and was so severely ill that classmates took turns nursing him. One night in delirium Casey made some references to the Boyd affair that aroused the suspicions of his roommate, Cadet William J. Hamilton. The next morning, when Casey was again conscious, Hamilton questioned him. Casey confessed that he had stolen the various sums of money and valuables that Boyd had been accused of taking, and he told the entire story of hiding the marked money in Boyd's room.

This confession would have marked the climax of a King novel, but no public vindication of Boyd took place. Casey pledged Hamilton to secrecy, and Hamilton kept silent. Casey was in desperate straits. He had been secretly married, and if known this would have meant his immediate dismissal from the corps. According to accounts, his wife blackmailed him by threatening to announce the marriage, and Casey was forced to steal to meet her demands. King made use of this situation in his novel *Cadet Days*.

Hamilton, graduating two files ahead of Casey in the class of
1868, became a second lieutenant in the Fourth U.S. Artillery and
died January 22, 1872. Only a few months before his death he
called in Lieutenant Richard H. Savage of the class of 1868 and
told him the story of Casey's confession. By this time Casey was
dead, having been accidentally shot at drill by a soldier at Fort
Washington, Maryland, on March 24, 1869. Savage immediately
notified Boyd of the story told by the dying Hamilton.[13] Boyd did
absolutely nothing about it.

Savage went to the Orient and Europe for three years. On his
return he discussed the supposed Boyd vindication with Captain
Philip M. Price of the Engineers, a West Point graduate of 1869,
and learned that nothing was known about it. Savage immediately
prepared affidavits and sent them to Captain Boyd. Captain Boyd
calmly replied that his "character needs no present backing!"

Boyd died "in the field" on July 25, 1885, at camp near Grafton,
New Mexico, of an inflammation aggravated by hardships during
an expedition of the Geronimo campaign. It was not until then
that the truth was known to many of his classmates. Savage
prepared an obituary that was published by the Association of
Graduates of the United States Military Academy, with additions
by its secretary. Here, finally, the sad story was told.

Academy life had its lighter side too, as shown in King's account
of an ancient institution known paradoxically as the "Stationery
Riot." No, not a stationary riot. This annual affair occurred early
in Cadet King's plebe year. The way having been duly prepared,
the cadet captain was wont to announce: "All members of the
fourth class who desire stationery for the ensuing month will call
at the Quartermaster's tent right after supper."

It can readily be imagined that there was a grand rush for the
free stationery, for every cadet had much writing to do this early
in his career. Charles King, in on the secret, warned a few of his
companions, and this little group did their running in the opposite
direction. But it was useless. A stern cadet lieutenant halted them
and ordered them to join their comrades. King protested that they
wanted no stationery.

"Then it is your duty to notify the Quartermaster," they were
told. Of course the quartermaster was nowhere around when the
torrent of plebes descended upon the supply tent. The quartermaster sergeant professed great alarm and appealed to the cadet
sentry, and the sentry, posted on what to do in case of riot or
disorder near his post, immediately called loudly for the guard.

The guard was suspiciously ready to act, and in a short time the entire plebe class was herded into a column of twos and marched in arrest to the guardhouse.

But on this occasion the plot was a little too successful. Some forty plebes were herded into one small tent, and it could not stand the strain. The rotten old canvas split in all directions, allowing most of the rioters to escape. And, King records gleefully, the plebes did not have to pay for the tent.[14]

Charles King mentioned a few other interesting incidents of his cadet days. He recalled one war scare that no doubt seemed very real at the time. During the draft riots in New York City in July 1863, the regular army garrison of West Point was sent to the metropolis, leaving behind only about twenty-seven cadets of the first class and sixty of the third to guard the Military academy, the second class being in camp and the fourth not yet in uniform. Then came a rumor that a band of southern sympathizers had secured a steamboat and were coming up the Hudson to destroy the academy. For the first time in history cadets were issued ball ammunition, and two squads were detailed to man twelve pounder Napoleon guns. King was chosen corporal of one of the batteries, his first promotion. But the steamer failed to arrive, probably much to the disappointment of a number of excited young warriors.[15]

King always liked to recall the peculiar honor he devised for Lieutenant General Winfield Scott, who lived at West Point after his retirement. Scott was the author of a tactics system the army used for thirty years, but it had been superseded, and among other changes the stately old grenadier salute had been replaced by "a jaunty, graceful, finger-tip touch of the cap visor, with a downward and forward sweep of the hand and arm." King conceived that Scott did not like the change, and

> remembering the old-time Mexican war salute Scott himself had taught me when a little shaver of five, I made a suggestion to a few cadets—like Churchill, Capron, Heintzelman— whose fathers had fought under Scott. The next time we saw the General's carriage approaching, instead of walking straight ahead and passing him with the cadet salute of the day, we "lined up" along the roadside several paces apart, and as he came nearly opposite, each in turn squarely faced him, raised the hand, palm to the front, fingers extended and joined, the tips just touching the visor, in the rigid, ramrod

salute—his own salute—of the days of our fathers; it was a joy to see his instant recognition of our purpose, and his obvious delight in our homage. General Cullum, then superintendent and long a member of his staff, told relatives of mine who came up for a visit, that nothing had given the old warrior such pleasure as the sudden and unexpected salute tendered by the young soldiers of the Corps of Cadets. In June, 1866, we fired the last volleys over his grave.[16]

King, demoted as a result of the Boyd affair from his high post of adjutant, the office he had regarded with childish wonder at the age of five as one of the grandest positions to be attained by man, nevertheless was chosen as one of two cadets to be retained at the academy as instructors in tactics during the summer encampment. At the same time he was commissioned second lieutenant of the First U.S. Artillery on June 18, 1866.

An Initial Experience

Charles King had occasion to rail against those relatives whose opposition had kept him from entering West Point before 1862, for the graduates of 1865 were immediately commissioned first lieutenants and some of them became captains within two years, whereas the unfortunate class of 1866, King included, took rank as second lieutenants behind all the volunteer officers commissioned in the regular army at the close of the Civil War, and many of them "marched meekly in the line of file closers until they were grandfathers."[1]

At first the prospects seemed bright enough. A month after Charles was commissioned, Congress vastly increased the army, from nineteen to forty-five regiments of infantry and from six to ten regiments of cavalry, although the artillery, in which King served, remained at five regiments. The cavalry was enlarged because of troubles on the western plains, where restless Indian tribes had become much emboldened by their comparative immunity during the war. The large westward migration that followed demobilization of the armies caused new friction with the Indians, and there had been some serious outbreaks. But this had less to do with the increase in the army than with the supposed necessity for keeping large garrisons in the South. It was to this field of duty that King was sent.

A "massacre" occurred at New Orleans only two days after Congress passed the army bill, and it concerned the light battery that King was assigned to. The governor of Louisiana had called upon the 1864 constitutional convention to reconvene. The mayor of New Orleans declared he would not permit such a meeting. A mob moved on the Mechanics' Institute in Dryades Street, where the delegates, mostly blacks, were to assemble, and as a result forty-eight persons were killed and a large number wounded.[2]

The commander of Light Battery K urged that King join with-

out delay, so the young lieutenant left West Point, visited his
family in Milwaukee for a week, and joined his first regular army
organization in the fall of 1866. In those days, and for many years
thereafter, it was an obsession for company officers to join their
commands whenever the latter were about to perform hazardous
field duty; this was a point of honor rigidly adhered to. ·

The First U.S. Artillery dated from 1821 when it was organized
from existing companies, many of them much older. It existed
until 1901 when regimental organization was discontinued for
artillery. At the time of King's service a regiment of artillery
consisted of twelve batteries; two of these were known as "light
batteries," that is, field artillery, and the others were assigned to
coast defense or other service. King's first assignment was to
Light Battery K. Later he served for a time in a heavy battery, C.

For the time being there was no serious need of the services of
the artillery. The Ku Klux Klan was beginning its activity, and
that was not an institution that so thorough a Yankee as Charles
King could approve, though he had no direct interest in its work at
this time. But generally he found less to condemn in the South
than he had expected, after fours years of white-hot war propaganda against these supposedly wicked people. In fact he discovered, much to his surprise, that the schoolbook had not been
far wrong, and that the wealthy classes, now not very wealthy,
were well educated, possessed cultivated minds, and were still
noted for their hospitality, though a bit distrustful of a blue uniform at first glance. And with reason. King also found a number of
persons from his own section of the country who were not above
exploiting the lawless and devastated condition of the invaded
states.

The backcountry of Louisiana was a somber region of hopeless-
ness and desolation, in no way helped in its troubles by the Reconstruction policies of the government. Under the conditions that
existed it is not surprising that epidemic was added to the burden
borne by the South. Yellow fever was especially virulent that
year, and Charles was one of its victims. Sent north on sick leave,
he was ordered not to return until frost set in, which was rightly
believed to put an end to the spread of the disease. After some
time in Milwaukee, he returned to New Orleans by way of New
York, bringing a large party of recruits from the East.

The troubles in the South rose to a peak in 1868, the year
Ulysses S. Grant was elected president over Horatio Seymore of

New York. Riots were frequent as the election drew near, and Lieutenant King had much to do with these, for he was probably the first officer to command the recently invented and since famous Gatling gun on riot duty.

The "Gatling battery," as it was sometimes called, was a legitimate ancestor of modern machine guns; in fact it was described in 1867 as "an American automatic machine-gun" by an English expert who also referred to it as "an infernal machine, combined of six large needle guns and a Colt's revolver."[3] The "needle gun" notion derived from the needlelike firing pins used by the Gatling and the newly adopted Springfield breech-loading rifles and carbines. The weapon had from six to ten barrels, depending on caliber, which kept up a continuous fire as long as they were turned by a hand crank. Invented by Dr. Richard J. Gatling of Indianapolis during the Civil War, a few Gatling guns were in the hands of Major General Benjamin F. Butler's Army of the James during the closing days of the war, but there is no record of their having been used in battle.

The Gatling gun of 1867 is described as of one-inch caliber, although later models were made in .45 and .50 caliber to correspond with production rifles and carbines. Unlike modern machine guns, the Gatling was considered an artillery weapon, and the usual form of organization for its use, until after the Spanish-American War, was a platoon of light artillery. So in 1868 the junior lieutenant of Light Battery K, First Artillery, who happened to be Charles King, was given command of the new platoon of Gatling guns.

The Gatlings were mounted on wheels and formally had their carriages, caissons, harness, and horses like any other piece of artillery. And when the state election drew near, these "bullet squirters" were stationed in an abandoned cotton press on Canal Street to answer riot calls, just as a fire engine company answered fire alarms. The crackle of revolvers and shotguns was the signal to dispatch these guns on the run, and King records, "Never once had we to fire, though often it was 'Front into Battery' at the gallop. The rioters, black and white, had an idea those guns would belch lead that would sweep the streets from curb to curb, and the crowds scattered like sheep at the sound of our bugle, and the cry, 'Here come the Gatlings.'"[4]

In army annals the following year, 1869, is known as the "Consolidation Year."[5] The elections were over, the South was "recon-

structed" at least until another election was due, and it mattered
little to congressmen that Red Cloud, an Oglala Sioux chieftain,
was raiding on the northern plains or that there had been such
events, still famous in frontier annals, as the Wagon Box Fight
and the Fetterman "Massacre." One of the last acts of the dying
Congress, on March 3, was to slash twenty regiments of infantry
from the army list and to provide that there should be no new
commissions and no promotions until a surplus of 17 colonels, 18
lieutenant colonels, 20 majors, 177 captains, 211 first lieutenants,
and 55 second lieutenants had been absorbed. These were indeed
gloomy days for a junior second lieutenant. The army was not
increased again until the Spanish-American War was imminent,
and for more than two decades it stood at a constant figure of
27,000 men.

Sometime during 1869 Lieutenant King was sent to Cincinnati
on recruiting duty. Under the consolidation plan it could not have
been a very busy assignment, so he found time to join the Cincinnati Red Stockings, organized that year as the first professional
baseball team in the United States. Cincinnati sports fans, a term
probably not yet invented, were tired of the talk about "ringers"
and "professionals" in the so-called amateur teams of that period,
and the financial backers decided on the bold experiment of hiring
an out-and-out professional team. George Wright, all-time all-
American shortstop as listed by Albert G. Spalding, was hired at
an annual salary of $1,400 and given free rein to organize a team.
His brother Harry was captain and center fielder, and among
other players were Charles (or George) Gould, first base; Andrew
Leonard and Calvan McVey, fielders and leading batters; Douglas
Allison, catcher; and Fred Waterman and Charles Sweazey.[6]

The team won a number of games against others in the vicinity,
and world championship aspirations arose when it defeated the
"Buckeyes" by the stupendous score of 103 to 8. It decided to tour
the East and challenge all comers. All went well until Cincinnati
met the "Unions" of Morrisania, New York, where the Red Stockings were given a surprise. Pitcher Martin was the first curve-ball
pitcher known to baseball, and he himself could not explain how he
did it, but the champion Cincinnati batsmen were baffled by the
strange course of the ball. Nevertheless they squeezed out a
victory, closing the season with a record of fifty-five games won,
one tied, and no defeats.[7] Charles did not finish the season, so he
did not get the regular salary of eight hundred dollars paid most of

these pioneer professional athletes for their work from March 15 to November 15. In August King was again detailed to West Point, this time as assistant instructor in infantry, artillery, and cavalry tactics.[8]

This comprehensive title does not explain the whole of his duties. As a young person of great good nature and considerable social inclinations, he found himself in frequent demand to entertain the important personages who were continually visiting the institution, a duty agreeable enough had it not been that it was done at his own expense. His success in this line, however, led him into one even less agreeable—explaining to fond mothers the faults and shortcomings of their offspring. But the greatest trial of this period was the admission of the first blacks as cadets. [9]

One can imagine the excitement in those days of Reconstruction. Congress had determined that freedmen should be given full equality in government service and had specifically provided for their admission to West Point. It was a period when the Military Academy was under considerable fire in the halls of Congress, for had not that "aristocratical institution" provided the Confederacy with its greatest generals, even its president? Congress was full of war veterans, and many thought they had grievances against their comrades from the regular army who had held the more important posts and sometimes had enforced discipline more strictly than the volunteers had thought necessary. So the experiment of sending blacks to an academy that had been frequently denounced as pro-South was watched closely in anticipation of serious trouble.[10]

West Point, however, accepted the event calmly. The instructors and officers took the view that when the government established a policy it was not for them to object or question. When two Negro men arrived they were treated just like any other cadets, except that they were not subjected to the hazing with which "plebes," or fourth classmen, were always welcomed. One of the two was a good-natured Mississippian who unfortunately was unable to pass the entrance examination. The other was naturally aggressive and was encouraged to look for trouble by various organizations pretending to be friendly to his race. He refused to submit to discipline and was several times tried and ordered dismissed, but in each case he was ordered reinstated by higher authority because his retention had been made a political issue.

Only once was any violence offered him, and that occasion was never reported. One cold February night the student body turned out to fight a fire in the barracks. For three hours the cadets

manfully fought the blaze with hose, hand-pumped engine, and water buckets. One cadet was missing. The skulker was found by the warmth of a stove in the gymnasium and was booted bodily out of his shelter. After considerable newspaper furor and much wordy argument West Point at length dismissed this unfit cadet.[11]

The last commandant King served under at West Point was Emory Upton, lieutenant colonel and brevet major general, a famous name in the United States Army though little known to the public at large until Camp Upton was designated to honor him during the First World War. Upton was the hero of the "Bloody Angle" at Spottsylvania and was author of *Infantry Tactics: Double and Single Rank*, the standard army drill regulation for a generation. He is most widely known, however, for his *Military Policy of the United States*, the longhand manuscript of which was neglected in government archives until discovered in 1904, long after Upton's death, by Elihu Root when he was secretary of war. After it was carefully edited by the newly formed army general staff, Secretary Root succeeded in getting Upton's great work published by the government, and the ideas set forth there formed the basis for the National Defense Act of 1916, the Selective Service Act of 1917, and the organization of the army during World War I.

Upton was strict and exacting but never impatient or out of temper. He was a devout Christian but made no parade of piety. He was unpopular, however, because of his relentless discipline. He was austere and reticent, never referring to his heroic conduct in the war or to his having been wounded three times. Even in his own time he was little noticed, and it remained for military students of later generations to realize his impress upon the United States Army.

Charles King developed a warm friendship for Upton, which was reciprocated. Later Upton invited King to assist him in a revision of *Infantry Tactics*, a task that was never completed because Upton died in 1881.

About this time an elimination board went through the army list attempting to reduce the surplus of officers. It created more vacancies in the cavalry arm than in the other branches, and King, who had always preferred cavalry service, applied for transfer to that branch. He had become a first lieutenant May 15, 1870, and on December 31 of that year he was assigned to the Fifth Regiment U.S. Cavalry.

A Trooper Galahad

No other organization in the army had so prolific a publicity agent as the Fifth Cavalry had in Charles King, for his nine years' service in that regiment resulted in thirty or forty books celebrating its history. But the Fifth was notable long before this series of romances was written, though before King's time it was remembered more for the distinguished names of officers on its roll than for their services to the Union. The Confederate States of America commissioned eight officers as generals of full rank. Four of these came from the Fifth Cavalry. They were its first colonel, Albert Sidney Johnston; its first lieutenant colonel and second colonel, Robert E. Lee; a major, E. Kirby Smith; and a second lieutenant when the regiment was organized, John B. Hood. Then there was a lieutenant general, W. J. Hardee, author of *Hardee's Rifle and Light Infantry Tactics,* and two major generals, Earl Van Dorn and Fitzhugh Lee. To the Union cause the Fifth gave only one distinguished officer, but George H. Thomas, known as "Major Slowtrot" in the old regiment, proved more than a match for one of his former subordinates, Hood, whom he defeated in the annihilating battle of Nashville. The Fifth Cavalry dated from 1855, when it was organized as the Second Cavalry. During the Civil War it was renumbered the Fifth.[1]

When Lee resigned as colonel of the regiment to become a general of Virginia state troops, his place was filled by the promotion of William Helmsley Emory; ten years later Emory was still in command, and Charles King reported to him for duty at Fort McPherson, Nebraska. But Emory had not actually commanded the regiment during the Civil War; commissioned in the volunteer service, he had been adding to a collection of brevet commissions that was one of the most complete ever accumulated. The system of brevets provided a means of commissioning an officer in a grade where there was no vacancy. It provided an honorary title, but

34

with no advance in pay unless the officer was called to duty in his brevet rank. Emory entered the army as a brevet second lieutenant of artillery in 1831 because there were not enough vacancies in the rank of second lieutenant for members of his West Point class. He was breveted captain for gallant and meritorious service at the battle of San Pasqual in the Mexican War, promoted major for San Gabriel and the Plains of Mesa, and made lieutenant colonel for "meritorious and distinguished service as commissioner for running the boundary line between the United States and the Republic of Mexico in 1857."[2]

Emory was commissioned lieutenant colonel of the First Cavalry on January 31, 1861 and, foreseeing secession, he placed his resignation in the hands of his wife to be used in certain circumstances. She offered it while he was in the Far West extricating regular army units from the danger of being forced to surrender to Confederate forces. Since Maryland, his native state, did not secede, Emory asked that his resignation be withdrawn. The records show that it was accepted May 9 and that a new commission as lieutenant colonel of the Third (later Sixth) Cavalry was issued May 14. He became a brigadier general of volunteers March 17, 1862. A brevet as colonel followed, awarded for the battle of Hanover Court House, and subsequent commissions were as colonel of the Fifth Cavalry, brevet brigadier general, brevet major general of volunteers, brevet major general, and major general of volunteers. When mustered out of the volunteer service, he retained commissions as colonel of the Fifth Cavalry and brevet major general.

All was quiet in the valley of the Platte River when Charles King reported. Although four companies of the regiment were out on an expedition against maurauding Indians, there was no immediate active duty for King, so he took advantage of the opportunity for a buffalo hunt on the plains in company with William F. "Buffalo Bill" Cody, then chief of scouts of the Fifth Cavalry.

Technically, all the noted plainsmen who were used as scouts and guides were civilian employees of the Quartermaster Department, the only department authorized to pay outside workers. Considerable Indian restlessness blanketed the central plains in 1868. During successive maneuvering in Kansas, Cody brought an important message from Fort Larned to Sheridan at Fort Hays, a distance of 65 miles through a section infested with hostile Indians. No other of the many boastful scouts could be found to carry orders to Fort Dodge, 95 miles farther on, and Cody volunteered after four or five hours' rest. From Fort Dodge he returned to Fort Larned, then went back to Sheridan at Fort Hays, a total distance of 350 miles ridden in sixty hours, including rest, all through country so full of Indians that other scouts would not attempt it. It was for this heroic exploit that General Sheridan made Buffalo Bill chief of scouts of the Fifth Cavalry.[3] In 1869 Cody accompanied that regiment under its lieutenant colonel, Eugene A. Carr, to the fight against Tall Bull's band of Cheyennes at Summit Springs, Colorado.

On their hunt King and Cody forged what proved to be a lifelong friendship. But King was not to stay on the plains long at this time. In the fall, Colonel Emory was assigned in his brevet rank of major general to command the Department of the Gulf, with headquarters at New Orleans. Since Lieutenant King was familiar with conditions there and had made a favorable impression on General Emory, it was logical that he should be appointed aide-de-camp to the new department commander.

Returning to Louisiana, King found that state still being "reconstructed," with two legislatures and a confusion of state officials. Henry Clay Warmoth, a Republican and a Union war veteran, was governor, but apparently he was of a higher type than some "carpetbagger" and "scalawag" politicians of the period, and he was backed by some of the most responsible and respectable former Confederates. Among these was James Longstreet, who had been a lieutenant general under Lee but was now adjutant general of the state and wore the double stars of a major general of the United States in command of the militia, consisting of one regiment of former Confederates, another of blacks, and a battery of artillery.

General Emory's orders were to keep the peace and uphold the constituted authorities. No one was willing to define "constituted authorities," so he decided upon the expedient of "upholding the party that was attacked." This worked very well in preserving the peace, but it kept the controversy alive, and King thought it might have been well to let the factions fight it out. In pursuing his policy Emory kept in close touch with Longstreet, though unofficially, and the go-between or liaison was Lieutenant King. The young officer looked upon it as a great privilege to know the famous Confederate leader, and Longstreet himself appreciated the officer's friendship, for many former southern friends had cut

his acquaintance because of his services to a Republican governor.
Charles later regretted that he never screwed up enough courage
to ask the general about Gettysburg and Pickett's charge, the
great controversial question in his military career.

Street fighting was frequent in the revolutionary conditions
that prevailed in New Orleans, though it usually stopped as soon
as federal troops were reported on the way. There were no serious
clashes. At one time the Negro legislature was besieged in its
"capitol," but the most serious result of this was that the local pie
woman, who was the only source of supplies, refused to extend
credit until the gentlemen of the House and Senate settled their
arrears with her. In many ways social life went on in a quite
normal way, as it had during more disturbing upheavals than this.
Neither the French nor the Russian revolution halted the theater,
and New Orleans continued to have its opera and its Mardi Gras in
the throes of Reconstruction. In fact the Nineteenth U.S. Infantry formed the oriental guard for the carnival king at the annual
February festival, an incident that brought about much better
feeling toward the northern invaders.

Experiences during the reconstruction of Louisiana inspired
King to make his first venture into novel writing. *Kitty's Conquest*, written during 1872 and 1873, is one of the few among many
stories of the Ku Klux Klan that were written contemporaneously.
It was sent to a publisher and as promptly sent back. That is not
particularly remarkable; it happened, no doubt, to many a better
book. The unusual thing in King's literary career is that this was
the only manuscript he ever wrote that was rejected. It was
published in 1884, however, and is quite a readable story with
much historical value in representing the abnormal conditions of
the period. The Ku Klux Klan is by no means idealized in King's
novel—all the villains in the story belong to it—but much sympathy is expressed for the conditions that brought that organization
into being.

The civilian narrator of *Kitty's Conquest* is recorded as expressing astonishment at the military discipline that forbids the officer
hero to make any sign of recognition to "Kitty" when she attends
a review. Lieutenant King must have written this tongue in
cheek, for he has left on record his own lapse on a similar occasion.
The young artillery officer, riding at the rear of his battery as chief
of caissons, saluted Winfield Scott Hancock, commanding general
at New Orleans, and passed on. But his horse curvetted so as to

bring him directly facing Mrs. Hancock and a bevy of army girls, some of whom were waving handkerchiefs and laughing mischievously in greeting to the lieutenant, knowing the rules forbade his returning their greeting. But King could on occasion put a gallant courtesy even above a paragraph in army regulations, so his saber was presented and swept downward in full salute to Mrs. Hancock. Some giddy girl had to tell the general how beautifully it was done. So rumor has it that King's arrest was ordered, but Mrs. Hancock begged him off. The young ladies thought her intervention very necessary, since King had been picked to lead the "german," as it was called—or more properly in New Orleans the "cotillion"—at the general's quarters that night.[4]

Pictures of General King in his later years, when he had become a widely known novelist, might make one think he was a stiff and unsocial person. That he never was, and in this period at least he must be looked upon as an active and gallant figure. Some pictures make him seem large and imposing; actually he was rather under medium height and at this time weighed 147 pounds. But he always cut quite a figure among the ladies, and associates later recalled how girls hung on his every word when he had become a famous and elderly visitor to West Point. He did not attempt to deny that he liked it! One time, in describing General Sherman's habit of kissing every pretty girl he met, King regretted that he could not have remained in the regular army long enough to become commander-in-chief.

But King was no mere ballroom figure. In Cincinnati he had played professional baseball with the best team of his period, having learned the game at Columbia before the war, when it was very new. Now he tried to play again with the Excelsior Club of New Orleans, but he needed glasses and found himself no longer expert. There was one sport, however, at which he still excelled—horseback riding. During this era the Metairie Jockey Club at New Orleans controlled one of the most famous racetracks in the country. There, King records, he saw Sanford's Monarchist win the last four-mile heats ever run in the South. That occasion may be forgotten now, but one of M. H. Sanford's colts, Preakness, by Lexington out of Bay Leaf, trained by William Hayward, won the Dinner Party Stake at Pimlico in 1870 and gave his name to a race that is still famous. Preakness was named for the town in New Jersey where the Sanford stables were situated. King borrowed the Sanford name for the heroine of *Marion's Faith*, though he

only hinted that Marion Sanford might be connected to the family
of Preakness fame.

During the New Orleans racing season of 1872 there appeared
Captain George Rosenlecher of France and the Count de Cren-
neville, aide-de-camp of the Austrian emperor, who issued a challenge for an international race to be run on Ladies' Day, April 9. A
Mr. Stuart, formerly of the British Hussars, was ready to ride for
England, and a Mr. Ross, once of the Inniskilling Dragoons, for
Ireland. Paul O. Hebert, former brigadier general of the Confederacy and now president of the Jockey Club, and General
Westmore picked Charles King to ride for the United States. He
demurred; he was too heavy. Moreover, the jockey's silks, white
cord breeches, and fourteen-ounce top boots that would be demanded for the race cost a lot of money. But General Emory said,
"It is your duty, sir, to ride for the regiment," and the matter was
settled. After three weeks' training King's weight was somewhat
reduced, perhaps because he rose each morning at 3:30 and
walked six miles to the track.[5]

The day of the race dawned bright and fair, as it always did in
horse-race melodramas, and of course all the beauty and chivalry
of the Old South were in the stands, as was to be expected on such
an occasion—more the precursor, perhaps, of the modern Olym-
pic games than of the present-day overcommercialized "sport of
kings." We know that among the entries were a Kentucky filly,
Rapidita, that had been clocked at 1:53, and General Buford's
Kentucky four-year-old, Nathan Oaks, which had won the two
one-mile heats the day before. Both these horses had beaten
Templo, the Natchez-bred five-year-old that King rode. Southern
belles, in courtesy to their guests, wore the colors of France and
Austria, and many wore cerise and blue for England or green for
Ireland. But only two wore the blue and white of Columbia Col-
lege for King. One of them, of course, was Mrs. Emory.

Even the smaller details of this race of one mile and eighty
yards have come down to us. As the drum tapped and the flag fell,
Stuart was seen to take the lead at the pole, and Templo, with
King up, was in the center, close to the flank of the leader. At the
turn King took the lead, and all five rode beautifully bunched to
the backstretch. There de Crenneville plied whip and spur to dash
out in front and take the pole. But it was a spurt, and at the turn
into the homestretch the Austrian rode so close to the fence that
he struck it with his knee and knocked off the pad he carried to

make up three pounds weight handicap. The loss of the handicap weight was of no advantage, for now King gave the word and loosened the reins. Templo's stride lengthened. He easily passed the leader and finished two lengths ahead of Ross, whose Nathan Oaks made a tremendous effort to be in at the finish. The others were left a half-dozen lengths behind.

There is no mention of a horseshoe wreath of flowers, but the prize awarded was a gold-mounted whip, and "in less than five minutes" it was resting in the lap of the other wearer of the blue and white, Adelaide Lavender Yorke, daughter of Captain Lewis S. Yorke of Carroll Parish, Louisiana. Captain Yorke had commanded a famous merchantman, the *Globe*, on which he had made the passage of the straights of La Maire, and he had been a widely known seaman before being commissioned acting assistant paymaster in the United States Navy in 1862, where he served until the close of the war. A brother of Adelaide's had served through the Civil War and risen to the rank of lieutenant colonel and brevet colonel in a New Jersey cavalry regiment. A younger brother later followed in his father's footsteps in the navy, serving as assistant paymaster from 1869 to 1887 and also during the Spanish-American War. The family settled in Louisiana after the Civil War, and the elder brother at one time served in the legislature.[6]

These details are given largely because General King, forever after, has little to say about Adelaide. He does mention that within a year the prize whip came back to him, with its owner. They were married in November 1872. But after a year of happy married life—and their entire married life down to her death in 1928 seems to have been ideally happy—he was forced to leave Adelaide and their infant daughter in Louisiana while he went to join his regiment, then in the field against hostile Apaches.[7]

The Way of the West

To be "an officer and a gentleman" has always involved something beyond the call of duty, and in the stirring days of the Indian Wars it meant a little more than it does now. Its code was much nearer that of chivalry than anything that has survived the mud and blood of twentieth-century warfare. Even the *code duello* was not extinct in the 1870s. In more recent times officers serve a tour of duty on the staff and then one with troops, and that is that. But when staff officers were detailed temporarily from troops, leaving companies woefully short of commissioned leaders, contempt was unhesitatingly expressed for one who would use political or family pressure to get an assignment to some center of pleasant social activity while his regiment was in pursuit of Apaches or Sioux.

The staff duties Lieutenant King performed in New Orleans would hardly classify him as a slacker. Being selected as aide by his own regimental commander was a recognition of his soldierly qualities and an honor much to be desired. When he accepted the detail, Indian warfare had ceased in the valley of the Platte, and there was likely to be more risk and danger in mob-ruled New Orleans than on the plains. But as soon as King learned that the Fifth Cavalry had been ordered to the Arizona Territory and had begun active campaigning under General George Crook, he began to fuss and fidget until he succeeded in getting himself relieved and was actually en route to his regiment at Camp Verde, a post he fittingly dubbed for later fictional purposes "Camp Sandy."[1]

Railroads had crossed the continent in 1869, but not a single funnel-stacked wood-burning locomotive had turned a driver wheel in Arizona by 1874, nor had a single mile of track been laid in that territory. The Southern Pacific made its advent in 1877. Meanwhile, an army officer ordered to the Southwest from New Orleans went by transcontinental rail to San Francisco, then took a steamer around Lower California to the head of the Gulf of California, where he transferred to either the *Colorado*, the *Cocopah*, or the *Mohave*, the palatial and sometimes reliable steamers of George A. Johnston and Company. He then proceeded up the Colorado River, past Fort Yuma to Ehrenberg, where he found some form of land transportation to Prescott and Camp Verde. A mail route went part of the way, so there was a stagecoach, but King made the last leg of the journey in a buckboard, a common frontier wagon. Had this not been available he probably would have thumbed a ride in an army ambulance, which was used on many semiofficial occasions as well as for conveying the wounded, and which was much more comfortable for an able-bodied officer than for the victim of an Apache fight.[2]

Arriving at Camp Verde, King found to his regret that the present Indian war seemed at a standstill. But if he was disappointed, it was a needless worry. Many years would pass before hostilities with the Apaches were finally ended. These people were perpetually quarreling among themselves and were particularly hostile toward invading whites, though according to rumor and tradition the Apaches themselves were invaders, warring against the somewhat more peaceful Navajos, the Pueblo tribes, and other natives.

There are atrocity stories aplenty concerning the Apache wars, and frontiersmen found few traits to admire in these desert nomads. The warrior of the plains country recklessly rode his pony within shooting distance when opportunity offered and was usually ready to put up a fight. Apaches liked to make killing a sure thing. Adept in the use of natural cover, they never attacked except when the odds were overwhelmingly in their favor. Their habitations were so secret or so temporary that troops seldom found their foes. The Arizona Indians made their presence known by assaults on isolated settlers, on exposed sentries, or on stragglers, messengers, and detached soldiers. The Apaches perpetrated ingeniously horrible tortures on their captives, exceeding the Indians of the forests and plains in these inhumanities. And they were not romantic to look at wearing little finery, perhaps only a rag around the head and another around the middle.

Yet Charles King, and many other soldiers who fought against Apaches, found much good in these uncivilized foes. In *Tonio, Son of the Sierras*, King produced a James Fenimore Cooper type of Indian hero as an Apache-Mohave, and his *An Apache Princess* is sympathetically and realistically portrayed despite the extravagantly romantic plot. Some army officers took advantage of the Apaches' intertribal warfare to enlist them as scouts, though often with indifferent success. Others agreed with Major General E. O. C. Ord, an early departmental commander in Arizona, that the only logical policy was annihilation.

But this was not the idea of George Crook, who commanded in Arizona when Charles King arrived. Crook's sympathy toward Indians was not exceeded by that of the pious General Oliver O. Howard. Not even General Hugh L. Scott of a later day better understood the Indian nature. Nor was Colonel Nelson A. Miles more relentless in waging war against them when war had to be waged. As a lieutenant with Phil Sheridan, Crook had first come to notice in warfare against the Indians of Oregon and Washington before the Civil War. He had been a brigade and division commander under Sheridan in the Virginia campaigns and was remembered for suppressing guerrilla bands in the Shenandoah Valley. After the war he reverted to the rank of lieutenant colonel, but he was conspicuously successful against the Snakes, Bannocks, and Paiutes of the northwest and so was jumped over the heads of many colonels and given command in Arizona in his brevet rank of major general.

King tells how company commanders of the Fifth Cavalry "gathered, as they supposed, to receive final instructions before starting out on the campaign, and were quietly told that they would 'get them as we went along.'"[3] Crook took the field himself in 1872 and 1873 and rounded up most of the Apache bands after twenty-three fights. His rugged honesty won respect from his enemy, who soon came to know that his promises were always solemnly kept. He was known to them by a number of names. King mentions Hyas-tyee, Chinook for "Big Chief," and many times uses the term "Gray Fox," though he admitted to somewhat overdoing it.[4] He describes the general as "of iron frame, of almost superhuman endurance, shunning no exposure, dreading neither peril nor privation" and recounts that Crook "could ride from dawn to dawn without apparent fatigue, and dismount only because his horse or his followers could go no further. While they slept he would take rifle and hunt for game. Temperate to the verge of abstinence, he shunned even tea, coffee and tobacco. 'They spoiled the nerve,' he said, and would touch nothing that could impair his wonderful prowess as a shot." He outdid Taylor and Grant in his disregard for the regulation uniform, preferring a worn and patched old hunting suit. King knew Crook, at times intimately, for sixteen years, and records that he never saw the general in the proper uniform of his rank until he "lay garbed for the grave."[5]

It was under such a commanding general that King began his service in the Indian Wars. Crook's simplicity of dress was quickly copied by his followers, and when the young lieutenant turned out for his first scout with Company K he was inclined to think his men were trying to "put up a joke on him" when he found them lined up with hardly a single article of uniform equipment on or about them. The army-issue campaign hat, a wide-brimmed black felt, was almost universally discarded as unsuitable to the Arizona climate. Only two men were wearing the regulation carbine sling. Holsters were of every pattern and description except the type designed by the ordnance department. Moccasins and buckskin pants were favored, and it was the new young officer, in regulation uniform even to the saber, who was out of place in such a gathering. After some chaffing remarks from brother officers that the saber had proved too long and clumsy for a scalping knife, King decided to discard that article of equipment except for ceremonial purposes. But he could never bring himself to emulate General Crook's contempt for the uniform prescribed by army regulations.

This first expedition in which King participated was sent out to search for three hostile Tonto rancherias or villages reported by Apache-Yuma and Apache-Mohave scouts. One of these in the Mogollon Mountains was that of a band led by Eskeltsetle, or 'Skeltetsee. Additional information next sent the expedition against the band of Eskiminzin at Diamond Butte in the Black Mesa. The name Eskiminzin, or 'Skiminzin, was famous in Apache annals; a chief of that name, possibly the same man, was said to have kidnapped the beautiful Inez Gonzales, whose rescue by an American boundary commissioner shortly after the Mexican War was a favorite story in the Southwest. The Black Mesa, where Eskiminzin lurked, is shown on the maps of the period as running diagonally northwest and southeast between Camp Verde and the Mogollons. Unfortunately the name has since been attached to a spur known then as the Black Hills, directly south of Camp Verde, which is a bit confusing. Diamond Butte is south of the Black Mesa and the Mogollon range.

On the night of June 2, 1874, the troopers of the Fifth Cavalry scaled Diamond Butte and found their quarry, the Apache rancheria, in a cleft between two sharp ridges far up the mountainside. They decided to wait for dawn, and meanwhile the men were deployed so as to block the entrance to the rancheria that the troops had discovered in their ascent, though the "front door" to the stronghold was found to be at the other side of the mountain and could not be reached without detouring down the butte and up the opposite slope. It was too late to do this. As silently as any Indian, the troopers moved to their positions—canteens, cups, or anything that would rattle had been left behind—and as patiently as Apaches they awaited the signal for action. Just at dawn it came; an Indian left the camp, probably to gather firewood, and walked directly into the ambush. Quickly he was seized and made prisoner, but not silently, for there was a scuffle and a carbine was discharged. With this the troopers rushed in to do what they could. There followed fifteen minutes' sharp work with pistol and carbine; fifteen Indians were killed, three women and some children were taken prisoner, and the rancheria with all its supplies was captured. Two troopers were killed. Unfortunately Eskiminzin and most of his 150 warriors escaped. The expedition pursued them and, in a second action, punished this band so severely that it no longer was a menace.

In 1894 a bill was presented to Congress to grant a number of brevet commissions, for which recommendations had accumulated over many years since the Civil War. Included was one that Charles King be made captain for gallant and distinguished service at Diamond Butte. As he was already a captain, he declined the brevet of the same rank on the grounds that it was "of no value and brought no additional honor." Several other officers took the same stand at that time.[6]

This action at Diamond Butte was typical of the campaign General Crook had been carrying on since November 15, 1872. Small expeditions were sent out to harry the Apaches on every occasion. Notable among these raids was the virtual annihilation of one band of Indians at the Cave on Salt River, where seventy-six Apache-Mohaves were killed, eighteen women and children were captured, and only six or seven women and one man escaped the trap set by three companies of the Fifth Cavalry and Indian scouts under Captain William H. Brown. Another band of Apaches perpetrated the gruesome killing of a small party of emigrants at

Wickenburg and were trailed to the summit of Turret Butte by troops under Captain George M. Randall of the Twenty-third U.S. Infantry. These two actions, according to Captain John G. Bourke in *On the Border with Crook*, broke the Apaches' spirit, and under the leadership of Cha-lipun a number of bands surrendered to General Crook at Camp Verde on April 6, 1873, which was why the fighting seemed to be over when King arrived.[7]

General Crook lost no time in putting the Apaches to work, for he believed that even the wild wanderers of the southwestern deserts could be taught to become producers instead of destroyers. A tract near Camp Verde was set aside for their use. An irrigation ditch was dug under the direction of Captain and Brevet Colonel Julius W. Mason and Second Lieutenant Walter S. Schuyler of the Fifth Cavalry. Some thirty-seven acres were planted in melons and other produce, and the Apaches found it surprising that something edible should appear as the result of a new and strange form of exercise. Captain Bourke gives the cost to the government of this experiment as about thirty-six dollars, which was a bargain considering that these Indians would soon become self-supporting and that they were being withheld from destruction of property worth considerably more. But there were certain persons in Arizona at that time who found this procedure little to their interest, since their business consisted of supplying food to Indians on reservations. Contractors and civilian officials who looked with contempt on experiments in Indian education combined to represent the Camp Verde project in an unfavorable light. Unfortunately, the army of the frontier lacked a lobby and publicity service.

Sunset Pass

Lieutenant King looked up from his mapping board in annoyance and took up his field glasses again. A faint shadow of movement had caught his eye, a very slight disturbance in the topography of Camp Verde that he was trying to set down on paper. He did not so much see as feel that something was wrong with the landscape. Now as he looked through the glasses he indeed saw black specks moving across the countryside, distinguishable to a trained eye as horses. The apparent movement was slow; actually he knew it was very fast. Something must be wrong!

As he watched it became evident that four mounted men were approaching from the direction of the Indian agency where Lieutenant Schuyler was still carrying on his agricultural experiments. The lieutenant gathered up his board and drawing materials, untethered his horse, mounted, and rode toward the messengers. Could it be that the Indian wards had revolted? That Schuyler was in trouble? It seemed an interminable time, but at length the riders came within hail.

"Trouble?" "Trouble enough," they explained. They were herders from the agency. A band of Tontos had just swooped down from the Red Rock country and driven off a herd of cattle that had just arrived for the use of the Apache wards there. King rode in with the men to report the affair to Captain Mason, the Camp Verde commander.

"Ride at once to the agency," the captain ordered. "Find out all you can about the raid and see if Lieutenant Schuyler can let you have twenty Indian scouts who are good trailers. We'll see if we can run this band down before they get out of the country."

"May I go on the expedition?" implored King, who as acting post adjutant was ordinarily not available for detail with a detachment.

"Yes, if you wish. Get good scouts if there are any."

King rode off on the twenty-mile trip, and meanwhile the expedition was hastily organized. The post was garrisoned by Companies A and K of the Fifth Cavalry and two companies of the Eighth U.S. Infantry, but only one other cavalry officer besides King was available at the time—George Oscar Eaton, a second lieutenant, recently assigned, who was acting as commissary. Eaton was eager to go too, so he was given the assignment.

Although a West Point graduate of the previous year, 1873, Eaton was a veteran of the Civil War. He had enlisted in the Fifteenth Maine Infantry at the age of thirteen in time to take part in the closing campaign of spring 1865. After serving for some time in the army after the war, he received appointment to the Military Academy from James G. Blaine, eminent Republican leader. Lieutenant Eaton had joined the regiment the preceding December.

Twenty men from the two cavalry companies were chosen for the expedition, and everything was in readiness when King returned with the Indian scouts. The scouts, Apache-Yumas, were not entirely satisfactory—at least they were unproved—but were the only ones immediately available at the agency. The Apache-Mohaves used in previous expeditions had been able scouts, but unfortunately they had scattered to their camps far from agency headquarters. The Apache-Yumas seemed none too eager even before the expedition got under way, and they were very slow in returning to the post.

At dawn the little command forded the Verde River and moved up Beaver Creek. By nightfall of the day following the raid it was climbing the steep slopes of the Mogollon Rim. A smoke signal was seen, evidence that the band was not far away, but also an indication that the pursuers had been discovered. From then on they climbed by night and hid by day, pressing on relentlessly in pursuit of the Tontos, who were impeded by the stolen herd.

On the fourth evening, October 31, King's party saw signs that the band was not far distant. Without calling the usual halts for rest, they pushed on until after dark, when they caught sight of the Tontos and the herd near Snow Lake, on the divide of the Mogollons. The alert Tontos had also seen their pursuers and were already driving off the stolen herd. No time was to be lost. With a shout the twenty troopers and their two officers charged, firing pistols and carbines. The Tontos did not wait to receive them; abandoning the herd, they fled with the soldiers galloping in hot pursuit. But the Indians had too great a start, and in the darkness the troopers' fire was ineffective. King, seeing that the chase was hopeless, recalled his men. The Indian scouts had not been overeager to get at their ancient enemies, but the cattle, which were really theirs, interested them, and they had performed the useful though not heroic duty of rounding up the herd by the time the detachment returned to the scene. Four or five troopers and as many Indians were detailed to escort the herd back to the agency.

When King prepared to resume the chase, he found that the herd guard had become much larger than intended. Only a half-dozen of the Apache-Yuma scouts could be found to pursue of the outlaw Apaches. The rest had disappeared and probably had joined the party guarding the cattle. Those left displayed no great enthusiasm for meeting the Tontos. As the march was resumed at about 10:00 P.M., the Indians hung about the rear of the column and absolutely refused to go to either the front or the flanks to look for signs of the fleeing Tontos.

The expedition, however, pushed on for twenty miles, halting at 2:00 A.M. at Sunset Pass, where the Colorado Chiquito (also known as Jack's Canyon and Sunset Creek) goes between two high peaks. There camp was made until daybreak. As soon as it was light King turned out his scouts to look for the trail. The Indians said they could find no "sign" and insisted that the Tontos must have doubled back to Snow Lake.

"Nonsense!" exclaimed an old trooper. "Look there." He pointed to the bed of the stream, where moccasin tracks, undoubtedly made by the Tontos, were plainly visible. Eagerly the soldiers followed the trail. It ran along the edge of the stream, then turned away and led up the side of the mountain to the south.

"Like as not they're watching us from up there right now, Lieutenant," one of the soldiers suggested to King.

"All right! We'll go get them. Dismount!"

A small guard was left with the horses and pack mules. The soldiers, on foot, started the steep climb. The Yuma scouts huddled in the rear, but King drove them out in front and insisted they find the trail.

"No Tonto! No Tonto!" they insisted in terrified accents, but their fear made it evident that they had found signs of the enemy. The troopers soon pushed ahead, but King halted them, again driving his useless allies out in front. They could not be kept there. The troopers pushed on for half an hour through the timber until they came to a point where the trees stopped and they could see much of the face of the mountain ahead of them. Here the expedition halted while the two officers, together with Sergeant Bernard Taylor of Company A and Apache-Yuma scouts, made a quick reconnaissance. They found that the slope became steeper and steeper and that the mountain was covered with low, tangled shrubbery until near the top, where a vertical cliff of jagged rocks stretched right and left as far as one could see. Lieutenant Eaton, over protest, was ordered to return to the command at the edge of the timber, ready to come on at a signal, while King proposed to drive the Indian scouts ahead of him and rout out the Tontos he was sure were at the top of the mountain. King and Sergeant Taylor were soon out of sight of the command, and as usual the Indian scouts also were quickly lost from view, hiding out at every opportunity and attempting to drop back to the rear. King finally lost patience after nearly fifteen minutes of trying to push them on, and he went ahead with the sergeant, leaving the unwilling scouts to come on at their own pace, if at all. In another quarter of an hour he reached the ledge but found nothing.

King directed Sergeant Taylor to look toward the right for a path to the summit, and he signaled his scouts, now about fifty yards behind, to come on. He was about to move to the left when a Tonto arrow whizzed past his head and stuck quivering in a stunted oak. Almost as King watched it strike, a second arrow, better aimed, tore through the flesh and muscles at the outer corner of his left eye. He sprang for the edge of the shelf and crouched behind a rock just as two rifle shots were fired at him. He shouted for the Apache-Yumas to come on, but they had turned tail at the sound of the guns and fled down the mountainside.

King had a carbine, and he looked eagerly for a chance to use it. The whiz of another arrow drew his eyes to the left, and despite the blood streaming down his face, he was able to fire and hit one of the two Tontos he saw among the rocks. But as he started to reload there was a scattered volley from the hostiles. His carbine dropped to the ground and his right arm hung useless, shattered at the shoulder by a rifle bullet. There was nothing left to do but run in the hope that he could reach his men before the Tontos reached him.

King leaped from rock to rock, supporting his helpless arm with his left hand, but had gone only a few yards when his foot slipped

and, unable to catch himself, he tumbled eight or ten feet, cutting a jagged gash in his forehead. Blood rained down in his eyes and blinded him. He staggered on a few more steps but fell again, and now he felt he could not go on. He groped for his revolver but found the holster empty; the weapon probably had dropped out in his first tumble. Disarmed and helpless, he saw nothing to do but await his fate.

But King had forgotten Sergeant Taylor. Now he heard the sergeant calling his name, and he made a feeble response. Taylor heard King and came running up. It took him but a moment to see that the lieutenant was out of action and a few seconds more to swing King over his shoulder and start bounding down the mountainside. Closely pursued by the Tontos, he stopped, laid the officer down, and sent shot after shot up the hill. A tall Tonto dropped from a rock, and the pursuers were discouraged. Again Taylor picked up the officer and went dashing on, but as soon as he moved there was a shout from the Tontos, and these swift desert runners were close upon him again. Once more he stopped, put down his burden, and opened fire. Again he hit an Indian. Quickly hoisting King to his back, he ran on. The lieutenant's dangling arm gave him terrible pain, and he felt he could stand no more. He begged—ordered—Taylor to put him down, leave him, save himself, but the stout sergeant paid no heed.

Meanwhile, Lieutenant Eaton had not been idle. At the first sound of firing he spread his men into a skirmish line and dashed up the mountainside to the rescue. Skillfully the young officer took charge of the battle, ignoring the terrified Apache-Yuma scouts who came rushing through his lines. Just as Sergeant Taylor gave out after a three-hundred-yard run carrying the wounded officer, the troops appeared below them. In a few moments Eaton and his command covered the intervening space, and the two officers were united. King, still conscious, urged Eaton to push on, and the battle was continued. In ten minutes the Tontos had been driven back up the mountainside, scurrying for cover, and their dead and wounded were captured.[1]

King was made as comfortable as possible while a courier was sent to Camp Verde for assistance. Acting Assistant Surgeon Warren E. Day left immediately with an escort of nine cavalrymen and an ambulance. The shortest route was that taken by the troops, a journey of several days. He reached the head of Beaver

Creek the first night, but the next morning he struck a snowstorm in the Mogollons. In a letter written several years later, Day described his difficulties vividly:

Reached Pine Springs the second night and the snow was then three or or feet deep. It was so cold the ambulance driver was badly frozen and I had to drive the ambulance myself. I had nine men. The animals were put into a corral that night. About four o'clock the next morning the men came and woke me and said the mules had all got out and wanted to know what to do. There was one horse that did not get away. I took that horse the next morning and with my instruments in my hands rode on to Captain King, a distance of twenty-two miles.

I found King lying in his blankets badly shot with a compound fracture of the right arm between the elbow and the shoulder. Of course under ordinary circumstances it was an injury that would require amputation. Before I could get off my horse and could get to work King held up his left arm and said, "This is all right; if you want to take that off, take it first."

I told him he would do as I said. I would try and save the arm. I made a mule litter and packed him from Sunset Pass to Verde and took care of him in my quarters for about two months. We made the litter of poles and blankets and canvas and used the pack mules to carry him. We first tried to make a travois but found that would not work so we slung him between two mules. There was a wagon road all the way to Verde and I think we were about three days on the trip. It was in the neighborhood of one hundred miles from where he was shot to my headquarters.

My instructions to him were to drink a gallon of whiskey a day and remain in my quarters. If he had not had a good constitution and a good deal of courage and been a man of good sense we could not have done what we did. After his recovery he had a fairly useful arm.[2]

The mule litter, King later explained, was made by lashing two mules fore and aft between two saplings about fifteen to twenty feet long. The intervening space was crudely but comfortably upholstered with robes and blankets and "therein the invalid might ride for hours as smoothly as in a palace car."[3] In fact, he

says of his journey, "I never enjoyed easier locomotion—so long
as the mules behaved." With the travois only one mule was used. Two poles about twelve feet long, with one end of each dragging on the ground, formed an improvised ambulance that was even less comfortable than when the mules did not "behave."

After his two months' heroic treatment, King was given sick leave until September 1875. But the arm was a long time healing—for eight years an open, suppurating wound remained, discharging pieces of shattered bone and proving a continuous trouble. It was never entirely cured.

Sergeant Taylor was awarded the prestigious Medal of Honor for his courageous exploit in rescuing King, one of a small number given for action in the Indian Wars. When King left Camp Verde on sick leave he probably had little idea that he would never see his rescuer again, but the sergeant died at that post a few months later. Corporal Bryan Smith and Private Frank Biffer were named in orders for conspicuous bravery at Sunset Pass.

The other hero of the affair, Lieutenant Eaton, deserved great credit for his handling of a difficult situation on his first expedition, but his only military reward seems to have been assignment to command a second expedition against the same band of hostile Apaches. With twenty men from Companies A and K he was gone from November 17 to December 5 on what is recorded as the Snow Lake or Jarvis Pass expedition. Snow Lake does not appear on many contemporary or modern maps and may be the one now known as Hay Lake. Jarvis very probably is army Spanish for Chavez Pass in the Mogollons. "Eaton's Scout," as it was commonly known, resulted in two engagements with the Tontos, on November 25 and December 5. In the second of these three warriors were killed and several women and children were captured. Twice Eaton was nominated for a brevet as first lieutenant for gallant and distinguished conduct on this scout, but both times confirmation failed because the United States Senate adjourned, a common fate for such recommendations in those days, having no bearing whatever on their worth.

King later founded the character of Jack Truscott, hero of *The Colonel's Daughter* and a figure in several other novels, on Lieutenant Eaton, and during this year that young officer almost exceeded his fictional prototype in deeds of derring-do.[4] It was only a short time after these events that Eaton sought diversion by riding the forty miles from Camp Verde to Fort Whipple, near

Prescott. If Eaton was in search of adventure, he had come to the right place. An outbreak in the direction of the San Francisco Mountains had called off virtually all the troops from the post, and General Crook was anxious to send a message northwest to Camp Beale Springs, though he knew the road was blocked by hostile Indians. Eaton immediately volunteered to take the message without escort, explaining that he had noticed the road went a long way around and that he proposed to try a beeline route.

At daylight next morning Eaton started out with a Winchester rifle, a belt full of cartridges, a canteen of water, and a not-so-fresh horse. He soon learned why the road went the long way, and he met with a minor adventure characteristic of the period. The shortcut he was exploring crossed a succession of box canyons—three-hundred-foot-deep cracks through glasslike lava. As he came to each of these he was forced to hunt for a pathway to its bottom and then find a way up the steep opposite side. It was slow, hot work, and his canteen soon became very light. As he attempted to ration the remaining water, the distant buttes appeared to dance in lively fashion. He found a spring before his thirst became desperate.

He drank his fill, replenished his canteen, and started on, cheered that he seemed to have traversed the worst of his journey, but he had not gone far when he saw a party of five Indians at a distance. For a short time they only looked at him, but then, without warning, one raised a rifle and fired a shot that came close to Eaton's head. The lieutenant had his rifle lying in the hollow of his left arm, and without stopping to shift it he fired in the general direction of the group and had the satisfaction of seeing one of the Indians fall, to be dragged away by his companions. Eaton did not wait to see more; he spurred away and after a short gallop reached Camp Beale Springs. Its beleaguered garrison, knowing all the trails were blocked, was much surprised at the arrival of this unexpected messenger of aid.

Eaton's daring exploits continued into 1875, but in March of that year General Crook was relieved of command in Arizona and ordered to the Department of the Platte on the northern plains, being succeeded by General August V. Kautz. In May the Fifth Cavalry was ordered to the Department of Missouri on the central plains. In all these changes the closing operations were overlooked, and King and Eaton received little recognition for their considerable achievements.

Foes in Ambush

Service at the Kansas posts in 1875 seemed idyllic to survivors of the Fifth Cavalry. The sole summer expedition for that year was a small skirmish between a detachment from Company H and Indians along the Smoky Hill River. There was little intimation of the storm about to break upon the army, marking the nation's centennial year as the bloodiest in the annals of Indian warfare in the West. In King's later novels this year in Kansas marks the beginning or the end of love affairs. One gets an impression of dreamy afternoons and evenings, of dress parades, bands, and dances.

Lieutenant King returned from a long sick leave in September. His wound was not entirely healed—it never was—but he felt well enough that he thought he could resume duty. In fact, he managed to endure the hardships of several severe campaigns.

The regiment was typically under strength and widely scattered. Commanded by its lieutenant colonel, Brevet Major General Eugene A. Carr, its muster rolls showed a total of 783 names, including 172 recruits on the way. Headquarters was at Fort Hays, Kansas, where there were stationed the noncommissioned staff and band numbering 22; Company A, Captain Calbraith P. Rodgers, 45 men; the gray horse company, B, Captain Robert H. Montgomery, 41 men; Company D, commanded by Captain and Brevet Major Samuel S. Sumner, 56 men; and Company E, Captain George F. Price, 50 men.

King's Company K was at Fort Riley, Kansas. Its commander was the senior captain of the regiment, Brevet Lieutenant Colonel Julius W. Mason, and its strength was 53. Company C, the black horse troop, was at Camp Supply, Indian Territory, and its 50 men, who were largely Irish, were commanded by an old German soldier, Captain Emil Adam. At the same station was Company G, Captain Edward M. Hayes, 41 men. Company F, Captain

J. Scott Payne, 56 men, was at Fort Dodge, Kansas. Company H, Captain J. M. Hamilton, 46 men, was at Fort Wallace, Kansas. Company I was in Indian Territory, at Fort Gibson, under Captain and Brevet Lieutenant Colonel Sanford C. Kellogg, with a strength of 54. Company L, Captain A. B. Taylor, 52 men, and Company M, Captain and Brevet Lieutenant Colonel Edward H. Lieb, 45 men, were at Fort Lyon, Colorado.[1]

This statistical information may give some impression of the makeup and distribution of a cavalry regiment in the period of its greatest usefulness in the warfare on the plains. At that time cavalry was far from being the military luxury it was later considered, for the infantry seldom could find Indians to fight and was more useful in garrison than "pursuing and punishing." Even the cavalry had to add strategy to its speed to bring the Plains Indians to action. King, with all his admiration for the United States cavalry, particularly its Fifth Regiment, freely admits that "as light cavalry . . . the Sioux and Cheyenne Indians of our northern plains . . . are unequalled anywhere," an opinion echoed by such competent contemporary critics as Captain John G. Bourke and Captain Arthur L. Wagner.[2]

The Great Sioux War of 1876–77 was the concern largely of the Teton Sioux, whose "seven council fires" were those of the Oglalas, Hunkpapas, Sans Arcs, Minneconjous, Brules, Two Kettles, and Blackfoot Sioux. They were joined by other tribes, principally the Northern Cheyennes, Southern Cheyennes, and Arapahos, with smaller numbers of Yanktonai and Santee Sioux.

About the immediate causes of the war, the Indians seem to have somewhat the best of the argument. The confirmation of gold in the Black Hills by an exploring expedition headed by Lieutenant Colonel and Brevet Major General George A. Custer resulted in a stampede to an Indian-held El Dorado that by solemn treaty had no right to exist. The government seemed powerless to stop the gold rush and, following the usual policy of the period, attempted to buy out the Sioux.[3]

While not slighting legitimate Indian grievances, Charles King's writings recalled the army side of the conflict. King was not unfriendly to the Indians, but he notes that warfare was in their nature and that Indians were not pacifists. When cornered, a warrior merely surrendered and became "the recipient of more attention and higher living than he had ever dreamed of until he tried it." There existed friends of the Indians even in those days, particularly in the East, where well-meaning people had long

since forgotten the conduct of their own ancestors in a remote period when America's natives had been more of a menace than a "problem." So the Indians would be fed, clothed, and supplied with ample arms and ammunition during the winter—supplied, in fact, with repeating rifles thought widely but incorrectly to be superior to the armament of the troops. The weapons were meant for hunting buffalo, of course, but the Indians were ready to carry on a lively war as soon as the grass was green.

At times it seemed that this war was a controversy between the nation's War Department and Interior Department, which explains why the worst thing King could think of to say about an incompetent cavalry officer was, "He's as innocent and unsuspicious and incapable of appreciating Indian wiles as the average Secretary of the Interior." King barely exaggerates on this point. General Crook, no trouble seeker, said as much in his official congratulatory order issued at the close of the 1876 Big Horn and Yellowstone campaign:

> Indian warfare is, of all warfare, the most dangerous, the most trying, and the most thankless. Not recognized by the high authority of the United States Senate as war, it still possesses for you all the disadvantages of civilized warfare, with all the horrible accompaniments that barbarians can invent and savages execute. In it you are required to serve without the incentive to promotion or recognition; in truth without favor or hope of reward.
>
> The people of our sparsely settled frontier, in whose defense this war is waged, have but little influence with the powerful communities in the East; their representatives have little voice in the national councils, while your savage foes are not only the wards of the nation, supported in idleness, but objects of sympathy with large numbers of people otherwise well-informed and discerning.[4]

Nor was it realized then by their "friends" that Indians enjoyed fighting. Sitting Bull and Crazy Horse sent contemptuous answers to an early request that they come to Nebraska's Red Cloud Agency to discuss ceding the Black Hills. In March 1876 General Crook directed an expedition against a camp believed to belong to Crazy Horse, under the immediate command of Joseph J. Reynolds, colonel of the Third U.S. Cavalry and brevet major general, who led five companies of his own regiment and five of the Second U.S. Cavalry. The colonel's weathered reputation was by no means improved by his lackluster conduct in the fight. In fact Reynolds soon found it expedient to apply for transfer to the army's retired list. The Sioux and their allies, the Cheyennes, were much encouraged.

The unfortunate end of the Powder River affair, where the Indian village was captured but then given up with considerable loss to the troops, made it necessary for Crook to assemble nearly everything he could find in his Department of the Platte for a second expedition. This attempt involved fifteen companies of cavalry and five of infantry, representing the Second and Third Cavalry regiments and the Fourth and Ninth Infantry regiments, along with a number of Crow and Shoshone scouts. The Shoshones, incidentally, were described by Captain Bourke as putting on a perfect and well-practiced cavalry drill under their chief Washakie.[5]

At the same time two other expeditions moved against the Sioux. From western Montana came Brevet Major General John Gibbon, the same officer who commanded the "Iron Brigade" in the Civil War. And from Minnesota and Dakota Territory came Brigadier General Alfred H. Terry, hero of the assault on Fort Fisher during the Civil War. It had been intended to give command of this column to George Custer, but that officer had incurred President Grant's displeasure by appearing prominently in the investigation of irregularities of William W. Belknap, secretary of war, who later resigned. Custer had not improved matters by returning to his command without authority, but Grant had finally consented to allow him to go on the expedition, though only in command of the Seventh U.S. Cavalry.

Terry's column left Fort Abraham Lincoln, Dakota Territory, on May 17. Gibbon's column had been in the field since March; it arrived at the mouth of the Rosebud on the Yellowstone River May 28 and there was joined by Terry. Crook's second expedition started May 26. Terry, ever generous in the finer points of military rank, divided his combined forces between Gibbon and Custer after the two columns united. Custer perhaps had in mind the spirit of the orders withdrawing him from general command when he retained only twelve companies of his own regiment and rejected the "Montana Battalion," comprising Companies F, G, H, and L, Second Cavalry, and the three Gatling guns manned by

soldiers from the Twentieth U.S. Infantry, which Terry had
wanted to add to his column. Instead this force went to Gibbon, who retained the six companies of his own Seventh U.S. Infantry and received six companies of the Seventeenth U.S. Infantry. Terry accompanied the Gibbon column.

King records that Brigadier General John Pope, commanding the Department of Missouri, had won the hearts of the ladies of the Fifth Cavalry that spring by predicting that there would be no campaign during 1876, which goes to prove that Pope's ability to estimate a situation had not improved much since Second Bull Run. When King's Company K found itself transported by railroad from Fort Riley to Fort Hays in early June it lost faith in General Pope's prediction. Troops were not moved by railroad in those days unless they were needed someplace in a hurry.

King himself had been hunting stampeded horses along the valley of the Saline and reported to Lieutenant Colonel Carr, then commanding the regiment, at Fort Hays. Carr had just expressed his belief that Crook would mount a big campaign and that the Fifth would be needed when a messenger rode up with dispatches. King describes the scene as officers and men watched Carr read three pages without comment. They dared not ask questions, though they knew something was up despite Carr's matter-of-fact air. But even the thoroughly military Carr could not resist saying to King, "Well, what did I tell you?" Orders had arrived to take the field.

Company E was ordered to remain in garrison, while A, B, D, and K were sent by railroad through Denver to Cheyenne. At Cheyenne Major John J. Upham joined them with Company I, and in a week the five companies were off for famous old Fort Laramie, a landmark established by mountain men long before the army guarded the overland trail. Life at this post after the cavalry left in 1876 furnished Charles King with inspiration for one of his earliest and finest stories, *Laramie; or, The Queen of Bedlam*. The crazy structure known as Bedlam, still a landmark in Wyoming, was the bachelor officers' quarters, so called because of the "bedlam" that traditionally went on in such an abode. During the 1876 campaign officers at Laramie were few and officers' wives and families many, so Bedlam was temporarily invaded by femininity and could have a "queen."

It was at this stage in the summer war that Crook's column fought a major action, the battle of the Rosebud, on June 17. Here

Crazy Horse, with a considerable force of Sioux, attempted to lay a trap; but from a perch overlooking the scene Crook tended battle lines that stretched for miles along Rosebud Creek, and his troops successfully parried several Sioux onslaughts. For a few minutes in the engagement the company of Captain Peter D. Vroom was completely surrounded and was rescued only by a charge of the reserve battalion of the Third Cavalry under Lieutenant Colonel William B. Royall and Captain Guy V. Henry. Henry, who had won a brevet as brigadier general of volunteers in the Civil War, was shot in the face, losing the sight of one eye. A final charge by Captain Anson Mills ended the action and the Sioux withdrew, leaving thirteen dead on the field. Crook's Indian scouts behaved well; among them was Plenty Coups, later a famous man among the Crows.[6] Crook's loss was nine men killed and twenty-four wounded. He held the field after six hours of fighting, and his control of the action was admirable. But at the same time he was prevented from pushing on to Terry. Thinking that his present force was not adequate to accomplish anything, Crook withdrew to his base in Wyoming to await reinforcements and further word from Terry.

On June 22 Carr's Fifth Cavalry was ordered northward from Fort Laramie to cut the trail between the Red Cloud and Spotted Tail agencies and the camps of Sitting Bull and Crazy Horse. On the same day Custer's Seventh Cavalry, far to the north, left Terry and Gibbon to look for Sitting Bull's camp.

Two days later the Fifth passed the Cardinal's Chair at the head of the Niobrara River and moved into the valley of Old Woman's Fork of the South Cheyenne River. There Lieutenant King was assigned to command an escort for Major Thaddeus H. Stanton, the paymaster, who at this time was not concerned with the payroll but was in effect Lieutenant General Philip H. Sheridan's liaison with the column. Stanton had particular instructions to find out how many of the supplies so generously issued to the reservation Indians were being used to support the northern Sioux. The escort consisted of Lieutenant Edward W. Keyes, forty men of Company C, and the scout Baptiste Garnier, known as "Little Bat." Little Bat figures again and again in King's novels and is not to be confused with "Big Bat"—Baptiste Pourier—also mentioned frequently in the literature of the period. King refers to them both as Indians, though they were in part of French trapper descent.

Stanton's party, well in advance of the regiment, proceeded rapidly but with caution, Little Bat far in the lead, acting as "point" in modern military parlance and creeping cautiously up every low ridge for a look about before signaling "come on." Late in the afternoon he was seen to stop and dismount, and King rode forward to find the first Indian trail that the Fifth struck on the campaign. At about the same time, away to the north Custer's Seventh had also struck an Indian trail. In a few minutes King saw two smoke columns in the hills to the northwest and knew that his party had been discovered. Nevertheless it proceeded, relying on the fact that Carr's command was close at hand.

Soon Little Bat, again in the lead, was seen to circle his pony to the left, signaling "a discovery." He had found the recent trail of about fifty warriors, headed for the Big Horn Mountains according to Little Bat's diagnosis. The escort made camp in the valley of the Cheyenne and built fires of sagebrush, despite seeing five signal fires. An alarm caused by a timid sentry firing at a coyote provoked such usual army badinage as, "Hi Sullivan, if it was two cayotes would you advance the saynoir or the junior wid the countersign?"

In the first gray dawn the scouting party moved on looking for water, but both the South Fork and the Mini Pusa branch of the Cheyenne were dry. Major Stanton found a small water hole, and the party was able to proceed. Before noon a broad beaten track "that looked like a highway" was seen in the valley of the Mini Pusa, just as Sheridan had predicted from his office in Chicago. It was the route of supplies from the agencies to the northern Indians.

But on this Sunday, June 25, 1876, the broad highway was deserted. All the rest of that day the Stanton party watched it, but not an Indian did they see. Toward evening someone spotted a solitary buzzard through field glasses, far, far to the north. That was the only hint of what was happening well beyond in the valley of the Little Bighorn. For on this day Major Marcus A. Reno's battalion of the Seventh charged into an immense Indian village and was brought to a halt that soon became a rout as the Sioux scattered Reno's Ree scouts before them and then stampeded his troopers. The battalion broke for the hills, losing many of its men. Then came Captain Frederick W. Benteen's troops, to find Reno besieged. The third detachment of the Seventh Cavalry—five of its twelve companies, more than two hundred men—then rode with Custer into the valley of the Little Bighorn. Not one came back.

The solitary buzzard that King saw on this Sunday meant nothing to him. All the next day the seven companies under Reno remained besieged, awaiting the advance of Terry and Gibbon but not knowing what had happened to Custer. All day King and Stanton again watched the trail, with no result. That day they were joined by Carr with the rest of the Fifth, and for a week the watch continued. But for the time being there was no need for the Indians to rush reinforcements and supplies to Sitting Bull and Crazy Horse. The Sioux had won their greatest victory.

On July 1 the Fifth Cavalry was joined by its new colonel, Wesley Merritt, successor to General Emory. Merritt was a brevet major general and had won six brevets for gallant and meritorious service in the Civil War, during which he had served conspicuously with Custer as a cavalry commander in the Army of the Potomac. He had been assigned to the Second Dragoons after his graduation from West Point in 1860, and since the war he had been lieutenant colonel of the Ninth U.S. Cavalry. It is notable that he joined the Fifth Cavalry on the Mini Pusa in eastern Wyoming on the very day of his official assignment to that regiment as colonel.

A high sense of duty often brought officers to their commands when an expedition was in prospect, even though other assignments would have excused them. Buffalo Bill Cody had left the Fifth Cavalry when it was ordered to Arizona in 1871, and he had been under no obligation to it or to the government in 1876, since his only official status at any time was as a temporary civilian employee. But as soon as Cody heard that the Fifth was to take the field in 1876 he closed his show—he was onstage in a melodrama at the time—at Wilmington, Delaware, and in four days he had tendered his services and been warmly welcomed and reinstated in his old position as chief of scouts for the regiment.[7]

When Merritt, two days after joining, ordered the first chase of Indians, Buffalo Bill rode with Captain Mason and Lieutenant King of Company K and Captain Kellogg and First Lieutenant Bernard Reilly, Jr., of Company I. The thirty-mile dash wore out several horses and failed to catch any Sioux, though it compelled the Indians to abandon a considerable quantity of supplies. Its principal result was to show that the Indians knew the regiment was on the trail and that little more could be accomplished there.

Accordingly the regiment, now with eight companies assembled, since C, G, and M had joined, was marched in three columns

toward Sage Creek, where the entire command encamped on July 6 while a courier was sent to Fort Laramie for further orders. What came back was startling. It was from Buffalo Bill that King and the younger officers heard the words, "Custer and five companies of the Seventh wiped out of existence. It's no rumor—General Merritt's got the official dispatch."

King described many times the gloom that met this news. In the small army of those days officers knew each other well, and those in the Fifth Cavalry had many friends in the Seventh. One can imagine the fearful alarm with which the women of the Fifth received this sorrowful message, for their husbands and fathers were exposed to the same peril. And it is perhaps impossible to describe the scene at Fort Abraham Lincoln, where so many wives of officers and enlisted men of the Seventh became widows. For more than half a century, until her death in 1933—the same year as General King—Mrs. Custer was a sad figure whose name recalled that fearsome tragedy.

There was no officer of the Fifth Cavalry who did not know what the news meant to him. That night First Lieutenant William P. Hall rode in alone with more dispatches, one of the perilous trips that King commemorated in his character "Billy Ray." On July 10 Merritt was ordered to return to Fort Laramie and prepare to join Crook by way of Fort Fetterman. On the same day Merritt was notified that Cheyennes living at the Red Cloud and Spotted Tail agencies were preparing to go north to the war camps. Until July 14 the Fifth moved toward Fort Laramie, but on that day came definite news that the Cheyennes were kicking over the traces. Merritt immediately halted at Rawhide Creek, sending Company C to watch the crossing of Running Water, a branch of the Niobrara, while Major Stanton, the ever-busy paymaster representative of Sheridan, went to Red Cloud Agency to investigate.

The next day—Sunday, July 15—Stanton reported that some eight hundred Cheyennes were on their way to Sitting Bull. Not only would they add to the Sioux force in the field, but their movement probably would endanger the road to the Black Hills settlements. Merritt thought it worth a week's delay in joining Crook to stop them. He started a "lightning march," the first of many he led with the Fifth Cavalry, not in direct pursuit of the Indians but to cut across their trail and turn them back. The distance, eighty-five miles, was covered in thirty-one hours.[8]

One of the remarkable feats of this march was the performance of the wagon train commanded by Lieutenant Hall, the regimental quartermaster. Merritt had instructed Hall to make the best speed he could, but he had not expected the wagons to keep up with the troops. At 10:00 P.M. on the first night the regiment halted at Running Water after a march of thirty-five miles. Two hours later, while Captain Edward M. Hayes and Lieutenant King were on guard, in rolled the wagon train. When the troopers were roused at 3:00 A.M. they found breakfast awaiting them before their start at dawn on the final fifty-mile dash. At 10:15 A.M. there was a halt at the head of Sage Creek, and at 8:00 P.M. the regiment reached its goal and went into bivouac along Warbonnet Creek, Nebraska.[9]

Even though he had been on guard the night before, Lieutenant King was detailed to establish before daylight on July 17 an outpost toward the southeast, the direction from which the Cheyennes were expected. Although the Indians had only thirty miles to go to the troopers' eighty-five, at dawn they were not yet in sight. Lieutenant King described the position he took as a little conical mound at the foot of a wave of prairie that descended gradually from the southeast, while to the rear rose the line of bluffs that marked the tortuous course of the stream. From the south not even an Indian eye could tell that close under those bluffs seven veteran companies of cavalry were crouching, ready to spring. At 4:30 A.M. Corporal Thomas Wilkinson of Company K, with King, sighted Indians along the ridge to the southeast, and word was sent to Merritt. During the next thirty minutes a half-dozen parties were seen in that direction, two or three miles away. These Indians apparently were concentrating their attention upon something to the west, making no attempt at concealment from the direction where the cavalry regiment lay in ambush.

Not far away was another eyewitness to the entire action. Chris Madsen, at that time a trooper of Company A and in later years a notable peace officer in Oklahoma and one of Roosevelt's Rough Riders, was a signalman, assigned to be a connecting link between the pickets and headquarters. He had spent the night on the top of a neighboring hill, with signal flag and torch at the ready. About daylight, according to his account, Cody came in from a scouting trip, "directly to my post and told me to notify the command that he had been close enough to the Indian camp to see them preparing to move. However, he hastened to camp, and before the signalman had time to make his report, he [Cody] was at Merritt's headquarters, and made his report personally."[10] Within a few minutes of this incident the Indians first came into sight.

Colonel Merritt arrived at King's outpost at 5:15 A.M. with Carr, Major Upham, First Lieutenant William C. Forbush, the regimental adjutant, Second Lieutenant J. Hayden Pardee of the Twenty-third U.S. Infantry, an aide-de-camp, and other members of his staff. It seems important to identify as many as possible who were present at this stage because of the numerous self-styled eyewitnesses who later appeared. The picket was entirely from Company K; Sergeant Edmund Schreiber was sergeant of the guard. Among several officers who came forward to look the ground over, later rejoining their companies, was Captain Samuel Sumner, commanding Company D. The scouts of the command were present, with Cody as chief—one named Tait, Jonathan White, better known as "Buffalo Chips," and possibly Baptiste Garnier or Little Bat.[11]

Soon the Indians' preoccupation was explained by the appearance, a little to the west, of the white tops of army wagons. Lieutenant Hall, by traveling all night, had nearly caught up with the regiment. This alone would have caused little perturbation, since Hall had a train guard, but Merritt immediately instructed Forbush to convey orders to the troops to saddle up and wait in a close mass under the bluffs.[12]

Cody, who had remained at the observation point, was first to notice an unusual scurrying among the Cheyennes; a dozen or so whipped up their ponies and started toward the bluff where the observers were hidden. This was soon explained by a survey of the Black Hills trail, where two couriers were seen approaching ahead of the wagon train. They were later identified as Troopers Henry Anderson and George Keith of Company C, which had been sent to the Niobrara crossing of the Camp Robinson trail; they were bringing dispatches to Merritt, having ridden some twenty-five miles farther than the regiment during its lightning march.[13]

A group of perhaps seven Indians was advancing down the ravine, intent on cutting off the two couriers. To reach them the Cheyennes had to pass near the hill where King was watching. Buffalo Bill first recognized and seized this fortuitous opportunity.

"By jove! General, now's our chance," he exclaimed. "Let our party mount here, and we can cut those fellows off!"[14]

"Up with you then," ordered Merritt. "Stay where you are, King. Watch them until they are close under you; then give the word. Come down, every other man of you."

King was thus left alone on the hilltop to give the signal for this picturesque piece of western business. Cody, since he had conceived the plan, was given the honor of leading the party, which also included the scouts Tait and White and five or six private soldiers. Adjutant Forbush and Lieutenant Pardee were crouched out of sight on the slope, ready to pass along the signal, while Sergeant Schreiber and Corporal Wilkinson remained nearby.

His audience was small, though it burned with the enthusiasm of intimate concern; yet the artifice of the stage or Wild West show had never granted Buffalo Bill a more spectacular setting for deeds of heroism. This happy chance in actual warfare was by no means foreign to Cody's stage experience, however, for he was gorgeously dressed for the part. While the regiment was in its working clothes of buckskin or blue wool, Buffalo Bill shone forth in one of his stage costumes, donned perhaps to legitimize the myth he had been perpetuating in the East that this was the customary garb of a "scout of the prairie," or possibly just because he had no other clothes at hand. He wore a brilliant Mexican vaquero outfit of black velvet splashed with scarlet and trimmed with silver buttons and lace.

Cody's resplendence was matched by that of his opponents, the Cheyennes. They approached with the sun flashing from polished armlets and lance heads, bearing gaily painted rawhide shields, the wind making their long warbonnets stream out behind them. Intent on getting the scalps of the two couriers, they failed to observe King peering over the hillcrest with his binoculars, the only thing possibly visible to them in that still-peaceful landscape.

"All ready, General?"

"All ready, King. Give the word when you like."

King waited until the Indians had turned away from a direct approach toward the hill and were swinging toward the couriers.

"Now, lads, in with you."

Cody led his little band against the Indians while Merritt and the others sprang to the top of the slope to watch the action. For a moment both parties were out of view. Two shots were heard. Suddenly Corporal Wilkinson pulled at the general's sleeve, excitedly pointing to the front, where a single Indian, following the original party, had halted and was trying to make out what was going on.

"Shall I fire?" Wilkinson asked. The general assented, and at the shot the Indian swung down in his saddle and sent an answering shot whistling past the general's ear—fired, King believed, from under the horse's neck.[15]

Just as these shots were fired, King saw the main body of Indians rushing down the ravine and appearing by scores along the ridge. Upon his shout of warning, Merritt quickly ordered the first company up and sprang to his saddle, followed by his staff officers. The first company was King's K, commanded by Captain Mason, and King rushed back to mount and join them. His horse had broken away from the orderly, and King was perhaps three-quarters of a minute in running him down. Then King's crippled right arm caused him further delay in mounting, but despite these difficulties he was in time to join the first squad of his company as it came up, and it was only a moment later that he charged past Cody, who was standing over an Indian he had killed, waving a handsome warbonnet and shouting.

Cody and the leading Cheyenne warrior apparently had seen each other at the same time and fired simultaneously, Cody's shot piercing the Indian's leg and his pony's heart. The scout was not hit, but at almost the same instant his horse stepped in a rodent hole and threw him. He got up, recovered his rifle, and fired again, killing the Indian, who was lying wounded perhaps not more than fifty feet away. Cody appears to have run forward, and seeing that the Cheyenne really was dead, for the benefit of the oncoming troopers he raised the feather bonnet into the air with the cry—as he always told the story—"The first scalp for Custer!" The soldiers cheered as they galloped past.[16]

Whether or not these words gave him the idea, it seems clear that at some point Cody drew his knife and, as he told it to King, used it to scalp the Cheyenne. King later positively stated that Cody could not, as he claimed, have taken the scalp in the short space of time before the cavalrymen rode past, and King was sure there had been no scalping. But the signalman Madsen, still at his post on the butte, saw the scalp being taken. Later, passing close to the dead Cheyenne, he confirmed this for himself, and a Sergeant Hamilton of Sumner's company, who stopped near the body to adjust his saddle, also saw that the scalp was gone.[17]

The Indian was identified as Hay-o-wei, a young Cheyenne leader. Little Bat translated his name at the time as Yellow Hand, and so it appears in virtually all the Buffalo Bill stories about the affair. Since then other authorities have stated that it actually meant Yellow Hair, possibly referring to the scalp of a white woman he had taken.

As Company K topped the ridge the Indians fired a volley, but when they saw the gray horse troop, Company B, under Captain Montgomery, about sixty yards to the rear and Company I, Captain Kellogg's men, coming front into line at a gallop about the same distance to the left rear, they wheeled and scattered. The troops advanced cautiously in open order to the ridge, but after gaining it they saw the Cheyennes unmistakably fleeing in all directions. The regiment pursued them for thirty-five miles back to the Red Cloud Agency but were unable to catch up with them. At the agency it was impossible to tell which Indians had so recently been on the trail and which had remained there, so no attempt was made to punish the war party. As a result of the action the Cheyennes took flight no more that summer. It is one of few cases where a large party of Indians was successfully ambushed by troops, and it seems even more remarkable considering that the same organization had failed in a similar effort less than two weeks before.

Campaigning with Crook

The wife of a commuter who bolts for his train, leaving breakfast on the table, may sympathize with Lieutenant Hall, who saw the troops of the Fifth Cavalry galloping away just as he and his wagon train had caught up with them after an arduous effort. But the troopers were in much sadder state than the commuter, for there was no restaurant along their route where they could grab a cup of coffee. There was no doubt that Hall would now give up the hopeless effort of trying to keep up with them, and they saw no recourse at the Red Cloud Agency but to beg supplies from the agent or be "attached for rations" to the small force of infantry at nearby Camp Robinson. In any event they expected a long rest while awaiting their wagon train.

But Hall seemed to be about the best mule driver the army had ever developed. Despite the rough country full of ravines and "breaks," he drove in with his wagon train by noon the following day, and it was not necessary to borrow rations. Also, it was possible to move on toward Fort Laramie and the Crook expedition, and within two hours the troops were on the move again up the valley of the White River. They reached Fort Laramie July 21, and two days later eight companies were on their way to Fort Fetterman. Here wagon trains, new horses, recruits, and officers were waiting to join the Fifth in its march to General Crook, and Merritt was able to organize an "unattached" force to accompany his regiment. Among the officers joining were Calbraith P. Rodgers, recently promoted captain, and George O. Eaton, who had given up a leave of absence to get in on the campaign, quite in the manner of King's character "Jack Truscott." Two officers of the Fourth U.S. Infantry, Robert H. Young and Satterlee C. Plummer, had received permission to accompany the Fifth as volunteers, and another in the same category was a navy lieutenant, William C. Hunter, who had come west for a buffalo hunt with his cousin, Captain Rodgers, and decided to try an Indian campaign instead. He was given the facetious brevet of "commodore" by officers of the expedition.[1]

The column left Fort Fetterman the day after the regiment arrived, not even waiting for Company E, Captain George F. Price, and Company F, J. Scott Payne, which were hurrying to join. After two days of marching, on July 28 King was aroused from sleep in the pitch dark of the valley of the north fork of the Mini Pusa by Lieutenant Pardee and Colonel Merritt, who thought they heard trumpet calls from beyond the camp. The officers went out beyond the line of sentinels to listen, and soon "Officers' Call" was heard distinctly, but far away. The same call was immediately repeated by Merritt's trumpeter, and thus Companies E and F were guided to the command. From that night on, sounding "Officers' Call" as a signal became an accepted tradition of the Fifth Cavalry, and it was used dramatically some years later by the same officers when Merritt rescued Captain Payne, besieged by Ute Indians in Colorado after the killing of Major Thomas T. Thornburgh.

The Fifth now numbered ten companies, C having been gathered in after its side travels during the lightning march to the Warbonnet. Only H and L were missing, and they were in the field but unfortunately arrived at Fort Laramie too late to join.

The trail of the Fifth was dotted with names famous in western annals: Powder River; Fort Reno, named for Major General Jesse L. Reno, killed at the battle of South Mountain in the Civil War; Crazy Woman's Fork; Clear Fork or Lodge Pole Creek; Lake De Smet, recalling the famous missionary priest; and Fort Phil Kearny, named for the dashing cavalry general killed at Chantilly in the late War and, with Fort Reno, ordered abandoned after Red Cloud's War of the late 1860s. Near it lay scenes of the Wagon Box Fight and of the Fetterman defeat. Then they reached Tongue River and finally junction with Crook at Goose Creek, Wyoming, on August 3.

A day was spent in organizing the Crook column. Merritt now became chief of the cavalry brigade, temporarily relinquishing command of the Fifth to Lieutenant Colonel Carr. The Fifth was formed in two battalions, Major Upham commanding the first, Companies A, C, G, I, and M, while King's former company commander Mason, now promoted major but temporarily remaining with the Fifth, took charge of the second battalion, B, D, E, F, and

K. Captain Albert E. Woodson now commanded Company K, and

King was temporarily appointed regimental adjutant, a post he
was named to permanently on October 5. The former adjutant,
Forbush, acted as adjutant for the brigade.

Lieutenant Colonel William Royall of the Third Cavalry, who
had served with the Fifth in Arizona, commanded the remainder
of the cavalry, three battalions of the Third, which was complete,
and one battalion of the Second, four companies. Royall and Carr
were of the same rank, but Carr had several years' seniority and
in addition was a brevet major general, whereas Royall was only a
brevet colonel. In about 1890 he was given a brevet as brigadier
general for services at the battle of the Rosebud. For many years
Royall, as major, had served under Carr. Now it was Royall's
delight to speak pompously of his "brigade," for it was made up of
parts of two regiments, and slightingly of Carr's "detachment,"
the incomplete Fifth.

Major Alexander Chambers commanded the infantry, fourteen
companies from the Fourth, Ninth, and Fourteenth regiments.
This is a body of men to whom all commentators on the campaign
pay tribute, for they outmarched the cavalry—but with good
reason, since the Sioux had set fire to all the grass, forage had
been exhausted, and the horses suffered severely in the extended
march. In his earlier move to the Rosebud Crook had mounted
some of his infantry on mules, but this was not attempted as the
Big Horn and Yellowstone Expedition was renewed. The only
mules now used were in the pack train; all wagons were held back.

King tells an anecdote about the start of the ten weeks' march.
The colors of the Fifth had been left behind in care of the band,
and Merritt and Carr had adopted signal flags, red with a white
square in the center and vice versa, for their headquarters' use.
The Crow and Shoshone scouts had been told that these were
"talking flags," and they gathered around with great interest. To
show them how the flags "talked," Carr directed their use to
order certain movements of the regimental herds. The Indians
were amazed but not dumbfounded by the prompt result; being
adept signalers themselves, they speedily saw the possibilities. A
number of white towels hung out to dry promptly disappeared,
and they were found to have been appropriated by the newly
formed Indian signal corps. When the Indian allies paraded for the
start, every warrior had provided himself with some sort of signal
flag.

Merritt's delay in joining Crook, though fully justified, gave the Sioux time to break camp at Little Bighorn and get away. For six days the Big Horn and Yellowstone Expedition moved down the valley of the Tongue and Rosebud. On August 7 the troops passed the site of a huge Indian camp, and the trail outward appeared not to be very old. Early on the morning of August 10 there was great excitement, for it was believed that the main body of Indians had been sighted. The Crows and Shoshones stripped for action, and the troops were extended in battle formation, ready for the mass of Indians seen approaching. But behind the Indians they saw blue-coated troopers swinging into line, and King, far in advance, recognized the remnant of the Seventh Cavalry left after Custer's defeat. Buffalo Bill was first to welcome Terry's force and, riding like the wind down the column, to report its presence to Crook. The Sioux had slipped out from between Crook and Terry.

Terry also had awaited reinforcements, and the Fifth U.S. Infantry, commanded by Colonel and Brevet Major General Nelson A. Miles, had joined his Dakota Column for the second campaign. Neither side had expected this meeting; both generals had been sure the Sioux were between them. And they had been, for the trail was quickly found, crossing the Tongue River away from the point of junction. This meant that Sitting Bull might be headed for Canada, but he might cause trouble on the way. Within an hour Miles's Fifth Infantry was sent back to watch the Yellowstone.

There was quite a contrast between the two columns. Terry's forces had a large wagon train, bearing all the luxuries that usually accompanied an army in the field. His officers and men were dressed in their proper uniforms, their horses were well fed, and in fact his entire column looked just as it would at drill in an eastern post. Crook had only a pack train; his officers and enlisted men wore a combination of old clothes and Indian and frontier costume suited only for campaigning far from civilization. So far had this gone that even Charles King was ridiculed by West Point classmates in Terry's column, who had never seen him in such disreputable garb. Crook's horses were lean, for they had been marching over a country where much of the grass had been burned off by the scattering Sioux and no grain could be carried.

Nevertheless, Terry was impressed with the businesslike appearance of the Crook column and desired to emulate it. His own pack train was a sorry-looking affair compared with Crook's, and he was eager to learn Crook's methods. So he decided to send his own wagons back, realizing that the chase now would be long and difficult, needing great speed if the Sioux were to be found at all.

Crook's pack train was reloaded from Terry's wagons before they were sent away, and King says the men of his command now began to realize it would be a long time before they had even the comforts of camp life again. The combined columns bivouacked along the Rosebud, but during that night the herds of Companies A, B, and M of the Fifth Cavalry stampeded and were brought back only after a long chase. During the excitement Lieutenant Eaton's revolver accidentally discharged and tore off part of his index finger, a wound that forced him to leave the expedition two weeks later.

The Indian trail led toward the valley of the Tongue, and the combined columns marched east to that river August 11. Now day after day it rained a deluge, while the troops plodded down the valley of the Tongue, northward to Pumpkin Creek, then east-ward again to the Powder and down the Powder to the Yellow-stone. There the command bivouacked while awaiting a report from Buffalo Bill, who had gone on a scout sixty miles down the Yellowstone through the Badlands to the Glendive to see if the Sioux had crossed the river. The steamer *Far West*, famous as the first to carry the story of the Custer disaster to civilization, brought a small amount of supplies, and the pack trains were reloaded. Now all disabled men were weeded out and sent back, among them Lieutenant Eaton. Buffalo Bill had returned to re-port no sign of the Sioux, and he too now left the expedition, somethat reluctantly, though he believed most of the fighting was over. He had theatrical engagements in the East for the fall and winter that he could not afford to forgo. Most of the correspond-ents with the two columns also left, feeling that the excitement was over, but John F. Finerty of the Chicago *Times*, who had been with the Crook expedition from the start, continued to share its hardships to the end.

There were many conferences between Terry and Crook during the wait at the Yellowstone from August 17 to 24, though their purport is not known. There is indeed some mystery about the generals' parting. Crook's column marched up the Powder River August 24; for two days Terry's cavalry followed, then it marched back to the Yellowstone. It has been intimated that Crook left before he could receive orders placing him under Terry's command, a point Terry would not insist on. In any case Terry turned back with a view toward protecting the Black Hills settlements and other parts of Dakota from the Sioux, while Crook continued on in the hope of overtaking Sitting Bull or Crazy Horse.

Crook's column struck out due east along the trail that Terry and Custer had followed in June, across the west fork of O'Fallon Creek, Dry Fork, and Cabin Creek and north on Beaver Creek. There the column halted for muster on the last day of August; the formalities required by army regulations must be observed even in the field. Captain George M. Randall and the scouts were sent toward the Yellowstone to look for supplies. Presumably some arrangement had been made with Terry, though nothing was found. Then the column resumed its march down Beaver Creek, east along Andrews Creek, and across the Little Missouri and Davis Creek to Heart River, reaching there September 5.

At the start of the campaign the infantry had moved out early in the day and the cavalry, starting later, had passed them on the way. Long since, this had been reversed. Now the cavalry started early, dragging their worn out, starving, sore-backed animals, to be passed in a few hours by Chambers's swinging infantry force, whose members sarcastically offered a "tow" to their mounted comrades. The entire command was approaching the starvation point. Rations were left for only two and a half days. It was 160 miles, five full marches, to Fort Abraham Lincoln, Dakota, on the Missouri River. It was 200 miles, seven marches or more, to the Black Hills. In Crook's view, to go to the fort was two weeks' dead loss; to go to the Hills meant some chance of catching the Indians. But the correspondent Finerty was amazed at the decision.

"You will march 200 miles in the wilderness, with used-up horses and tired infantry on two and one-half days' rations?" he asked Crook.

Crook explained that he had asked General Sheridan to arrange for supplies at Crook City or Deadwood, and that if this failed something could be purchased from civilian sources; also, half rations would be issued and they might find some game to help out.

"If necessary," he added, "we can eat our horses!"[2]

It proved to be eight days to rations, with torrents of rain all the way. After two days the order was issued to slaughter three horses in each battalion every night and use the remains of these poor skeletons as food. After their scanty meal the men dropped to the drenched prairie and slept, soaked to the skin, without even removing their boots, for most of them could not remove them with any hope of ever getting them on again.

From the Third Cavalry the 150 men with the most serviceable horses were chosen to make a dash to the Black Hills. This picked force contained some notable names. Captain Anson Mills, commanding, was a prominent figure in both the Rosebud and the forthcoming Slim Buttes fights and was soon better known, perhaps, as the designer of the Mills web belt and other practical field equipment later used by the United States Army. One of his lieutenants on this dash was Emmett Crawford, to whose memory King dedicated *Marion's Faith*. Crawford was killed while commanding a company of Apache scouts in an unfortunate encounter with Mexican troops while both detachments were in pursuit of Geronimo. This unfortunate affair led to Crook's resignation as commander in Arizona in 1885. Another lieutenant with Mills was Frederick Schwatka, who in later years led a notable expedition to the Arctic to discover the fate of Sir John Franklin. A third was A. H. Von Luettwitz, soldier of fortune, who had served in the Prussian and Austrian armies and whose personal battle flag, had he been given one, would have borne honors for Montebello, Magenta, Solferino, the Italian campaign of 1859, Gettysburg, and several other battles of the American Civil War.

The chief scout of this party was Frank Grouard, one of the most notable frontiersmen of the period. He was of Polynesian descent and had been captured by the Sioux. He had lived for many years with Sitting Bull's band and married an Indian woman, but he had finally escaped and eventually became Crook's favorite northern plains scout. Grouard was given full credit for the escape from annihilation of Lieutenant Frederick W. Sibley of the Second Cavalry and a detachment from Company E, sent out in hope of finding Terry shortly after the battle of the Rosebud. The men of "Sibley's Scout" were completely surrounded by a large Sioux band and were extricated only by Grouard's expert woodsmanship and knowledge of Sioux tactics.

Another notable scout with Mills was Captain Jack Crawford, the "poet scout" remembered for many exploits during the campaign, who for many years recited his verse before Chautauqua audiences and from other lecture platforms.

A third, riding on his last scout, was the friend, partner, and imitator of Buffalo Bill Cody who had won the sobriquet "Buffalo

Chips." King gives James White as his real name, and Finerty refers to him as "Charley, alias Frank White," but his tombstone at Slim Buttes bears the name Jonathan White. King says of him, "a simpler-minded, gentler frontiersman never lived. He was modesty and courtesy itself. . . . I never heard him swear, and no man ever heard him lie."[3]

Mills's race for rations was destined to be interrupted. Two days after his departure, September 9, George Herman, a packer, dashed up to General Crook to report that Mills had captured an Indian village of forty-one lodges, a pony herd, and some supplies but was surrounded by the Sioux. General Carr had ridden forward to get the news. He immediately returned to the regiment and ordered King to "throw out every horse that can't carry a rider three miles at a trot," for the Fifth was to make the twenty-mile ride to the rescue.[4] King describes the sudden change in the men from dejection and disgust to anticipation and alertness; all were eager to fight after the long chase. He tells how one very slight man wanted to take the horse of a stouter comrade when the heavyweight doubted his horse would carry him so far. By 10:00 A.M. the Fifth reached Slim Buttes and relieved Mills. Merritt accompanied them, but they made no effort to dislodge the Indians from the surrounding hills until the main body of Crook's force arrived at about 3:00 P.M.

Mills had struck the Sioux trail the previous afternoon and had bivouacked within four miles of the village. During the night he and Grouard had reconnoitered, and at dawn Schwatka and twenty-five mounted men, the only men to fight mounted during the entire day, were detailed to round up the Indian pony herd, while Crawford and Von Luettwitz led the rest of the force, on foot, against the village. The attack, just before dawn, had been so great a surprise that the Sioux had to slash openings in their tepees to escape. The Indians had retreated to the bluffs and kept up a lively fire for a while, but it had fallen off by the time the Fifth arrived. Mills had promptly sent for more ammunition and reinforcements.

When the Fifth Cavalry reached the scene, King notes, Mills warned the men to avoid a small ravine where two or three wounded Indians were keeping up a spasmodic fire. While awaiting the arrival of the main force, a few scouts and other adventurous spirits decided to dispose of these "two or three" Sioux and were answered by a ringing volley that showed a formidable force was concealed there. Crook, arriving on the scene, took charge of

what King calls "one of the liveliest side shows to an Indian battle."[5] Finerty tells how the general exposed himself, display- ing "to the fullest extent his eccentric contempt for danger."[6] Private John Wenzel, alias Medbury, of Company A, Third Cav- alry, was killed in the first volley, and when Crook arrived his body was still where it had fallen. Private Edward Kennedy of Company E, Fifth Cavalry, was also killed and now, not even ten paces away from Crook across the ravine, Buffalo Chips, peering over the edge to locate the Indians, was shot through the heart and instantly fell dead. Several men were wounded.

Finerty also notes that Charles King was among those who "took desperate chances in true 'forlorn hope' fashion," and he also mentions in this connection Captains William H. Powell, Samuel Munson, and Daniel W. Burke of the infantry, Captain Rodgers of the Fifth Cavalry, and Lieutenant W. Philo Clark of the Second. Baptiste Pourier, Big Bat, succeeded in fighting his way into the ravine, seized a woman, and used her as a shield while he killed one of the warriors and then escaped. Crook or- dered up a considerable force to surround the place and throw in a hail of shots. As soon as this was done the women started the death chant, and a number of children began to wail loudly. This was the first intimation Crook had that women and children were in the ravine. He immediately ordered the firing to cease, and Grouard and Big Bat were directed to offer to spare the lives of the noncombatants. This was accepted by the Sioux, and Crook himself handed out one old woman from the mouth of the ravine. She clung to the general's hand and refused to free him until assured again and again that she would not be tortured or killed. Eleven women and six children surrendered, but the warriors elected to fight on, and the attack was renewed. For two hours they sustained a "rain of hell" so courageously that even the soldiers were willing to grant them mercy, despite the three comrades killed. Crook called another parley, and the chief, Amer- ican Horse, mortally wounded, agreed to surrender if the lives of those with him were spared. This was accepted, and it was found that only two were alive.

The captives refused to tell where the main Sioux band was now encamped, although a guidon of the Seventh Cavalry, a pair of gauntlets recognized as belonging to Captain Myles Keogh, killed with Custer on the Little Bighorn, and other pieces of cavalry uniform proved that American Horse's band had taken part in the Custer fight. King noted one "grinning, hand-shaking vagabond" wearing the uniform of one of Custer's corporals. Doubtless that corporal's scalp was somewhere in the warrior's possession, King added, "but he has the deep sagacity not to boast of it; and no man in his right senses wants to search the average Indian."[7] But American soldiers were civilized and magnanimous; they ignored these grisly relics and treated their prisoners in humane, even friendly fashion, though they well knew what would be the fate of any soldier captured by the Sioux.

While all this was going on, there had been little firing from the surrounding buttes, though Mills had been under heavy fire from there early in the day. At 5:00 P.M. it became evident that the Indians had been gathering reinforcements, and now heavy fire opened all along the line, manned by the main body of the Sioux under Crazy Horse, Roman Nose, and other leaders who hoped to dispose of Mills as they had Custer, not knowing about the arrival of Crook's main body. King dashed to Carr's headquarters and heard the commander order Trumpeter Bradley to sound "To Arms" and "Forward," opening an hour's battle. Although King called the Warbonnet fight "the most spirited, thrilling, pictur-esque warfare," he had seen that summer, "this late afternoon affair in the dripping mists that hovered over the sodden prairie of Slim Buttes was on a grander scale, where numbers at least were concerned. . . . Sioux by the hundreds came dashing down upon our lines, their first and fiercest efforts apparently aimed at the herds of the 3rd and 5th Cavalry."[8] All the herds were safely driven in except those of the gray horse company, Company B of the Fifth Cavalry. These grays were still in good condition— Captain Montgomery had not lost a horse in the entire cam-paign—and were ready for a gallop, even though unfortunately they chose to gallop toward the Indians. But Company B was a crack outfit, and Corporal Clanton was equal to the emergency. He galloped out in front, turned the leaders, and brought back all the horses in a five-hundred-yard circle, an exhibition of skill and daring that won mention in Carr's report. Upham's battalion of the Fifth scrambled up the ridge to the west, Mason's battalion to the front, and the Second and Third Cavalry to his right, all fighting dismounted. Back of them came the long line of infantry with heavier rifles, but all were firing rapidly and not hitting much, especially when a daring warrior galloped along the line

Charles King at age fourteen. (Courtesy of the Milwaukee County Historical Society)

Rufus King's Milwaukee home, built about 1845, at the corner of Mason and Van Buren streets. Charles lived here as a youth, and on this corner he presided over the locally notorious "King's Corner Crowd." (Courtesy of the Milwaukee County Historical Society)

General Rufus King, Charles's father, first commander of the famous midwestern "Iron Brigade" and later United States minister to Rome. (State Historical Society of Wisconsin)

Cadet Charles King, United States Military Academy. Admitted in 1862 as one of President Lincoln's at-large appointees, King graduated in 1866, ranked twenty-second in his class of forty-one cadets. (United States Military Academy Library)

Lieutenant General Winfield Scott, once commander in chief of the United States Army and long a personal friend of the King family. (Paul L. Hedren)

Officers and an enlisted man of the First U.S. Artillery, 1867, while on duty in New Orleans. Left to right: First Lieutenant Ballard S. Humphrey, Private and color bearer John B. Charlton, Captain William M. Graham, Second Lieutenant Charles King, and First Lieutenant John J. Driscoll. Graham commanded Light Battery K, First Artillery, King's company, during the New Orleans "riots." (Fort Laramie National Historic Site)

First Lieutenant Charles King, First Artillery, 1870.
(United States Military Academy Library)

Sergeant Bernard Taylor rescuing King from Apaches at Sunset Pass, Arizona, November 1, 1874. This heroic episode is depicted by the well-known military artist Rufus F. Zogbaum as the frontispiece to Theophilus F. Rodenbough's 1886 book, Uncle Sam's Medal of Honor. *(Paul L. Hedren)*

"Old Bedlam," the bachelor officers' quarters at Fort Laramie, Wyoming, as seen in 1876 during the fateful Great Sioux War. (Fort Laramie National Historic Site)

The "first scalp for Custer" at Warbonnet Creek, Nebraska, July 17, 1876, as depicted by Robert Lindneux in 1928. King, after strained involvement with Lindneux, came to despise this work. (Courtesy of the Buffalo Bill Historical Center, Cody, Wyoming)

"The Dandy Fifth" in 1876. Dakota photographer Stanley J. Morrow posed the officers of the Fifth U.S. Cavalry for this end-of-campaign remembrance. King is in the center, his arms folded across his chest. Colonel Wesley Merritt is seen at lower right wearing a light-colored scarf, with his right elbow on his knee. (Harry H. Anderson)

Captain Charles King, 1879, on the occasion of his retirement from the Fifth U.S. Cavalry. (Paul L. Hedren)

A King family picnic in the late 1880s. Left to right: daughter Carolyn, son Rufus, daughter Elinor, and wife Adelaide. (Ellen Macneale)

Charles King and his cousin Eliza Ida Eliot in an amateur production in Milwaukee of The Mikado. *(Courtesy of the Milwaukee County Historical Society)*

Teatime at the King residence in the early 1890s. Left to right: daughter Carolyn, King's sister Fannie Ward, son Rufus, daughter Elinor, and Charles's wife Adelaide Lavender Yorke King. (Ellen Macneale)

CAPTAIN CHARLES KING

A Goudey's Indian gum card likeness of Captain Charles King, ca. 1930s. King's appearance on a youth's collectible is unique testimony to his enduring public appeal among young and old, despite the quality of the card's reproduction. (Paul L. Hedren)

General Charles King, United States Volunteers, center front, and staff
during the Philippine Insurrection, 1899. (National Archives and
Records Service)

"Great Material for My New Military Novel." Despite meritorious service as a combat officer, King forever was better known as the army novelist. *(State Historical Society of Wisconsin)*

*"The Soldier Leaped from His Saddle," as depicted by Frederic
Remington to illustrate King's 1903 novel,* A Daughter of the Sioux.
*The setting is faithful to the actual Fort Fetterman, Wyoming,
prototype for "Fort Frayne" in that story. (Paul L. Hedren)*

Left: Carolyn Merritt King (1877–1953), Charles's second daughter, seen here in the mid-1890s. (Ellen Macneale)
Right: Elinor Yorke King (1881–1940), Charles's third child, as seen about the turn of the century. (Ellen Macneale)

Rufus King (1885–1975), Charles's fourth child. A 1908 graduate of the United States Naval Academy, Rufus later served in both world wars. (Ellen Macneale)

Left: William F. "Buffalo Bill" Cody in 1909. Lifelong friends, Charles King and Bill Cody shared manly exploits on the Plains. Forever after, both men successfully popularized the American West, on stage and in print. (Courtesy of the Buffalo Bill Historical Center, Cody, Wyoming)

Right: General William Carey Brown, one of King's closest friends, as seen in retirement in the 1930s. (Western Historical Collections, University of Colorado Libraries)

King and his horse Star, in Milwaukee on Memorial Day 1926.
(Paul L. Hedren)

King and two grandchildren, namesake Charles, son of Rufus King, and Betty Simeon, daughter of Elinor King Simeon, about 1928. (Paul L. Hedren)

*Brigadier General Ralph M. Immell and Major General Charles King
at Camp Douglas in 1931. On this much-publicized ceremonial
occasion, King donned vintage articles of uniform dating to his father's
early career and his own. (State Historical Society of Wisconsin)*

The King Medal, authorized by the Wisconsin National Guard on June 15, 1929, recognized perfect attendance at the guard's armory and camp exercises during a training year. Issued in bronze, silver, and gold, the medal bore King's relief portrait on the obverse and was suspended from a dark blue silk ribbon with stripes of Medical Department maroon, Infantry blue, Cavalry yellow, and Artillery scarlet. The award was discontinued after World War II. (Paul L. Hedren)

just out of range, calling out insulting remarks. Bourke, King, and

the other staff officers galloped along the line in an effort to get the men to conserve their ammunition. The infantry maneuvered to flank the Sioux on the bluffs, and just at sunset the Indians were driven off.

At dawn next morning—Sunday, September 10, 1876—Crook's column moved on toward Deadwood and rations, for the supplies captured in the Indian village did not go far. Upham's first battalion of the Fifth, dismounted, was designated the rear guard, with orders to burn the Indian village and all it contained and then to cover the departure. As soon as the main body moved away the Sioux returned to the attack, and the retiring battalion of the Fifth was forced to fight its way from ridge to ridge, the Indians being greatly encouraged at seeing the soldiers fall back before them.

As soon as Company G left a ridge it was covered with swarming Indians; the troopers quickly halted, dropped to the ground, and fired a volley that cleared it. Carr saw an attempt to break through the line of skirmishers connecting the rear guard with the main body two miles away. He sent Adjutant King galloping to Major Upham, and Kellogg's Company I was turned to the right to meet the attack. But it was time to break off this fighting. Carr again sent King to Upham with orders. As the next ridge was reached, a few sharpshooters were left behind to hold off the Indians while the companies raced across the boggy ground to a height a short distance away. As soon as the companies were placed, the sharpshooters were signaled. They came in with a rush. The Sioux quickly followed, and as they reached the vacated ridge they were met by a withering volley that emptied several saddles. This ended the fourth and last phase of the fight at Slim Buttes.

Sunday afternoon was spent devising means of caring for the wounded. Beside the three killed at the ravine, one man was reported missing and ten severely wounded. Finerty collected a list of fourteen slightly wounded men, not including several among the infantry. The best that could be done for the severely wounded, including Lieutenant Von Luettwitz and Private Charles Foster, who had legs amputated, and Sergeant Edward Glass, whose right arm was shattered, was to improvise litters between two mules. Those less seriously hurt but unable to walk had to be content with Indian travois, poles lashed at one end to a mule, the other end dragging the ground. During the halt most of the soldiers were busy fashioning moccasins from skins captured in the Indian village.

September 11 opened the last stage in the dash to the Black Hills. King described the disappointment that day when after a long and weary climb they reached an elevation from which they could see a considerable expanse of country. The valleys were covered with fog, but as they watched the fog cleared away, only to show a seemingly illimitable expanse of badlands, a "ghastly compound of spongy ashes, yielding sand, and soilless, soulless earth, on which even greasewood cannot grow, and sage-brush sickens and dies . . . , the meanest country under the sun."[9] The "Deer's Ears," buttes midway to the Black Hills, were not yet within view of field glasses. That night the expedition bivouacked in the rain along Owl Creek.

Tuesday, September 12, was the black day of the expedition. From Owl Creek to Crow Creek the starving soldiers, ill nourished on a diet of horsemeat, stumbled through the badlands until noon, then left them only to follow a trail along muddy and boggy streambeds. Worn-out mules, dragging travois carrying the wounded, stumbled and fell, tumbling the agonized men into mud and water, their companions almost too weak to give adequate aid. At dawn Upham's battalion had been ordered out on the last scout of the campaign. Mills again had been sent forward to hurry the provisions. But the main column was near its last gasp. During this march seventy horses were lost, according to Finerty. King says "scores," but he probably did not stop to count.

During this terrible march King commanded the rear guard, picking up and driving in stragglers. Despite his slight physique and his troublesome Apache wound, he was one of the giants of this test of endurance. Finerty pays this tribute to him:

> One of the most cheerful men I marched with, amid the pelting rain, was Capt. Charles King, now celebrated as a military novelist, who was then, if I mistake not, a lieutenant and regimental adjutant of the 5th Cavalry. He was full of anecdote, but complained occasionally of the effect of serious wounds which he had received while fighting the Apaches in Arizona, and which subsequently compelled his retirement from active service.[10]

It was after midnight when the rear guard finally reached Crow Creek, and still many men were scattered along the way, stagger-

ing on as best they could, sustained by the knowledge that the
Belle Fourche River was only a few miles beyond and that sup-
plies would probably reach them there from Deadwood in the
Black Hills.

But all night it rained torrents, and by morning Crow Creek
was flooded, its one available ford, between steep banks, dangerous because of high water and quicksand. Bourke says the
dangerous approaches were "corduroyed and placed in good order
by a party under Lieutenant Charles King, who had been assigned
by General Merritt to the work."[11] King's own account is not so
optimistic about placing it "in good order." He remarks that
General Merritt assigned him to put the ford into shape and gave
him Lieutenant Young and fifty men to do the work, "but there
were no tools and the men were jaded; not more than ten or twelve
could do a stroke of work. We hewed down willows and saplings
with our hunting knives, brought huge bundles of these to the
ford, waded in to the waist, and anchored them as best we could to
the yielding bottom; worked like beavers until noon, and at last
reported it practicable despite its looks."[12]

But this engineering triumph won no praise from General
Crook, who decided to find a crossing for himself. Expert horse-
manship brought him to the opposite bank, but one of his escort
went under, plunged toward the shaky causeway, and was saved
by scrambling upon it. The rest of the column stuck to King's ford
and found it adequate.

There remained a march of five or six miles to the Belle Fourche
or North Fork of the Cheyenne River, and it also had to be
crossed, but there the bottom was solid and the men were able to
get over safely by wading, swimming, and clinging to their horses'
tails. Camp was made, and within a short time the wagons of
rations from Deadwood arrived. Then came a wild scramble for
bacon, flour, and coffee, and for the moment discipline was forgotten. But there were no casualties.

The next day only the cooks had to work, according to King's
account, and the day was spent in feasting—probably not a bad
idea. Upham's battalion came in, not having seen an Indian during
their scout, though Private Alfred Milner of Company I was killed
by Indians while pursuing an antelope a half-mile ahead of the
column. Lieutenants Keyes and Plummer were sent back to
gather ammunition and other material cached along the way, and
while awaiting their return, and afterward, the expedition moved

leisurely through the Black Hills, first attention being given to
rehabilitating the horses. Oats and corn still were not to be had,
though small amounts were borrowed from an artillery train met
in the Hills. The artillerymen, spruce and trim from the western
coast, could hardly believe that the collection of scarecrows they
saw was really a part of the United States Army.

But all cavalrymen will go to great lengths for their horses, as
King records in his sketch entitled "Van," the story of a racehorse
that made the 1876 campaign. At one time King traded off his
entire supply of tobacco to provide oats for Van and for Donnybrook, a mount who was among the unfortunate ones whose sad
fate it was to be eaten during the march for the Black Hills and
who was referred to in an atrocious pun as "Donnybrook fare." At
another time King swallowed his pride and begged his colonel for
a small measure of oats for Van. And Van survived so well that
Spotted Tail was ready to trade four Indian ponies and a woman
for him at the close of the campaign.[13]

Crook had gone on to Fort Laramie to report to General Sheridan, leaving the command to Merritt. After visits in Crook City,
Deadwood, and Custer City and other mining towns in the Black
Hills, a long rest was taken on French Creek, where a formal
check was made of losses. Captain Montgomery of Company B
reported that not only had every one of his gray horses survived
the campaign, but not a saddle, bridle, nosebag, lariat, picket pin,
sideline, or any other article of horse equipment was missing—a
remarkable showing. King chuckles that while the "B fellers" had
gained some reputation for their ability to find things that nearby
companies lost, they "could not acquire gray horses at the expense
of the rest of the regiment, whatever they might have done in side
and other lines."[14]

But horses and recruits were on the way, and the troopers
moved to Amphibious Creek to meet them. Only one more move
remained for the "B.H.&Y.," as the Big Horn and Yellowstone
Expedition was commonly known. On Friday, October 13, the
command started a scout down the valley of the South Cheyenne,
but without result. Soon the expedition proceeded to the Red
Cloud Agency, where it proposed to seize the arms and ponies of
the resident Indians. But most of the Sioux and Cheyennes there
had taken alarm, and only a few ponies and guns were found. On
October 24 Crook issued an order dissolving the expedition, and
the Fifth Cavalry was ordered to posts along the Union Pacific
Railroad.

The campaign, however, had been far more effective in pacifica-

tion than its indecisive fights might indicate. Crook's men had not
starved in vain. The relentless pursuit forced Sitting Bull's huge
concentration to break up into small parties, and the scattered
Sioux never again reassembled to do battle as they had on the
Rosebud and with Custer. It was three or four years before all the
Sioux were gathered up, but the trouble was nearly ended.

Trials of a Staff-Officer

Exceptional as was the Great Sioux War of 1876 in the extent of its operations and in their importance, the disbanding of the summer expedition meant that troops could again settle down to winter barracks, officers could send for their wives and families, and the staff could begin untangling the red tape that had wound itself around regimental and personal affairs during the long absence. Headquarters and six companies of the Fifth Cavalry were to be stationed at Fort D. A. Russell, Wyoming, a famous frontier post established in 1867 to protect a division point of the Union Pacific Railroad at Cheyenne. The fort was named in honor of Brevet Major General David A. Russell, a notable hero of the Mexican War and Civil War who was killed at the battle of Opequon, Virginia, September 19, 1864. Still in use today by the United States Air Force, in later years it was renamed Fort Francis E. Warren and again Warren Air Force Base in honor of the senator from Wyoming.[1]

Officers' quarters were built in 1868 of one thickness of pine boards set on end, with cracks battened inside and out. King had vivid recollections of life in such a habitation when blizzards swept the plains, and readers of his many novels describing life at this post find few that do not feature howling winds. By the time King came to occupy one of these establishments, "officers' row" was a curious hodge-podge, for accommodating quartermasters had allowed the addition of sundry kitchens, lean-tos, and spare rooms, built for the most part of scrap lumber, old packing boxes, or anything else that came to mind. It must have looked anything but military. King had his "workshop" in a lean-to or "linter," as they seem to have been called, where he did much of his paperwork. But it was not long before he suffered one of those misfortunes he so frequently describes in his stories, being "ranked out of quarters." According to that old army custom, a new officer arriving at a garrison had the right to choose any quarters occupied by an officer junior to him in rank. Of course the man ranked out could select desirable quarters occupied by his immediate junior, and so on down the line to the lowest-ranking second lieutenant. In army society "moving day" was frequent and annoying. King's new quarters had no "linter," so he fenced off a section of the hall for an office. It was not until about 1885 that brick buildings were erected at Fort D. A. Russell, too late to do King any good.[2]

Barracks for enlisted men looked little better, or even worse, than officers' row. Also, there was a hospital of twenty beds, a guardhouse, a headquarters building, corrals for the animals, a bleak-looking parade ground marked by a flagpole, and buildings used as storehouses. "Fort" in the Far West implied no fortification, and commonly the sole artillery was a small piece used only for salutes. Stockades and blockhouses were rare in warfare on the plains, and attacks by plains tribes were even rarer.

But despite its discomforts, or perhaps because of them, frontier army life was as gay and as active as limited numbers could make it. Lieutenant Eben Swift, writing in 1891, spoke of "the well-remembered days of song and dance at Fort D. A. Russell."[3] In his book *Captain Blake*, King gives some idea of a winter's social program. When the regiment arrived at the fort the infantry officers threw a party in honor of the new arrivals. Then the bachelor officers of the garrison gave a party for the ladies of both regiments. It then was the turn of the officers of the "–th Cavalry" to entertain their hosts. And the ladies of the –th Cavalry could not be outdone; in fact, they brought this phase of the social season to a climax by giving a "german." By this time a change from dancing was in order, and amateur theatricals were next on the program. In *Blake* we are given the name of the play, *Caste*, initially produced by T. W. Robertson in London in 1867 and called the first modern realistic play. It was performed in the same hall where the german had been held, and King's readers are informed that the management had carefully taken up the canvas covering the floor so that the dancing surface would not suffer.

Thus it was that life at an army post, even on the frontier in winter, was not entirely flat, and not all the time was spent chasing Indians. Wives joined their husbands for the winter, knowing it was not probable that sudden orders to take the field would arrive during that season; the officers were ready for a certain amount of skylarking after their summer handships, and perhaps at no place in the country were parties and dances more thoroughly enjoyed. In fact, officers' wives would often bring with them younger sisters and other relatives, and King hints strongly at the dark design of marrying off some of these damsels to the younger officers who were joining every summer from West Point.

Although King wrote mostly about officers, whose society was of course a thing apart, enlisted men also had their gay times. In that benighted era there was still government pay and allowances for a certain number of women designated officially as laundresses, and in the course of time all laundry work was performed by the wives and daughters of enlisted men. Hence the quarters of the sergeants and corporals who had families, and of other married enlisted men, were known collectively as "suds row," and many a merry dance was enjoyed by the Bridgets and Betsys of the washboard, recruited by the maids of officers' wives and other available soldier sweethearts. There were not many male servants in an army post, except for a few retired enlisted men who had served faithfully for many years as "strikers" and were retained after their usefulness to the army was over. In those days enlisted men were glad to serve as officers' servants for a compensation and were regularly detailed for that service, though probably never unwillingly. The term "dog robber" was an opprobrious epithet, and occasionally its use was forbidden in formal orders, but it was mostly looked upon as a comparatively harmless employment. But enlisted men of the 1870s, many of them Irish and German immigrants, had little objection to doing servants' work, especially when it carried extra allowances.

King himself had little time for social gaiety that winter of 1876–77. On October 5 he was formally appointed adjutant of the Fifth Cavalry, a post bringing considerable honor and some perquisites. The adjutancy was open to both second lieutenants and first lieutenants, though according to King most colonels held that appointing a second lieutenant would be a serious reflection on the competency of all the first lieutenants in the regiment. But it was the most important position a lieutenant could hold, for as the executive of the commanding officer he could give orders to all captains and majors of the regiment. Although he had no authority in his own right over any of his superiors, the adjutant could arrange for many desirable details and assignments. It was usually expedient for officers to keep on his good side. At the same time the position called for considerable ability and tact. Army laws recognized its importance by granting each regiment an extra lieutenant for appointment to that office.

But in 1876 the position of adjutant had only disadvantages for King. During the campaign against the Sioux the field desk had been left behind, and among the first mail to greet the returning heroes was a series of angry demands from the adjutant general's office—and all the intervening adjutants' offices, including that of the department the Fifth had left in June—demanding the regimental returns for June, July, August, September, October, and probably a couple more months—King says seven, and it probably was bad enough without exaggeration. Undoubtedly these official letters had been forwarded from time to time all summer to troops in the field. High-ranking staff officers far from the scene of action could not understand the criminal neglect of the adjutant of the Fifth Cavalry in not replying to their repeated orders!

King thought he was badly used and, in turn, could not understand why adjutants general failed to realize that a soldier had great difficulty preparing regimental returns on horseback or while curled up under a sagebrush. But before he could get around to clearing up this accumulation of statistical reports, Companies H and L, the troops that had missed the summer campaign, were ordered out on Crook's third expedition. On November 25 and 26 the cavalry force under Colonel and Brevet Major General Ranald S. Mackenzie, brilliant colonel of the Fourth U.S. Cavalry, struck the village of Dull Knife's Northern Cheyennes. Dull Knife's village was captured, his band broken up, and much material identified as having belonged to Custer's lost battalion recovered, all in subzero temperatures. Then the captains of Companies H and L were met by demands from Adjutant King that they immediately submit returns for their companies so that the regimental papers could go forward. And *they* wondered how an adjutant, sitting comfortably in quarters at Fort D. A. Russell, could expect them to make out muster rolls on horseback at thirty degrees below zero!

Besides compiling these multitudinous reports, the regimental adjutant rose at 5:30 A.M., took the reveille report of the band, reported the results of the roll call to the colonel, got breakfast in time to see that the trumpeters sounded stable call promptly at 7:00, superintended the grooming of the horses belonging to the band and noncommissioned staff, saw sick call sounded and put the regimental clerks to work, and then changed into full dress uniform for morning parade at 8:00 and then attended guard mount, for the adjutant had important duties in both those ceremonies. Between 9:30 and drill call at 10:15 he had leisure to attend to his office work after he changed his uniform again, and then he attended battalion drill until noon. From 1:00 to 2:00 P.M. he was present at recruit drill, and from 2:00 to 4:00 he was again in his office. At 4:00 another stable call sounded, followed by retreat and evening dress parade at sunset. On Monday evenings there were recitations of officers, and on Tuesday and Fridays noncommissioned officers' classes.

But King did not ask to be relieved of any of the duties connected with drill and instruction. The regiment was sadly in need of "straightening out," since most of its men had seen nothing more complicated than a company drill for several years. The first evening dress parade displayed a wide variety of errors in the finer points of tactics. As just one example, King records that the first sergeants of the six companies reported as follows:

"Company 'O,' present or accounted for, Sir."
"Company 'R,' all present or accounted for."
" 'T' company, present or accounted for, Sir."
" 'U' company, all present, Sir."
"Sir! two privates are absent."
" 'X' company, all are present, Sir."

All were different, and not one used the correct form, which was "Company A present or accounted for" or "Company A two privates absent."

These minor details may seem trivial, and evidently most of the officers of the regiment paid them little heed. But King was something of a martinet in insisting on the finer points of the regulations, his view being that since these things were prescribed as disciplinary exercises, discipline would be most highly developed by strict adherence to the letter of the law. To scoff at such manifestations of the military mind ignored the reality of war, where exactness in phrasing an order could mean the difference between life and death.

But in addition to all these trials, King had others. Among his heaped-on duties, the lieutenant was regimental ordnance officer. This all started near the very beginning of the Fifth's service in 1876. King was ordered to issue certain needed supplies during a pause in the Warbonnet campaign. When the Fifth joined Crook's expedition, King was put in charge of all ordnance issued to the entire column. The term ordnance, as all soldiers know, covers a wide variety of matériel, including rifles, carbines, revolvers, sabers, ammunition, cartridge boxes and pouches, holsters, haversacks, bridles, halters and straps, lariats, nosebags, saddles, surcingles, saddle blankets, sidelines, and very much more. When the campaign was over there were scouts and guides and teamsters and soldiers scattered all over the wild and woolly West bearing arms and equipment for which Lieutenant King was personally and financially responsible.[4]

It seems this ought to have been trouble enough, but King immediately let himself in for more. At about the time Fort D. A. Russell was established, a quartermaster depot was built nearby. Known as Cheyenne Depot, it became the second largest such station in the United States, furnishing supplies for twelve army posts, some of them four hundred miles away. It was also thought necessary to establish an ordnance depot there as a substation to the arsenal at Rock Island, Illinois. As an example of the efficiency of the period, King points out that though no officer of the ordnance department was sent to Fort D. A. Russell, supplies were shipped there, and often shipped halfway back, with only some temporarily appointed officer responsible for distribution.[5]

This responsiblity, which amounted to $700,000 worth of property, was vested in the commanding officer of Fort Russell, Colonel J. J. Reynolds, former corps commander of the Army of the Potomac, who had been so unfortunate in the first Crook expedition of 1876. For his conduct in the Powder River fight Reynolds had been acquitted by court-martial, but he had applied for retirement. He had been granted a leave of absence pending final review of his case by the War Department, and now he was only awaiting a relieving officer to quit Fort Russell. The Fifth Cavalry arrived in command of Major Upham, but he also was expecting a leave of absence and refused to sign for the ordnance property. Now Reynolds's position was that of a "lame duck," so when Merritt arrived he had no compunction in also refusing to sign for the ordnance property, going so far as to state that he also would demand a leave of absence if the order were insisted upon.

Reynolds begged and pleaded for something to be done. His baggage was aboard a steamer, and his family in New York awaited his arrival for a trip abroad as soon as he could be relieved of responsibility for this tremendous lot of ordnance. Adjutants were supposed to be capable of all sorts of odd jobs, so it occurred to someone to suggest King for the position of division ordnance officer. King almost rebelled. He thought of appealing over the heads of the whole flock of brevet generals to Phil Sheridan himself, but Reynolds put up such a sad story that King finally weakened and signed the official receipts.

This being satisfactorily settled, Merritt was ready to do everything in his power to obtain relief for his overworked subaltern. He immediately wrote a letter demanding the appointment of an officer from the ordnance department to accept this responsibility, and in due course, after seventeen months and several Indian campaigns had again scattered these supplies far and wide over the plains, this very reasonable request was granted.

But long before this happened it was discovered that $600,000 rounds of ammunition were stored in a makeshift warehouse used as the ordnance depot. Merritt, worried about the danger of fire and explosion, ordered this matériel placed in a magazine about a mile and a half from the fort. For a while a guard was posted at the site, but Merritt felt sorry for the men detailed to walk this post in zero weather and ordered them relieved. Promptly a party of citizens from Cheyenne appeared at the magazine and helped themselves to whatever they could carry. King trailed them, recovered some of the ammunition, and had one man arrested. A jury of fellow townsmen promptly acquitted the culprit, and King offers his opinion that in those days no jury could have been found to convict any civilian of a crime against United States property or even the murder of one of Uncle Sam's soldiers.[6]

Indeed, robbing of Uncle Sam's warehouses seems to have been a popular diversion, to judge from the many times such incidents figure in King's novels. Just to prove he was not exaggerating, he records that one night a wagon was backed up to one of his warehouses and loaded with government property. Fortunately the thieves mistook boxes of picket pins for ammunition, so the loss was not heavy, and King was somewhat comforted by reflecting on their disappointment. There was a guard, of course, but it was a very dark night, and the sentry was supposed to be in charge of a coal shed, a commissary storehouse, two quartermaster storehouses, a saddler's shop, and a few loads of hay.[7]

By this time most of the $600,000 or $700,000 worth of equipment must have been charged against King's pay, but it happens there is an ancient and honorable institution in the army, still in existence, known as a board of survey. Such a board is made up of officers, usually those near at hand who know the circumstances, and it has power to charge off items lost, strayed, or stolen so long as reasonable evidence can be produced that the responsible officer exercised proper care and vigilance.

Officers farther from the scene are sometimes less lenient. King relates the story of a glass inkstand that performed its final duty by removing a howling cat from a brick wall. Two years later, while King was lying wounded in a hospital after his fight at Sunset Pass, he received a letter from the office of the quartermaster general informing him that his pay would be stopped if he did not immediately account for this piece of property. Such inkstands were worth about six cents a gross, according to his estimate. But the department commander disposed of this case.[8]

In the midst of these tribulations came other campaigns. The first orders of the year 1877 were for a new kind of duty for the Fifth Cavalry, one not then customary for the regular army. Early in that year occurred the great railway strikes, starting in the East, where rioting soon developed that the state militia could not effectively cope with. President Rutherford B. Hayes called out regular troops from the South and from the plains as the strike spread westward. General Sheridan was called on to preserve the peace in Chicago, and among the troops hurried there by the Union Pacific Railroad were the Indian fighters of the Fifth Cavalry, with Merritt in command and King as his adjutant general.

As the troop train approached the western outskirts it was reported that Chicago was in the hands of the mob and the train would not be allowed to enter. A flatcar was placed ahead of the engine, and on it was mounted a Gatling gun, which had by this time had even more of a reputation than it had in New Orleans in 1868. Supporting it was a guard of sharpshooters, recruited from the best of the men who had chased Sitting Bull. Mobs were gathered along the right-of-way, but only at one point was an attempt made to stop the train. One man rushed toward a switch, planning to turn the train aside. Not a word was said, but three or four soldiers on the flatcar raised their carbines and took careful aim, ready to fire if he touched the switch handle. Friends of the rioter shouted a warning; he saw the carbines pointed at him and left so hastily that he rolled clear down the embankment, jeered by the mob. At the station the troopers quickly left the train and marched through the streets.[9]

Needless to say, the mobs did not wish to test these soldiers who were visiting Chicago merely as an interlude in Indian warfare. Doubtless the Fifth Cavalry looked tough, perhaps a little tougher than the plug-uglies who were causing the trouble. The troopers had expected action and were in campaign garb; there was little of dress parade about them, and their businesslike appearance was all that was needed. It was characteristic of the times that everyone from the president on down was happy the trouble was ended, and little attention was given to the grievances that had brought it about. In any case, suppressing disorder was the business of professional soldiers.

The Fifth's stay in Chicago was not long. Almost immediately came word that of a new Indian war was breaking out, one that threatened to be of major proportions. The Nez Perces, with whom the United States had never before had any trouble, were on a rampage. And from all available evidence it seemed they were completely justified. A treaty had been signed by which the Nez Perces agreed to give up their ancestral lands, but there was dispute as to who signed the treaty on behalf of the Indians. At all events very able leaders—Looking Glass, White Bird, and Joseph among them—refused to acknowledge it and prepared to resist. At White Bird Canyon, Idaho, the Nez Perces fell upon Companies F and H of the First U.S. Cavalry and killed an officer and 35 enlisted men out of a total force of 110. At Craig's Mountain they killed to the last man a scouting party from Company L of the same regiment. Brigadier General Oliver O. Howard attacked Joseph with a large force, capturing the camp, but the Indians slipped away and started a long flight with many members of the tribe. By this time troops from all directions were being hurried to intercept the Nez Perces. Colonel Gibbon had a lively fight at the Big Hole in western Montana but was unable to halt their flight. Brevet Major General Samuel D. Sturgis, colonel of the Seventh Cavalry, covered Clark's Fork; Major Verling K. Hart with five companies of cavalry was at Stinking Water River; and Merritt with ten companies of the Fifth Cavalry was rushed by rail from Chicago to take part in the supposed roundup. After a short stop at Fort D. A. Russell, Merritt led his regiment by another "lightning march" north to Wind River, where he was given command of a column consisting of the Third and Fifth Cavalry, with King again as his adjutant general.

The arrangement was expected to halt the Nez Perce movement northward to Canada. But the Seventh Cavalry was unfor-

tunate again and was lured from its position in the blockade, allowing the Nez Perces to slip through. The Seventh made a rapid pursuit and caught up at Canyon Creek, Montana, where an all-day fight took place but had no effect in halting Joseph's march. The move had left Merritt's column far behind, and it did not get in at the finish, the surrender of the Nez Perces being forced by Colonel Nelson A. Miles's column of Fifth Infantry at the Bear Paw Mountains, Montana.

During this campaign Mrs. King and other women and children of the Fifth Cavalry were left behind at Fort Russell with only a doctor, a sergeant, and sixteen enlisted men to guard them. In the midst of this trial Lieutenant King's second daughter, Carolyn, was born. Little did he know that his regular army career was drawing near its close. In 1878 the Fifth Cavalry was out again, after Bannocks this time, but during that year surgeons told King he could never pass a physical examination for promotion and "could never swing a regulation saber again. The War Department was most kind and let me hang on until I reached my captaincy," he says, which is more heart than might be expected from an institution so concerned about the fate of an inkwell.[10]

He became Captain Charles King, commanding Company A of the Fifth Cavalry, on May 1, 1879, and was placed on the retired list for "disability resulting from wounds received in the line of duty" June 14 of the same year.[11]

Between the Lines

Probably the popular conception of a retired officer is of a gentleman seated comfortably in an easy chair in some downtown club, sipping liquor, smoking cigars, and spending little money but much time in spinning long yarns of his military career to whomever will listen.

Perhaps Captain King would have enjoyed just that. But he could not afford to do much of it on $2,100 a year, the retirement pay of a captain. That sum was not large, even in those days, for a man with a growing family. He had found the active duty pay of a first lieutenant little enough, considering the constant changes of station required of him and his family. He needed money. And King, despite his injuries, had tremendous vitality, requiring constant activity of mind and body, a characteristic that never left him even in advanced age. The many tales fleshed out in his book *Trials of a Staff-Officer* exemplified King's life after leaving the regulars. For despite his complaints in that volume, which were largely intended to be whimsical, it is obvious that he really enjoyed having a great many challenges and experiences.

For the rest of his life, though he never had any regular occupation for an extended period—at least in a traditional sense—he always had two, or three, or four, or five concurrent duties and obligations. These may be roughly divided into two categories. The one placed him before the public in a number of military and political-military offices, bringing him considerable local newspaper publicity, but little notice beyond the borders of Wisconsin. The other, carried on simultaneously, was his literary work, which soon brought him national and even international fame. For King military pursuits were nearly inseparable from his writing, but by reading "between the lines" of his many books one sees their influence in shaping his career.

There is evidence that these literary pursuits were among the first occupations he considered after retiring from the army. Since collecting his first and only rejection slip in 1873 for the story that finally appeared as *Kitty's Conquest,* he had done little writing except keeping a diary and attempting one brief newspaper story, telling about Buffalo Bill's exploit at the Warbonnet, published in the New York *Herald* on July 23, 1876, only six days after the fight.[1] Now upon retirement he thought again of the story long kept in the bottom of a trunk, and he submitted it to an old Milwaukee friend, Colonel George A. Woodward, then editor of the *United Service Magazine* in Philadelphia, a military periodical that published some valuable contributions to the military history of the United States. Colonel Woodward thought the story could be published as a book if King would put up four hundred dollars. But King was looking to get money, not pay it out, so he rejected the offer.

While considering his qualifications for civilian life in 1879, it occurred to him that his knowledge of engineering, acquired at West Point and demonstrated at the bridging of Crow Creek and elsewhere on the frontier, might be applied to railroading. He applied to friends for employment on one of the midwestern railroads, but no job developed.

There is a story that King started his literary career because of a slur on the military profession. The tale has as its scene a downtown club in Milwaukee, in summer or early fall 1879. Captain King is exemplifying the popular conception of a retired army officer, undoubtedly smoking a cigar, and very probably sipping a glass of Milwaukee beer. Several other gentlemen are seated in easy chairs, which one imagines are upholstered in red plush. So far King has never bored his mates with any stories of his army life. But one of these gentlemen unwittingly is looking for trouble. He indulges in the small boy's favorite complaint of "nothing to do." And really in those days, before there was golf or even very much baseball to talk about, one wonders how gentlemen ever managed to pass the time. But this witless person had the ill grace to opine that Captain King might have some special secret for doing nothing gracefully—that he should be experienced and expert in the art of loafing.

"Why?" was Captain King's crisp response to this suggestion, in a tone that carried enough dynamite for a considerable explosion.

"Oh, I don't mean anything personal. But I have always supposed that an army officer has little do do except play cards and drink whiskey."

"So that's your idea of army life is it? Now just let me tell you something. On the first day of June in 1876, just three years ago, the Fifth Cavalry. . ."[2]

We have just read the story of the Sioux campaign, but that small audience knew little about it. There had been some scattered accounts of Indian campaigns in their newspapers, but the men had paid little attention to them and had little conception of what they signified. But now they listened, fascinated, while King talked hour after hour. And far from being bored, they begged for more.

There was present a member of the editorial staff of the *Milwaukee Sentinel* who was planning a new Sunday supplement to that newspaper.

"That was a very interesting story, Captain King," he suggested. "Why don't you write it out? I believe we could use some of it in a feature article. Were there any Wisconsin men besides yourself there? Build the story around them."

The result was "The Fight of the Rear Guard," the story of Major Upham's combat of September 10, 1876. One finds it, "local angle" and all, as chapter 9 of *Campaigning with Crook*, for King did little revising of the newspaper version when it appeared in the book. There is mention of the "Badger State Benefit"—Major John J. Upham of Milwaukee in command, Lieutenant Hoel S. Bishop of Fond du Lac, First Sergeant John Goll of Milwaukee, and various other Wisconsin men, including the adjutant who had been "marker of our Light Guard years before"—King, of course. And the chapter ends with Upham's remark, "Eight o'clock here; church time in Milwaukee," and King's comment, "Who would have thought it was Sunday?" stamping it as a Sunday supplement article.

The first story attracted notice, and the *Sentinel* asked for more. Buffalo Bill Cody happened along and suggested an account of his friend "Buffalo Chips," and that became the second article. By this time King had written all around "The Combat at Slim Buttes," so it seemed fitting to include it as the third of the series. In time there followed the rest of the chapters of *Campaigning with Crook*, except the last, "Dropped Stitches," added when the *Sentinel* decided to reprint the series as a pamphlet of five hundred copies. It was called *Campaigning with Crook*, with an overtitle at the top of the page, "The Fifth Cavalry in the Sioux War of 1876." Its preface bore the date May 25, 1880. Many of the copies went to officers of the regiment, and the largest single order came from Fort Laramie, where the Fifth Cavalry was then headquartered. The pamphlet sold out within a year and is now a highly prized first edition.

This small paperback was the first of King's books to be printed, is one of his best known, and is still regarded as one of the most useful accounts of Indian warfare on the plains. Ten years later *Campaigning* was reprinted with three additional "stories of army life," one of which, "Captain Santa Claus," both King and his wife regarded as the best short story he ever wrote.

In 1881 Colonel Woodward asked Captain King for a serialized story of army life to be a companion piece to a story of naval life by an admiral that was soon to be published in the *United Service*. The slur about army officers having little to do except play cards and drink whiskey rankled King, and he had determined to tell a story of the everyday life of the army. The result was a serial that ran in the magazine during most of 1881 and 1882 under the title "Winning His Spurs." It was published as a book by the J. B. Lippincott Company in 1883 with a new name, *The Colonel's Daughter*.[3]

This book was an immediate literary success and was taken seriously by many reviewers. The *Army and Navy Journal* found it "a charming work, worthy of achieving a permanent place in literature." The *Chicago Tribune* declared it "the first American military novel," and the *New Orleans Times-Democrat* compared it to the work of Sir Walter Scott. Both the *New York Tribune* and the *Milwaukee Sentinel* hoped it would be followed by many others from the same pen. They were not to be disappointed.

However romantic and sentimental *The Colonel's Daughter* may now appear, it was the height of realism in its own day. King, in his preface, remarked that he had written no conversations worth reading, for he found himself quite unable to attribute to his characters the colossal wisdom exemplified by those of Augusta J. Evans's *St. Elmo*. He feared that his soldiers talked quite prosaically. But they became known to a wide circle of readers. *The Colonel's Daughter* made the reputation of "Captain Charles King, U.S.A.," and by it he was known for the remainder of his life.

King still had faith in his previously rejected manuscript, and

Kitty's Conquest, his second novel to be published, appeared in 1884. Meanwhile he had been urged by a subscription book publisher to write the series of sketches that became *Famous and Decisive Battles of the World; or, History from the Battle-Field*, which also appeared in 1884. This made a weighty volume of 752 pages, discussing forty-five battles from Marathon to Plevna. It was long favorably known to military students and was reprinted several times, and it even suffered the doubtful honor of being "pirated."

In his preface to *Marion's Faith*, the first sequel to *The Colonel's Daughter*, King recalled the story of Sam Slick, who at a first shot knocked the cork out of a bottle floating some distance away and never again could be induced to handle firearms, knowing he could not improve on his first attempt. Some readers agreed that King never improved on *The Colonel's Daughter*. In his first story he had drawn upon his Arizona experiences, but *Marion's Faith* carried the "–th Cavalry" into the campaign of 1876 on the northern plains. Few readers failed to identify King's Fifth Cavalry.

King's stories attracted a wide circle of followers, for they had both adventure and love interest, were well written, and contained certain elements of real value. The bookish plots, characteristic of almost every work of fiction in that day, may seem unnatural now, but King presented an accurate picture of contemporary society, one that has become historic.

He is perhaps unique in that with the single exception of *Kitty's Conquest*, King never wrote a book that was not commissioned by a publisher. These requests usually specified the type of story and nearly always the length. Captain King never denied that he was writing for financial remuneration, and he made little pretense of being a literary personage. Interviewers always found him much more ready to discuss military affairs than his books. His "favorite book"—evidently a frequent question from newspaper interviewers—was either *The Colonel's Daughter*, *Between the Lines*, or the title most recently published.

One can readily imagine that King did not long receive serious consideration from reviewers. But it did not matter. The curse of that day was to be popular. One best-seller was all any writer was allowed, and after that he was ignored by the literary fraternity. Captain King added nothing to his reputation by his prolific production. It was not long before his "novel factory" rivaled that of Dumas.

In 1887 appeared *The Deserter* and *From the Ranks*, short novels of the plains, published separately and also combined in a single volume by Lippincott. *Harper's Weekly* solicited a story for serial publication, and King wrote *A War-Time Wooing*, the first of his many stories about the Civil War. It was issued in 1888 by Harper and Brothers with illustrations by Rufus F. Zogbaum, a noted military artist of the period whose work is to be found in several of King's novels as well as in the books of Elizabeth B. Custer, General Theophilus F. Rodenbough, and others. *A War-Time Wooing* sold "beyond expectations," and Harper asked for another of double the length, received delivery the same year, and brought out one of King's most widely read stories, *Between the Lines*.

This Civil War tale provoked one of the finest contemporary tributes to King's work ever to appear. An editorial in the *Boston Transcript* declared:

> There is an excellent American story teller who has gained great popularity, but has not earned the critical approval that is his due, Captain Charles King. His novels of army service in the war and on the plains are stirring stories, with the narratives moving in answer to the trumpet call. They are well written, and the fact that their plots are not peculiarly original does not work against them as stories. Captain King is not as "slaughterous" as either Dumas or Stevenson, but that may be because he has with his own eyes seen "the red blood flow." "Between the Lines" is a novel of which any writer might be proud. Lord Wolseley says the description of the cavalry fight at Gettysburg is the best thing of the kind he ever read. Captain King's books are stories; he is wise not to seek to make them anything more.[4]

The year 1888 also saw completion of another Arizona story, *Dunraven Ranch*, one of King's novelettes that was coupled with an 1890 production as *Two Soldiers and Dunraven Ranch*.

How did he do it? One suspects fortitude and perseverance rather than ego, particularly after reading of the tribulations that beset him despite "The Advantages of One's Own Workshop" set forth in *Trials of a Staff-Officer*. There he reveals that *Marion's Faith*, a book of 446 pages, was completed in ten weeks, *The Deserter* in three, and *From the Ranks* in four. But the children in the backyard, the telephone, and other interruptions delayed

Dunraven Ranch to four months instead of the expected four weeks. King's workshop was a masculine den in his Milwaukee home. The house had been completely furnished by *Between the Lines*, he says. The King family also frequently stole away to a summer cottage on Lake Pepin, near Frontenac, Minnesota.

Laramie; or, The Queen of Bedlam, another famous number in the King repertoire, appeared in 1889. To this era belongs also the inception of a series of volumes "edited by" Captain Charles King. The first of these, *The Colonel's Christmas Dinner*, appearing in 1890, used the interesting device of presenting connected, contributed stories as though they were told by a group of army people gathered fortuitously around the Christmas table at "Fort Blank," an isolated frontier post. The methods used to give a festive air to unattractive quarters, and the problems of inviting, seating, and providing food for unexpected Yuletide guests throw additional light on western conditions and social life. King's contribution to this volume, in addition to an introduction and connecting passages, was the "Adjutant's Story," a "true ghost story" from his own experience and a yarn he liked to tell when there were ladies present. It was really a kitten that made the chair rock so mysteriously, not the ghost of a man who, it turned out, had failed to die as expected. A second title of this series, *By Land and Sea*, was published in 1891; *An Initial Experience* followed in 1894 and *Captain Dreams* in 1895.

King inscribed a copy of *Captain Dreams* to his secretary, Lucille Rhoades, "with the regards of the alleged editor, who never saw a line of the other stories or read proof of his own." To these collected volumes King generally contributed an introduction and one short story, the remaining pages being filled with stories by army and navy men and a few by women. It might seem that Captain King by now headed a military school of literature. Some names in these books are occasionally seen elsewhere— novelist Alice King Hamilton; Major William H. Powell, compiler of army and navy directories; and Lieutenants Alvin H. Sydenham and John P. Wisser, among others.

The first big production year for the King writing factory was 1890. In addition to *The Colonel's Christmas Dinner*, which contained little work from his pen, *Campaigning with Crook and Stories of Army Life* was published, as were *Starlight Ranch and Other Stories of Army Life on the Frontier, Two Soldiers, Sunset Pass*, and *An Army Portia*. Actually, his literary labor was not as concentrated as it appears. *Campaigning with Crook* had been written ten years before, and the three stories printed with it had appeared from time to time in magazines, as had the *Starlight Ranch* collection. *Two Soldiers* was a story of modest length, *Sunset Pass* was a juvenile, and *An Army Portia* was another half-book. Still, literary effort of any type required focused attention.

If we admit that King operated a "novel factory," we must also give the captain credit for his pioneering use of the latest technology. Thomas A. Edison invented the phonograph in 1877, and in the list of uses he thought this device might be applied to there appears: "Letter writing and all kinds of dictation without the aid of a stenographer."[5]

The first attempt to make commercial use of the phonograph was for letter writing, and the patents were sold to a company in Philadelphia whose chief promoter was a Mr. Lippincott, perhaps the head of the publishing firm. King undoubtedly heard of the invention at that time, but the project was unsuccessful, and Edison's biographers indicate that the field was inactive for years.[6] An early enthusiast was Henry D. Goodwin, a court reporter in Milwaukee, who began training stenographers to use the dictating machine about 1887. Goodwin persuaded King to try the idea, pointing out that it would relieve the captain's wounded arm. King experimented and thought the idea feasible if he could find a competent stenographer. Goodwin recommended Lucille Rhoades, and thus began an association that lasted forty-three years.[7]

Even if the mechanical stenography had not been practical, it might have been valuable for publicity, for Captain King, as the first author to use a dictating machine, was the subject of many newspaper and magazine articles. Of course, that a writer should merely "talk off" his stories did not add much to his literary reputation. It was not quite that simple, however, as Miss Rhoades explained:

He selected the theme, worked out the general trend of the plot, and determined how many chapters there were to be, in conformity with the number of words the publisher had ordered. Then, in his own study and working alone, he roughly sketched each chapter. He used a block of ordinary paper and a pencil. Sometimes he wrote an entire dialogue; again he may have set down only the high points. But he had enough to guide him in the dictation. His mind was highly trained and perfectly orderly, so that the first copy was almost exactly as it afterward appeared in print.

There were a number of little items, however, that I always watched. For instance, he sometimes forgot what color eyes he had given to a heroine. And if they were blue in the first chapter it was my job to see that they remained blue all the way through.

Once, in writing a chapter, I was startled to find that he had alluded to the "children" of a couple whom he had previously described as childless. When I called his attention to the mistake he said, "Well—scratch out the children."[8]

Sunset Pass was the first product of the dictaphone.[9]

In the midst of this flurry a letter from Major Henry E. Noyes of the Fourth Cavalry appeared in the *New York Journalist*. Noyes took King to task in rather sharp terms, which may be worth recalling as an example of the least favorable comment made at the time. Major Noyes, who had campaigned with King during the Great Sioux War, branded the "scurrilous and defamatory articles" that Captain King has written "concerning army life in general, and individuals in particular" as "simply disgusting to intelligent army readers. If we have no such paragons of men as he describes, we certainly have no such women as are some of his female characters." This lambasting rose to real heights as Noyes objected "to having a distorted image [of army life] displayed by such mental strabismus as Captain King's works exhibit." *St. Elmo* could hardly have improved on "strabismus."

This view was supported by the journalist Reuben B. Davenport of New Haven, Connecticut, who endorsed the letter as illustrating "to some extent the contempt in which King and his trashy and ephemeral stuff are held by some of the best class of army officers."

Literature was taken seriously in King's day, and the captain hardly took this all lying down. *An Army Portia*, founded on a notable court-martial case from the era, strongly reflected King's unfavorable opinion of the newspaper business.[10] But this attack from an army source was fire from the rear, and he needed to rally reserves. He prepared a printed form letter, in which he copied all the unfavorable comments, and sent it out to army friends. "For ten years," it read, "I have been led by the letters of many score of officers, many of them of high rank, and most of them personal friends to be sure to believe that I was doing a good work, 'making the Army known to the people,' and that my books gave much satisfaction to my comrades. I could attach no literary merit to them, nor could I hope to please everybody." But if these allegations are true, "I want to know it and at once, for orders for future work press upon me." In such a case, "he that is not with me is against me," in Captain King's forthright opinion, so "I beg you not to spare my feelings in this matter, but to say frankly that your views are coincident with those of the gentleman who at last has broken the ice; or, if you do not wish to speak, I will accept your silence as confirmation of his opinion.",

Captain King was overwhelmed by no conspiracy of silence, and evidently friends sprang to the rescue in such a vigorous counterattack that the original sniper was annihilated. None of King's friends recalled the incident in later years, and it might have been forgotten had not a copy or two of his statement survived. The form letter was dated February 28, 1891, and that year saw publication of one of the most popular and successful sequels to *The Colonel's Daughter*, the lengthy *Captain Blake*, concerned again with affairs of the –th Cavalry upon its return from the Sioux War, and its campaigns against the Nez Percés and Bannocks, but more particularly with life in garrison at Fort D. A. Russell. *Trials of a Staff-Officer* was also an 1891 production.

Foes in Ambush, another tale of the –th Cavalry followed in 1893, and in that year *A Soldier's Secret* appeared as companion to *An Army Portia* in a thick volume. *A Soldier's Secret* introduced the then imaginary Twelfth Cavalry in the Sioux Outbreak of 1890 and contained some strictures on the press reports of that campaign. So timely was it that it even contained a description of the funeral of General Sherman, which took place in 1891. *An Army Portia* has its hero in the Eleventh Cavalry and is perhaps the only one of King's stories of army life on the plains in which no Indian outbreak figures. It was a "novel with a purpose," an attack on the contemporary methods of the press, and was dedicated to Mrs. Custer.

In 1894 Captain King returned to Reconstruction days in Louisiana for the background of *Waring's Peril*; the same scene and some of the same characters are used in *Captain Close*, which also appeared that year. *Sergeant Croesus*, the pendant piece for *Cap-*

tain *Close* in a double volume, was written in 1893. It had the plains for its setting.

Cadet Days: A Story of West Point was a boy's tale of 1894 that won great popularity and became one of King's best-known works. It was one of few books kept in print by Harper and Brothers or any of his other publishers after his death in 1933, and it went far to justify the contemporary opinion of the *Boston Transcript* that "since the immortal 'Tom Brown' there has appeared no volume which will make more appeal to boyish hearts, whether these hearts can boast sixteen or sixty years' experience of life." But by this time King seemed to be a prophet with little honor in his own country. Of a production of 1895, *Under Fire*, described by the author as "the fourth of what may be called 'The Colonel's Daughter' series,"[11] the *Milwaukee Sentinel* complained of his "confining his efforts to frontier life as the enduring blue that envelops his troopers on dress parade." The paper advised him to enlarge his scope as a writer, because "one blizzard is too like another," and remarked that his "little bit of scandal is perfectly harmless in these days of *The Second Mrs. Tanqueray* and *Trilby*." Possibly it was the critic who lived too soon. *An Initial Experience* brought the year's total to four.

Perhaps Captain King took the criticism to heart, for later works in 1895 and 1896 do show some new themes. *A Tame Surrender* was a story of the Chicago strike of 1893, and *An Army Wife* told of contemporary life in Arizona, with little reference to Apache troubles. *Trooper Ross and Signal Butte* were another pair of twins, the first following the lead of *Cadet Days* in being a story of schoolboy life, with episodes from the plains. *Signal Butte* was another Apache war story. Other efforts included *Captain Dreams* and *Rancho del Muerto and Other Stories from Outing*, the latter a publication by a magazine that included Captain King's name but contained only one story by him, with Arizona again as the theme. The year 1895 was doubly important because of King's association with the New York publishing firm of F. Tennyson Neely and the appearance of their first joint effort, *The Story of Fort Frayne*.

The Story of Fort Frayne

In an era when the stage produced such masterpieces as *Shenandoah, Michael Strogoff, The Count of Monte Cristo, The Great Divide,* and *Jesse James,* Captain King's novels were ideal for dramatization. Yet the only play he had anything to do with was *Fort Frayne,* which was written originally as a drama, in collaboration with Evelyn Greenleaf Sutherland, a drama critic known to readers of the *Boston Journal* as Dorothy Lundt, and Emma V. Sheridan Fry, an actress remembered for her portrayal of Rebecca in *Dr. Jekyll and Mr. Hyde.* Of King's lone dramatic effort, one critic was so unkind as to say that the soldier-novelist-playwright had produced his work "under soothing influences of pink tea."

However that may be, few plays have had greater vicissitudes. In the first place the three authors seem to have produced only one copy of the manuscript among them, and in the course of sending it around to gather opinions and seek out possible producers it was lost in the mail. By this time several people had seen it, and with its whereabouts suddenly unknown, someone suggested that King protect his rights by copyrighting the story as a novel. Accordingly he hurried *The Story of Fort Frayne* into Neely's hands in 1895, and curiously it became one of his most successful novels, with eleven thousands copies sold and twenty-five thousand more struck off in a new edition before the play was produced on the stage two years later.

But the troubles with *Fort Frayne* were far from over. In March 1897 the play was accepted for production at the Broadway Theater in New York by the Actors' Society of America. Simultaneous presentation in London was planned. *Fort Frayne* was selected in competition with a number of other plays as this organization's first production for the benefit of its fund. A notable cast was assembled, including such luminaries as Minnie Dupree and Mrs. Thomas Wiffen, along with Frank Mordant, Herbert Kelcey,

W. J. Le Moyne, Joseph Wheelock, Jr., Edgar L. Davenport, James A. Barrows, Lawrence Hanley, Mary Shaw, Annie Clark, Grace Atwell, and Lucretia Fenton.

Trouble developed when Charles Frohman and other producers did not endorse the appearance of their stars under the auspices of this society. Less than three weeks before the premiere, the society begged off its contract. Although Annie Dupree happened to be one of the innocent causes of this collapse, she did create the part of Kitty Ormsby after all, when *Fort Frayne* was produced on August 30, 1897, as the opening bill of a newly organized stock company at the Schiller Theater in Chicago. For this second attempt other actresses included Elita Procter Otis, Kate Denim-Wilson, Minnie Radcliffe, and Mattie Earle, along with actors Robert Drouet, Herbert Carr, George R. Edeson, Percy Bowles, George W. Leslie, Bert W. Wilson, Benjamin Horning, and Charles H. Peckham.

The acts were pure King and pure melodrama: "Act I. A cloud rises over Fort Frayne. Act II. The storm gathers. Act III. The storm breaks. Act IV. Love and sunshine." The musical program included "Life in Camp" by Keler Bela as an overture, excerpts from Rubenstein's opera *Feremores*, selections from Chaminade and Dvořák, the latter's name being misspelled in the program, and as a grand finale, Sousa's "Stars and Stripes Forever." The time of the play was given as 1895, not 1897, the date of production.

Fort Frayne was favorably received by critics and the public. Chicago dramatic writers contributed a column and a half each in the *Inter-Ocean*, the *Times-Herald*, and the *Evening Post*, while the *Chronicle* thought nothing of devoting one column to a debate on the military authenticity of the production—a rather touchy subject, one would think, to take up with Charles King. In another three-quarter-length column the *Times-Herald* acknowledged the remarkable speed Miss Dupree displayed in changing costumes, a matter of astonishment considering the clothes of the Gay Nineties. The newspaper gave Mr. Bowles credit for a similar accomplishment, suggesting him for the part of Rudolph Rassendyl in *The Prisoner of Zenda*, a famous double role of the period once played by E. H. Sothern. *Fort Frayne* was kept on the boards four weeks instead of three, as originally intended. Since the stock company had signed a resident contract the play could not immediately be taken on tour, but it was later seen in Milwaukee and notably in San Francisco during the time when King commanded a brigade of troops there in 1898 and 1899.[1]

Although *Fort Frayne* was Captain King's only contribution to formal drama, he participated in another type of entertainment popular in that period, the public lecture. There exist clippings and a program from an opening entertainment at a lecture course entitled "A Night with the Story Tellers" at the Academy of Music in Milwaukee. King made his debut on the dais with a reading of his story "Van," described as "a soldier's loving tribute to an army horse," and of course the same story appears in his book *Starlight Ranch*. He was introduced by George W. Peck, a former governor of Wisconsin who well deserved a place in the distinguished array, as author of *Peck's Bad Boy and His Pa* and other popular stories. Eugene Field recited his "Seein' Things" and other poems, and Opie P. Read gave sketches in black dialect and recited his "Bill, the Lokil Editor." To complete the evening, a mandolin solo was given by Sig. S. P. Fachutar and baritone solos by William Osborne Goodrich. The press gave very favorable notice to King as a public reader, but there is no evidence that he ever made further effort to enter this field, though he delivered many lectures on military subjects in later years and was a frequent after-dinner speaker.

Another curious entertainment of the day got extended notice in the tabloid *Peck's Sun*, perhaps because of the distinction of certain guests in one of the boxes. The three prominent men at this particular Press Club affair were James J. Corbett, champion heavyweight boxer of the world, Charles K. Harris, author of "After the Ball" and other "compositions of world wide fame," and Captain Charles King. The entertainment was the "picture play" *Miss Jerry*. In 1895 this was not yet a motion picture but a succession of photographic scenes, three hundred views all told, projected onto canvas while a pleasant story was recited.[2]

Despite this diversionary activity, Captain King continued to write books. During a trip to Europe in 1893 he discovered and translated from the German the story *Noble Blood* and added to it in 1896 his *A West Point Parallel*, a tale based loosely on the Boyd affair. The same year saw two more books about the plains, *Trumpeter Fred* and *A Garrison Tangle*.

Remarkably, one Friday in 1897 he spoke forty thousand words into the phonograph, leaving only ten thousand to complete *Ray's Recruit*, which ran complete in one issue of *Lippincott's Monthly Magazine* and was later issued both as a separate book and twinned with *A Tame Surrender*. "A Contraband's Christmas" was a short story for *Harper's Weekly* written at about the same time as *The General's Double*, a lengthy Civil War book that wound an unbelievable plot around his now-familiar "mistaken identity" theme yet contained some excellent descriptions of Stuart's cavalry raids in Virginia.[3]

The last years of the century saw publication of *A Trooper Galahad*, in which King sought a new background in Texas during the days of Reconstruction and payroll bandits, and two lengthy novels, *A Wounded Name* and *Warrior Gap*, which appeared as perhaps the most curious pair of sequels ever written. *A Wounded Name* introduced an Arizona scene, while *Warrior Gap* was set at "Fort Frayne" on the northern plains during the Sioux War of 1868. In these stories the tangled web of circumstances that involved the two soldier heroes was untangled by a single Indian battle in which both took part, and one villain served for both plots. Actually these two books were less sequels than contemporaneous plots that crossed each other.

By this time King's reputation had shrunken somewhat in the Milwaukee press. *Warrior Gap*, said one of his hometown newspapers in a review that contained scarcely fifty words, "answers to the popular craving for this gentleman's stories which two novels a week can hardly supply." It was hardly that bad, even counting his numerous short stories, but four novels in one year was something, particularly in 1898. Yet another of these, a book for boys called *From School to Battle-field: A Story of the War Days*, was written in a detailed and easygoing manner that suggests the utmost leisure and considerable time for research. Largely this one concerned King's school days in New York City just before the Civil War, but the information concerning volunteer fire-fighting companies of that era, with technical descriptions of their equipment and methods, and the amount of material about regimental movements in the Bull Run campaign, including mention of Lieutenant Upton, author of the famous *Tactics* and *Military Policy*, are amazing when we know that King produced other books that year and also donned the single star of a brigadier general of volunteers for the war with Spain.

From School to Battle-field, copyrighted in 1898 but probably not published until early in 1899, was about the last book to bear the familiar signature "Captain Charles King, U.S.A." Henceforth his followers would note the byline "General Charles King, U.S.V." But the jump from gold bars to a silver star was not as sudden as it appears.

By Land and Sea

In the summer of 1880 Captain King had been casting about for an occupation, and the sketches that became *Campaigning with Crook* had not earned enough to give him any idea that he could make a living by the pen. Friends suggested that he apply as a military instructor at one or two colleges, but at first that idea did not appeal to him. Upon his retirement from the army the year before, he had supposed that his military career was closed.

There was held in Milwaukee that summer a reunion and encampment of Wisconsin volunteers of the Civil War. Generals Grant and Sherman were present, and of course Captain King was much in evidence, renewing acquaintances with veterans of the "Iron Brigade." A grand military parade was a feature of the gathering—no reunion was ever held without one—and among the organizations appearing was the student battalion from the University of Wisconsin. To a soldier's eye it presented a sorry sight, its uniforms archaic, its arms antiquated, and its discipline almost nonexistent. In charge of the students were two old friends, Allen Conover, professor of civil engineering, and Chandler P. Chapman, an Iron Brigade veteran. They were doing their best but needed help, and they urged King to apply for a university position.

Their pleas were later reinforced by a letter from Wisconsin's adjutant general, Edwin E. Bryant, asking King to look over the situation at the university. He did, and he found a general apathy toward the whole question of military training. Elisha W. Keyes, head of the executive committee of the board of regents, was not enthusiastic, but he thought a salary of six hundred dollars, the difference between the retired and active pay of a captain, might be arranged at the January meeting. John Bascom, president of the university, was willing for King to have the position as professor of military science and tactics if there would be "no friction." Other members of the faculty cared little.

This indifference to military training was no surprise. Yet under the stimulus of the Civil War Congress had passed the Agricultural College Act of 1862, providing substantial land grants to schools that would give instruction in military tactics, and the University of Wisconsin had come under the terms of this act. After a time interest in the course in tactics had dropped. The Civil War was far in the past by 1880, and the gentlemen of the university saw no reason there should ever be another war.

"The result of my visit to Madison was that I came away convinced that in University circles the military department was looked upon as a detriment," King wrote long afterward, and "I determined to go back there and show that it was not." Of course he did. He found the college battalion drilling with cumbersome, antiquated Civil War muskets, and the rest of the equipment was "as antique an outfit as ever I set eyes upon." When he complained, the president said he "didn't know anything about it," and the chairman of the executive committee of the board of regents said that none of King's predecessors had made any objection.

Captain King also found reason to complain that he was ignored by other members of the faculty. But he soon found a way to correct this. According to the rules of the university, all first- and second-year students were required to attend drill, but King discovered only about half in attendance. Some went so far as to attend only as onlookers, making fun of their comrades who took the requirement seriously. Captain King procured a list of those students required to attend drill and began a roundup. This "military despotism" was much resented, but the captain stood by the university's obligation to the government, and in this he had the support of the president.

Members of the faculty quickly began to notice King. Many of them interceded on behalf of one student or another, but they had little luck getting any excused. After the Christmas holidays a new battle developed. Numbers of students had provided themselves with doctors' certificates saying they could not undertake physical exercise. King's investigation disclosed that some of these had been faked. In some instances there were no such doctors as the names signed; in other cases letterheads had been used without consent. One physical wreck, whose certificate seemed legitimate, was found on the baseball field. The president was informed that a few hours of drill would be no more strenuous than running bases, but he refused to overrule the medical certifi-

cate. Bascom also supported a conscientious objector, who would
have been expected to show up at this juncture, but the president
was later chagrined to discover that he personally had signed the
same student's request for a recommendation to the army signal
corps.

By this time Captain King had gained a considerable reputation
as a troublemaker, and when a student complained that "Professor King" had treated him harshly, it did not occur to Bascom
that another instructor of nearly the same name might be meant.
Accordingly, Bascom took Captain King severely to task and
warned him against violent language and display of temper, because they "weaken one's influence with young men." But their
interview was interrupted by a group of sophomores clattering
down the stairway, who scuffled and shouted just outside the
president's door. Dr. Bascom was much annoyed at this uproar; he
rushed into the hall, collared one of the ringleaders, and banged
the young man's head against the wall half a dozen times. The
crowd promptly dispersed, and the president returned to his seat.

"Er, what was it we were talking about?"

"The supremacy, Mr. President, of the *suaviter in moto* over
the *fortiter in re*."

Dr. Bascom looked up in astonishment, then laughed. "I didn't
know they taught Latin in the army," he remarked.

"They don't, sir, and you must pardon my Columbia pronuncia-
tion," was King's reply. The discovery that King had attended
Columbia and had even acted as secretary of the faculty there
made quite a difference to Dr. Bascom, and from then on the two
got along in a very friendly fashion. Soon, also, Bascom began to
note an improvement in the students' attitude. Captain King had
taught them to show respect to faculty members, state officials,
and other superiors. Among others to notice this was Governor
Jeremiah M. Rusk, whose attention was thus called to Captain
King.[1]

But the six hundred dollars in salary failed to appear—it was
paid many years afterward—so Captain King quit the university
in 1882 after an experience that had brought many trials, but
some pleasures.

Meanwhile he had begun an association with the state troops of
Wisconsin, first as instructor of the Light Horse Squadron at
Milwaukee in 1881. The next year he was appointed inspector and

instructor by Governor Rusk, with rank as colonel and aide-de-camp, and in 1883 was made assistant inspector general of the national guard. In 1885 King accepted a position as military instructor at St. John's Military Academy at Delafield, Wisconsin, an association that continued until his death. During one summer he devoted full time to a similar position at the Michigan Military Academy at Orchard Lake, Michigan, and his corps of cadets there won national honors in competitive drill.

As inspector King was in continuous turmoil, but he enjoyed it, and eventually Wisconsin's citizen soldiers enjoyed seeing him win for them. He early discovered that some of the state's companies were using outdated Civil War tactics, that some of the companies with men of German descent were using Prussian drill, and that other captains had ideas uniquely their own. King's concept of an inspection was to take charge of a company and discover what it knew of Upton's tactics, the official system used by the regular army and the one he had absorbed at West Point from Upton himself. It did not add to his popularity at the time, but gradually the Wisconsin National Guard began to make progress.

A test of the guard's proficiency came early. On May Day 1886 there began in Milwaukee a general strike, instigated by anarchists and accompanied by rioting, a plan on a national scale that resulted in Chicago's famous labor-driven Haymarket riot. King had been warned of the approaching trouble by the mayor of Milwaukee, who had noticed large sales of firearms by the secondhand shops. The militia companies were found to be very short of ammunition, and King urged the governor to order more. At first Governor Rusk doubted the seriousness of the situation, but after a visit to Milwaukee he became convinced that trouble was in the air, and he ordered arms and ammunition shipped secretly to the armories.

On the first day of the trouble the mob overran everything in its path without much opposition and without doing much damage. The sheriff and chief of police were confident they could handle the situation. But on May 4, the day of the Haymarket bomb in Chicago, riots broke out in several directions, the police were overwhelmed, and alarm bells called the militiamen to their armories. The most serious of the troubles was ended by a single volley. The governor ordered Colonel King to take the Milwaukee Light Horse Troop and two companies of infantry and break up the main body of rioters, who had gathered at a west-side beer garden and surrounded the police. The troopers charged into the crowd and extricated the police, while the infantry cleared space to maneuver. Then again the troops charged, and with them went the police, pulling out leaders of the mob and loading them into patrol wagons. This broke the back of Milwaukee's rioting.

This 1886 trouble is notable as one of the first instances where the newly invented telephone was used to direct troop movements. Companies of the national guard throughout the state were called out by telephone within a few minutes of the first alarm, and soon many were reporting by the same instrument that they were ready to move and in some cases were boarding trains. At central headquarters, where Governor Rusk soon arrived to take charge, constant reports on the movements of the guard were received by telephone. But if great advantages were found in the use of this new instrument, defects were also discovered. One gathers that King felt little love for the telephone operator. Besides reaching wrong numbers, after being cut off several times and suffering a series of crossed wires, King on one occasion took a taxicab to find out just what the governor really wanted.[2]

Colonel King was reappointed to his offices in the national guard by Governor W. D. Hoard in 1889, and in 1890 he was given command of the state's Fourth Regiment of Infantry, headquartered in Milwaukee. In 1892, at his request, he was retired with the rank of colonel.

For the second time King thought he was done with military service. This time he planned to go to Europe to live more or less indefinitely, since the financial success of his many books made this seem possible. But 1893 was a year of depression. Before leaving America he had arranged to send future writings to the Authors' Guild, a boom-time project that promised large royalties. This organization promptly collapsed. The bank in which King had deposited most of his money failed. A fire destroyed books and valuable papers that he had stored in a warehouse. His wife broke her leg and was confined to bed at Lausanne. There was nothing to do but return to Milwaukee, resume his literary affairs, and attempt to recoup.

By this time, of course, Captain or Colonel King had become a marked figure in the civic life of his home city. He was active in the affairs of the Military Order of the Loyal Legion and delivered several papers at its meetings. These subsequently were published with many others in three volumes of war papers. In addition to this Civil War veteran officers' society, King was also active in the Order of Indian Wars, and in later years he delivered many notable lectures before that group. Other activities along this line were typified by the announcement of an address before the Twentieth Century Club in Chicago titled "Coblenz and Chicago: A Comparative Study of Army Life."

In 1895 William H. Upham was elected governor, the same Upham who had been King's classmate at West Point and for whom King had once given up appointment by Abraham Lincoln to the Military Academy. One of Upham's first acts as governor was to name Charles King adjutant general of Wisconsin with the rank of brigadier general. His two years as head of the state's military forces brought the Wisconsin National Guard to a widely recognized high state of efficiency. In 1897 a new administration in 1897 replaced King as adjutant general with C. R. Boardman, who had been one of King's first students at the University of Wisconsin. It had been a custom of the National Guard Association to elect the adjutant general of the state as its president, but on Boardman's motion a high tribute was paid by instead electing the retiring adjutant general, King. Despite compliments and commendations, King retired for a third time in January 1897, now as a brigadier general of state troops.

This third retirement was a brief one. King had planned to go to Europe again in March 1898, but on visiting Washington he found intense excitement over the destruction of the *Maine* in Havana harbor on February 15 and became convinced that war would be declared against Spain. He canceled his sailing plans and returned to Milwaukee to await developments. Meanwhile his friends in and out of Congress lobbied on his behalf, hoping to get him a commission as brigadier general, with the expectation that he would be assigned to command a Wisconsin brigade.

No doubt the parallel with his father's career appealed to Charles King. General Rufus King had also been a West Pointer; he had been adjutant general of a state; he had commanded a Wisconsin regiment; and again he too had canceled a trip to Europe on the prospect of service in time of war. But King was not so eager for the tie-up with a Wisconsin brigade. He indeed wanted action, but he felt his chances would be better if his assignment were less definite. The Spanish American War began April 21, and

the first list of brigadier generals of volunteers bore the date May 115
4. These were nearly all regulars, and King's name was not in-   *By Land*
cluded. But a second list dated May 27 gave him the commission.   *and Sea*
Among his seniors on this list were Edwin V. Sumner of the old
Fifth Cavalry on the plains; Loyd Wheaton; and "King's Corner"
mate Arthur MacArthur. Others of this same date were Francis
Vinton Greene, of some fame as a writer on military subjects,
Frederick Dent Grant, son of the president, and Thomas L.
Rosser, classmate and friend of Custer.

Of the many telegrams of congratulation he received, undoubtedly the one that gave General King the most pleasure was one
from his old commander Wesley Merritt, now a major general in
the regular army, who wired on May 27: "Am delighted to hear of
your appointment. Would like to have you go with me to the
Philippines. Tell them so in Washington. Will apply."

And the next day this telegram came from H. C. Corbin, adjutant general of the United States Army: "I would like to know if
you desire service with General Merritt in the expedition to the
Philippine Islands." To this King replied: "Telegram received.
Glad to service with General Merritt, Philippines or anywhere."[3]

Within a few days, orders were received to report to General
Merritt at the Presidio of San Francisco. Brigadier General
Thomas M. Anderson had started for Manila with a lead brigade,
and General Greene was embarking a second brigade. King was
assigned to the division of Major General Elwell S. Otis, an 1876
Sioux War veteran, who assigned him to command the Second
Provisional Brigade, consisting of the First Idaho, Thirteenth
Minnesota, Twentieth Kansas, and First Tennessee. General
Merritt ordered that General King's brigade be next to sail.

Now occurred a series of complications over rank, precedence,
and fate that seemed to suggest some sort of ill luck attached to
the King family. General Arthur MacArthur arrived in camp without command; outranking King by four files, he claimed the next
command and got it. Orders were issued that King should certainly have the following contingent, but instead direct orders
from the president sent out the brigade led by Harrison Gray
Otis, King's junior but a fellow veteran of the Twenty-third Ohio
in the Civil War with President William McKinley. And when it
was King's turn again, Merritt sent notice that for the present he
had all the troops he needed in the Philippines. Obviously none of
these assignments were intended as an injustice to King, but they

cost him participation in the battle of Manila and probably a commission as major general.

There was other assorted ill luck. An old wooden railway coach bearing recruits caught fire in the desert at 2:00 one morning—obviously the fault of the railroad, King thought. Yet he was billed $5.85 for the breakfast served those men whose supplies had been lost in the fire.[4] Then one of his units seemed to be slipping. Merritt asked which Wisconsin regiment King preferred in its place. To have Wisconsin troops under his command was a wish dear to King's heart, but he wanted to think over until morning which regiment to choose. The next morning there arrived in camp the colonel assigned to command the forthcoming regiment, who had had a rather unsatisfactory time trying to tell Major Generals Nelson A. Miles and William R. Shafter something about Cuba. Within a week of the arrival of that Cuban filibuster, Colonel Frederick Funston, it became apparent that it would not be necessary to sidetrack the Twentieth Kansas, a unit that became perhaps the most famous of all the volunteer regiments sent to the Philippines, and whose commander was later the actual captor of Aguinaldo. Funston's opinion of King is worth quoting:

> General King's temperament was peculiarly suited to his task
> of commanding a brigade of raw volunteer troops, and direct-
> ing their training. His keen eye took in every defect and
> noted every improvement. In the former case the needed cor-
> rection or admonition was made in a way that left no sting, he
> never being either brutal or sarcastic. His readiness to en-
> courage or to praise stirred all to put forth their best efforts.[5]

A subaltern in the Kansas regiment, Philip Fox, later professor of astronomy and director of the Museum of Science and Industry in Chicago, recalled King's rising in his stirrups and expressing in his ringing voice at brigade drill, "Well done, Kansas. That is well worth seeing."[6]

And on the matter of praise, a letter received that summer read, in part, as follows: "I was greatly touched at your so much as remembering me. . . . Do you know, I never realized that you had known me when I was small. I did not think I had then ever been noticed by such a famous personage! When you return I must meet you; there are many things I wish to talk over with you." This letter was datelined "First Regt. U.S. Vol. Cav., in camp at Montauk Point, L.I." and signed by Theodore Roosevelt.[7]

By midsummer 1898 King and his Union Brigade, now consisting of the Fifty-first Iowa, First Tennessee, and Twentieth Kansas, seemed no nearer the Philippines, despite a renewed promise after a very fine review before Major General Henry C. Merriam that they should go there.

General Merriam sympathized with King in his many disappointments and thought he knew a way out. The *Arizona*, once a speedy liner of the Guion Line and the holder of the Atlantic passage "blue ribbon," was about to sail with replacements, Red Cross nurses, and other casuals, and Merriam suggested that King might go if he were willing to give up his brigade. He was more than willing to get overseas in any capacity, and he moved on board the *Arizona*. But an order came to await a shipment of guns before sailing. Though King stewed, there was nothing he could do but wait. At the last moment Merriam decided to go along, and there was yet another day's delay after the guns were brought aboard. This last day nearly finished King, for orders came holding him at Honolulu. The steamer finally started and Merriam refused to interfere, but he did hold King at Honolulu.

As a result King became the first commanding general of the Department of Hawaii, the islands having just been annexed by the United States. But this was an honor the general little wanted. By now the Spanish-American War was over. King felt sure that there would still be trouble in the Philippines, but for a time no one seemed interested in sending him and his replacements anywhere. Then General Otis, who had succeeded Merritt in the Philippine command, decided he needed King and his men, and he sent the *Arizona* after them. They sailed on November 10. But King's ill luck was not over. On arriving at Manila he was taken ill with an eczema that he attributed to an impure vaccine. He recovered by December 15 in time to review a new brigade to which he was assigned.

Found in the Philippines

A generation was familiar with the name and works of Captain Charles King, but that a retired officer of this rank should turn up in the Philippines as a brigadier general of volunteer troops was mystifying to many of his old comrades in the regular service. His long and sometimes thankless duty with the Wisconsin National Guard was little known, but now it was to serve him in good stead, for he was about to lead a brigade into a hotly contested battle that for some reason has found little space in historical writing since then.

The generation that lived through the Spanish-American War and the Philippine Insurrection learned something about the campaign from newspaper accounts that necessarily, and perhaps sometimes carelessly, were as distorted as newspaper accounts can be in wartime. Since then much has been written about the naval battles, and some about the siege of Santiago, but almost nothing about the campaigns in the Philippines.

Sir Roger de Coverley was not original in discovering that most disputes have two sides. But for some reason the propaganda department of the Republican party was not working well in 1899. True, a diversion was created by nominating Theodore Roosevelt for vice president in 1900 and concentrating attention on the charge up San Juan Hill. That worked so well that the Philippines could be conveniently forgotten. They have been forgotten much of the time since.

The Philippines, like Cuba, had had their rebellions against Spanish rule. In 1898 the most prominent Filipino rebel leader was Emilio Aguinaldo, then in exile in Singapore.[1] It occurred to someone that Aguinaldo, if turned loose on the island of Luzon, might be of material assistance to the American cause. That seemed a reasonable supposition, but it proved highly unfortunate.

After returning from exile Aguinaldo raised a considerable Filipino force and brought it to Manila to cooperate with the army of General Merritt, who was besieging the city. Merritt preferred to take Manila with American troops, and he did so on August 13, the day after the signing of a peace protocol with Spain. Cables had been cut, and he did not know about the peace.

Merritt rejected the assistance of the Filipino force because he knew the insurgents planned to loot the Spanish capital. They made no attempt to conceal this intention and were openly indignant that the American force prevented it. Behind them lay several years of intense hatred for Spanish oppression. But to General Merritt the surrender of Spanish lives and property into American hands meant that the American force was responsible for their safety, in accordance with what were regarded, in that quaint, old-fashioned era, as the rules of civilized warfare. So the Filipino army was barred from the city but remained on the outskirts, awaiting the outcome of the peace negotiations.

It is not to be implied that Aguinaldo was interested solely—or even at all—in looting Manila. But he was interested in Philippine independence. He probably knew little about the United States, and he certainly was not informed about the high idealism that actuated its government policies. He had not been told, presumably, that the sole purpose of this war with Spain was to rescue the sadly oppressed island of Cuba, and incidentally the Philippines. To him this was just a change of masters, and he would have none of it.

All idealism aside, the United States placed itself in an embarrassing position when it entered the Philippines. Having taken the islands away from Spain, it could not turn its Spanish population over to the mercies of a people then regarded as half-savage. Germany and certain other nations of Europe undoubtedly were willing to relieve America of its burden, but it was inconceivable that the United States would shift its responsibilities in so summary a manner. The only solution seemed to govern the Filipinos until they were capable of governing themselves.

It was hinted to Aguinaldo that it would be a good idea to let his troops go home, particularly now that all danger of Spanish tyranny was ended. But Aguinaldo preferred to keep his forces as near Manila as he could get them. Moreover, they began entrenching, threw up gun emplacements, and strictly forbade Americans to pass through their lines. But the American Eighth Corps, now commanded by General Otis, had strict orders to show no distrust toward the Filipinos. No American spade was to touch soil, not a gun was to frown on these apparent preparations for battle. Aguinaldo's officers and men were allowed to cross the American lines to visit Manila. This policy of trust was carried too far and became a political as well as a military error, since it gave the impression that the Americans had no intention of fighting and were overawed by the Filipino soldiery.

This was not so unreasonable a reaction as it may appear, for the army of the so-called Philippine Republic was no mere collection of guerrillas and bushwhackers. In it were several regiments that had been uniformed, drilled, and armed under the Spanish administration. Its numbers were estimated at twenty to thirty thousand, whereas Otis had some fourteen thousand American soldiers in Manila, of whom about ten thousand were front-line troops. The insurgents were armed with Mauser magazine rifles, generally superior to the .45-caliber Springfield black-powder rifles carried by most of the volunteers, and probably quite as good as the then new United States magazine rifle known as the Krag-Jorgenson.

The city of Manila lies along the Pasig River, which runs east and west to the sea through Manila from Laguna de Bay, the city proper being south of the river. The Spanish defenses had been created around a series of fifteen blockhouses that formed a semicircle around the city, terminating at Manila Bay on both sides. The Eighth Corps established an outpost line on the blockhouses, the troops being held at the edges of the city within easy supporting distance. The Pasig River was the boundary between two divisions, the First, commanded by Major General Thomas M. Anderson, being south and southeast of Manila and the Second Division of Major General Arthur MacArthur north and northeast of the city. MacArthur's First Brigade, commanded by Brigadier General Harrison G. Otis, held the left of the line with a battalion of the Third U.S. Artillery acting as infantry, the First Montana Infantry, the Tenth Pennsylvania Infantry, and the Twentieth Kansas Infantry. His Second Brigade consisted of the First Colorado Infantry, the First South Dakota Infantry, and the First Nebraska Infantry and was commanded by Brigadier General Irving Hale. The Battalion of Utah Artillery was attached to the division.

King commanded the First Brigade of the First Division. To

settle some embarrassing questions of precedence between regular and volunteer commissions, which he probably worried about
more than those serving under him, and also because King was
more familiar with state troops than the other brigade commanders, he suggested that his regular regiments be traded for
volunteers.[2] His command eventually consisted of the First California, First Washington, and First Idaho regiments of infantry.
The Second Brigade of the First Division, commanded by Brigadier General Samuel Ovenshine, consisted of the Fourteenth
U.S. Infantry, six troops of the Fourth U.S. Cavalry acting as
infantry, and the First North Dakota Infantry. One battalion of
the First Wyoming Infantry was added to King's brigade during
the coming action. Also attached to Anderson's division was Company A of the Battalion of Engineers and two batteries of artillery, one of 3.2-inch guns and the other of 3-inch Hotchkiss mountain howitzers, both manned by Light Battery F of the Sixth U.S.
Artillery, assisted by detachments of other regiments of the division.

As Filipino attitudes grew more and more threatening, on New
Year's Day 1899 the following order was issued to King's brigade:
"Keep men well in hand; need not be kept in quarters. But within
bugle call. Outposts to alert. Field officers of the day to visit
outposts at night as well as day."[3] It was a penciled scrawl, which
somewhat accounts for its faulty punctuation. Four times during
January General Otis was warned of a threatened uprising. Organizations of natives within the city planned to assist, and a strong
provost guard was kept within Manila. Meanwhile a presumably
friendly correspondence was maintained with Aguinaldo, but the
final outbreak seems to have been unexpected on both sides. A
complaint was made to Aguinaldo that a patrol of his men had
encroached upon the line held by the First Nebraska at the extreme right of MacArthur's division, near the bay. The insurgent
general promised to withdraw this force. Yet it was at this very
point on the evening of February 4 that a Filipino advanced upon
an American outpost, refused to halt when challenged, and was
fired on by a Nebraska picket. Immediately, firing broke out all
along the Second Division front.[4]

This was culmination of a long series of such incidents. Each had
been a supreme test of American discipline and a high tribute to
the recently raised volunteers, who had withstood insult and more
serious provocation in a continuous effort to cause them to open

the fighting. The insurgents succeeded in drawing the first shot from an American sentry only by a deliberate violation of military law. Private William Grayson received no reprimand for firing the first shot.

But despite a rain of rumors all day, February 4—of unusual movements in the insurgent lines, of an English residence having raised its national flag for protection—several general officers were in Manila that night, one being Ricarti of the insurgents, who was to oppose King, and another MacArthur, who was playing whist in his quarters. King says it was the last game of cards that officer could ever be induced to play. King himself spent most of the evening with Colonel William C. Smith of the First Tennessee, a Confederate veteran of A. P. Hill's division who died the next day of apoplexy while riding into battle at the head of his regiment. King was recalled from Manila by an orderly and hastened to get his brigade ready for attack.[5]

King's troops were in perhaps the least tenable position of any of the four brigades in the battle of Manila, but they were also in the position that had the greatest possibilities. Their left rested on the Pasig River at Pandacan Point, their right connected with Ovenshine's brigade at Blockhouse Twelve, and their center jutted out at an angle toward Blockhouse Eleven and the Concordia Bridge on the main road from Manila to Laguna de Bay. This salient angle resulted because the line followed the bank of the Concordia Estoro, and across the river were the insurgent forces, armed with two modern Krupp guns, ready to enfilade King's regiments occupying the sides of the angle. He was forbidden to change these dispositions before the battle opened, but he also knew there was no other practicable line, for the suburb of Paco was in his immediate rear.[6]

This was the most disturbing aspect of King's position. But immediately to the east of his line the Pasig River bent into a double horseshoe with the villages of Pandacan and Santa Ana in its angles. King knew that if his brigade could be swung to the left like a door on its hinges, the insurgent force fronting it could be enclosed in Santa Ana between the Americans and the river. Quick to see this opportunity, he proposed it to General Anderson but was told to make no attack until ordered.

Through the night and into the morning of February 5 the roar of fighting could be heard from MacArthur's position, while in front of Anderson's division all was ominously quiet. At 2:40 A.M.

the storm broke on the Washington regiment holding the main part of this line; the fire also reached the Idaho regiment coming up to reinforce the front. Again King begged to be allowed to attack at dawn. "Not yet," was the quick and curt response.

But at 8:00 A.M. General Otis authorized an advance, if not carried too far, and General Anderson, taking the Wyoming battalion with him as a reinforcement, delivered in person the "long-prayed-for order," as King called it in his official report.[7] Anderson records that King and Colonel James F. Smith of the First California "received this order with delight, and their troops with enthusiasm."[8] General Otis's report, noting that King had suggested movement, says "the Californias, Washingtons, and Idahos responded with great vigor," and the movement was attended with signal success. The insurgent casualties here were very heavy, and many were drowned attempting to cross the Pasig to escape punishment. Anderson directed the movements of the Californias and Wyomings from Battery Knoll, where Captain A. B. Dyer had his guns, while King led the Idahos to their place on the left of the line.[9]

The advance was made by battalion in echelon, a military maneuver somewhat resembling the staggering of stairsteps. The first step or rank, nearest the river, was the Idahos, the second rank the Washingtons, and the third and fourth ranks the two California battalions, with Wyoming as support. King's brigade executed its advance with precision and quickly squeezed the Filipinos between his troops and the river.

But the attack was not completed without difficulty. When Companies A, E, and H of California pivoted to face Santa Ana, their left flank was exposed. Wyoming was supposed to support but was slow to take up its position, and insurgents from San Pedro Macati, farther east along the river, attacked. Colonel Smith was forced to draw back his Company A and face it east, but at this juncture the company of regular engineers opportunely appeared to help out, and by a withering fire they kept the insurgents at bay until Wyoming reached its proper place in line.[10]

Meanwhile Idaho and Washington were having even greater difficulties. Between them was the Santa Ana road. Its Concordia Bridge was swept by the insurgents' most formidable battery, two Krupp guns, and was also under heavy rifle fire from enemy redoubts. Lieutenant H. L. Hawthorne's light battery of Hotchkiss mountain guns answered this fire as best it could, and pictures taken after the battle show the stone bridge chipped and riddled by bullets and shells.[11] King sent everything he could gather against the redoubts. Major Edward McConville was killed leading three Idaho companies against the Krupps, while Washington companies and even some stray California troops rushed in. The Krupps and the redoubts were taken, and Santa Ana was threatened.

Now General King worried that the Washington battalion under Colonel John H. Wholley would advance too far before making its turn to the left and thus leave a gap through which some of the insurgents could escape. King joined the Washingtons, and in his own words in the official report, "personally ordered the left to halt and, galloping along the line, by dint of much shouting, swung it around, pivoting on the left, until our right center broke through the native huts and entered the town to the south of the old church." The California battalions also made their swings to the left, and Santa Ana was taken. Many of the insurgents were driven into river. Particularly bloody was the attack on the redoubt on the extreme left, where insurgents had pretended to surrender and then shot down the first volunteers who climbed over the parapet. California now pushed on to San Pedro Macati and Guadalupe, establishing a new line far to the east. It had all been done in an hour and a half. As Anderson noted, it was an advance not by rushes, but with a rush. And General King is recorded as saying, "There goes the American volunteer—God bless him. All hell can't stop him."[12]

As for General King, he seems to have been everywhere, displaying the highest qualities of field leadership, and there are plenty of testimonials to his personal courage. He was the idol of his soldiers.

"You should have seen him in our fight around Manila," a private told Senator Albert Beveridge of Indiana.

> He was as pretty as a girl in springtime. He was dressed in a perfectly fitting fresh uniform, and I think even had patent leather boots on. And his gauntlets! he had a new pair, it seemed to us, each morning. He looked like a ballroom soldier; but great Scott! you should have seen him, I say. Until time to charge or do rush work, or things like that, he would make us all lie down or go behind a tree or a stone, while he himself would walk daintily along the line, a target for the

whole fire of the enemy, because of his conspicuous uniform,
and because he was the only one of us in sight. He was all the
time talking to us, and swore like—well he just swore, that's
all. "Lie down there, ——— it, my boy! Do you want to get
your head shot off? Be careful there; don't expose yourself
too much, man! Do you want to get what little sense you have
shot out of you?" and such talk, with the expletives in just
the right places and all the time the bullets whistling around
him. He put you in mind of a scolding mother, though he was
directing us how and where to shoot best; and you should
hear him order a charge; yes, and see him lead it, too. And all
this done so daintily that you kind o' felt as though there was
a lady around. Well, maybe the boys don't love General King.
We just felt we would not go out of our way to keep from getting killed, if we only knew that he could see us shoot.[13]

"That man will never see America again," another private told
a correspondent as General King passed by "immaculately attired
and calmly lighting a cigar, although the bullets were whizzing
around in a most reckless manner. And it's a shame, too, for he
might write some fine stories of this war," the private mourned.
The correspondent expressed the opinion that the novels could be
spared, but that cool-headed generals were not a glut on the
market. But the private stuck to his point. "He is as fine an officer
as he is a story-teller, and that's the best compliment I can pay
him," the soldier insisted as he "picked up his gun and quietly
followed along after the general, a self-instituted rear guard," for
he had explained that King was "perfectly indifferent to shooting."[14]

Not only was his courage recognized, his generalship also was
highly praised. General Anderson almost immediately recommended King's promotion to the rank of major general for "energy, bravery and efficiency in battle," and General Otis later
suggested recognition by brevet, remarking of Santa Ana that
"the movement was suggested by General King, effected under
his immediate supervision and he in person led it, at least in part, I
am sure, showing conspicuous gallantry and efficiency."[15] But no
brevet commissions were granted on this occasion, and the Senate's failure to act on the brevets recommended at this period
ended the brevet business forever in the United States Army.

The battle of King's brigade materially aided the advance of

General Ovenshine's troops, who previously had been held up by an almost inpenetrable thicket. The entire line of the First Division drove the insurgents far to the north. After San Pedro Macati and its English cemetery were taken, there was little further resistance to King's brigade. The headquarters papers of Pio del Pilar, insurgent division commander, were captured. Guadalupe—church, village, and convent—was taken, and the First Brigade pushed on and took the island town of Pasig and the villages of Paternos and Taguig, almost to Laguna de Bay. The Second Brigade of the division was held up near Pasay, having advanced only two miles to King's five and a half. MacArthur's division faced a strong enemy force at Caloocan. General Otis still had to maintain a heavy provost guard at Manila to watch for an advance until the arrival of new regular regiments, then on the way from the United States. King's line was dangerously thin, covering a front of seven miles, and General Otis ordered it withdrawn to San Pedro Macati, to connect with Ovenshine's brigade on a shorter line.

Little had been heard from the insurgents in King's front between the fifth and the thirteenth of February. On February 13 there was a considerable attack; a hastily scrawled field report says, "Insurgents are coming against our company at Pasig," but there was little difficulty in beating them off.[16] On February 14 Colonel Smith sent out a scouting party of Californians that stirred up insurgents in a brisk fight in which the gunboat *Laguna* took part. Another attack was made on February 15. These three days of fighting determined the immediate recall of the brigade.

It was in no very cheerful frame of mind that the Californias, Washingtons, and Idahos received the order to retreat. They were eager to push forward and end the fighting, and they knew that the enemy would regard the American withdrawal as a victory and come pouring over on them. General Anderson had carefully prepared a rear line of defense, throwing up earthworks across a valley in front of San Pedro Macati. King's brigade retreated fighting to this line, an affair of shovel and rifle that was something like a World War I engagement. Hawthorne's Hotchkiss guns provided the only artillery support. But it was a long-range battle until about 11:00 A.M., when the insurgents attempted a formal attack on the new line. With bugles blowing, fire by volley and fire by file, and all the panoply of nineteenth-century warfare, the Filipino lines advanced confidently until they came within close range of the Springfields; then they began to falter. A surprise attack struck them on their right. Guadalupe Church, a heavy stone structure, had been occupied by a battalion of the First California, Companies G, L, and M, commanded by Lieutenant Colonel Victor D. Doboce, with Companies C and D of the First Idaho under Captain Phil W. McRoberts in trenches nearby and in the vicinity of the convent. To the rhythm of "There'll Be a Hot Time in the Old Town Tonight," these companies opened fire across the Filipino flanks and forced their retreat.[17]

"I congratulate you and yours on your success today," wrote General Anderson. "I sincerely regret that orders prevented you from following it up." And he added the caution, "Do not fire away so much ammunition. The California people have used a large quantity."[18] But King's line was still very thin, and there were continual warnings of impending attacks. He knew his front must be held at all costs, and he fretted about a weak spot on the right. For three days Colonel Doboce's men held Guadalupe—"dead tired," he reported—but there was no one to relieve them.[19] On February 18 the Bureau of Military Intelligence warned of a serious threat against the left. General Anderson suggested that the five companies there be recalled to the main line and that the church be burned.

King afterward said this was the hardest thing he had to do in the Philippines. The church had a library of valuable books, many of them two centuries old, and its altar furnishings and other decorations were very fine. King put off the destruction as long as he could. He instructed Doboce to have everything ready, but not to move until he telegraphed the single word "Quit." A signal corps operator was in the tower, and the moment a campaign hat appeared the bells began to chime. The general himself heard this toll while under fire in the tower. There had been no letup in scattered firing for several days, and King later remembered that the nights were about as quiet as the Fourth of July at home. It was after 5:00 A.M. when a burst of volley firing began on the right, and preparations were rapidly made to meet the attack. The signal was sent to the church tower. And then, just as smoke began rolling from Guadalupe's windows, the firing ceased. It had been a false alarm. But it was too late. The church was doomed. Soon explosives demolished its roof, and a tall column of flame shot into the air. "It seemed like vandalism," sighed the general as he later described it.[20]

But King's thin line was able to hold on without much further fighting, and it was just as well, for at this period the general was stricken again with the eczema that had caused him trouble shortly after he landed in the islands. At the suggestion of General Anderson, he turned over the command of his brigade to Colonel Smith and retired to Manila for treatment. He was quite worried when he learned that Colonel Smith had been relieved by Brigadier General Loyd Wheaton, who had just arrived in the Philippines, but was reassured by General Anderson's writing, "I had no more idea of relieving you than I had of relieving myself," and that Wheaton's assignment would be temporary.[21] Soon Wheaton was leading a provisional brigade under General MacArthur, whose division now bore the brunt of the war along the Dugapan Railroad running north from Manila. King quickly recovered and resumed command of his brigade.

For a month or so all was quiet. Meanwhile Anderson, a major general of volunteers, was promoted brigadier general in the regular army and was ordered to the United States to take departmental command at Chicago. On March 17 Major General Henry W. Lawton assumed command of the First Division. As an officer of the Fourth U.S. Cavalry, Lawton had been prominent in the Indian Wars, particularly in the campaign against Geronimo, and he and King had been friends for many years. More recently Lawton had conspicuously commanded a division in the campaign of Santiago de Cuba, in which he had fought in the battle of El Caney. He had an utterly fearless nature and, like King, made his reconnaissances in person and far to the front. While on one of these, in a rather unimportant action, he was killed by a Filipino bullet, but not before he had led several successful expeditions against the insurgents.

When Lawton first appeared on King's front to inspect that part of his new command, the men of the brigade were much amused at the contrast their two generals made. Where King was "short and squat," to use his own words, and mounted on a nondescript pony, Lawton was a towering soldier. King ordered two companies to make a demonstration to the front so that the generals could have a look at enemy positions. Before it was completed Lawton strolled out to a rocky mount some three hundred yards ahead, where he was "perched like a lighthouse" calmly studying the insurgent trenches through field glasses. Indignant, King galloped out. Perhaps he felt no general officer more consequential than himself should be permitted to expose himself to enemy fire in that manner. He called Lawton down off the rock, remarking, "You'll break my heart if you persist in such performances; and the whole Army will damn me for letting you do it."

"But how else can I see what I need to see?" Lawton laughed innocently.

"What good will it do you or me if you get killed in seeing?" was King's unanswerable question, but it failed to reform Lawton, and in just such a look around he was killed the following December.[22]

In April Lawton organized his first expedition, its object being to capture the city of Santa Cruz on the southeastern shore of Laguna de Bay, the richest and most important city in La Laguna province. Lawton figured that its seizure would cut off the insurgents' retreat and would have an important effect on the native population.[23] King was assigned to the immediate command of the force, though Lawton planned to accompany it. The expedition consisted of one squadron of the Fourth U.S. Cavalry, two battalions of the Fourteenth U.S. Infantry, a battalion of the First North Dakota Infantry, a battalion of the Idahos, and a picket company of the Washingtons and two of Hawthorne's guns. General Ovenshine remained behind to command the old battle line.

The force assembled at San Pedro Macati, the town on the Pasig River that figured so largely in the earlier movements of King's brigade. There it embarked on the launches *Cascos* and *Bancos* to sail up the Pasig and into Laguna de Bay to Santa Cruz. A landing was made late at night on April 9 without mishap, but it was discovered that General King was too ill to leave the boat. This caused some "confusion and delay," but they were overcome.[24] The infantry made a charge across a bridge and the cavalry attacked from the beach, and in a short time the insurgents gave up the city.

Meanwhile General King was put on sick report by the brigade surgeon, Major George F. Shiels, who had long had the general under his care. He now declared that King's "physical condition renders him unfit for the hardships of the present campaign," the cause of his condition being diagnosed as "cardiac depression, probably due to fatty degeneration of the heart." Lawton immediately ordered that King be taken back to Manila for further treatment.[25]

It proved a somewhat inglorious end to a promising career as a battlefield general. At Manila the doctors felt King's only chance for recovery was to leave the climate of the Philippines. Orders were accordingly issued on April 18 relieving him of command of his brigade and ordering him to return to San Francisco. It is somewhat ironic that only five days later orders came from Washington reappointing King a brigadier general of volunteers, to date from April 15. He arrived in the United States June 1, a quick passage for a transport, but the captain of the *City of Puebla* was credited with hurrying things a bit in tribute to his distinguished passenger.[26]

Probably no army officer who had been in the Philippines was more widely known to the public, and he was one of the first to return. Newspapers were eager to interview him and devoted columns of space to whatever he had to say. Undoubtedly he was gratified at this opportunity to set right his journalist friends, for his old feud with the newspaper fraternity had been intensified by inaccurate accounts of his battle of Santa Ana. He states that "the maddest day I ever knew" was when he received at Manila the first accounts from the United States telling how his brigade had "massacred" and "slaughtered" the Filipinos.[27] "Native troops drown like rats," and "700 of these naked savages facing artillery fire with bows and arrows" were phrases that particularly stirred the soldiers' ire. King emphasized that every man killed on his front, except two Chinese who were innocent bystanders, was in uniform and armed with either a Mauser or a Remington rifle.

But during his short experience in brigade command, King had achieved an enviable record. "I cannot express to you how much I regret the necessity of your return to the United States at the time you did," General Lawton wrote.

> I want to say to you that you are the only general officer whom I know who possesses that peculiar faculty or that magnetism which attracts men to him; you are the only one of all the general officers who has excited among the men of his command any great amount of enthusiasm. I remember when you left your launch to come aboard the gunboat just before the attack on Santa Cruz, what a cheer went up from all the men in the transports; and you seem to possess that peculiar dash and spirit which carries men who follow you along with you in enthusiasm.[28]

And Loyd Wheaton wrote, "You have not left us until you have established a reputation for bravery, ability, and skill, that will make you honored by Americans while you live."[29]

For a time his conduct at Santa Ana became a legend among those he had commanded. In 1901 an Idaho newspaper correspondent recalled the figure of General King "rising in his stirrups, and whirling his sword above his head," while he called out, "Go it, you Idaho savages; all hell can't stop you."[30]

But there was a statutory limit on the number of brigadier generals, and King's place was needed. He was discharged from the volunteer service on August 2, 1899.[31]

Comrades in Arms

On the cover of the *Saturday Evening Post* containing the article on the Philippines by Senator Beveridge, there appeared a drawing of an immaculate General Charles King, standing erect, field glasses in hand, on the edge of a very shallow trench. His men watched and battle smoke wreathed him as he calmly surveyed the fighting. We know this picture is no exaggeration. But almost as accurate is a cartoon depiction of General King at Manila that appeared in the *Chicago Record* of February 11, 1899. Here King is represented standing among the guns on a battlement, shells bursting about his head, looking out toward a group of Filipinos as they were conceptualized in 1899—barefoot, dark midgets shooting guns wildly into the air. Under one arm King has a much-nicked sword; in the other hand he grasps a huge notebook and a splashing bottle of ink while he writes busily. The caption reads, "Great Material for My New Military Novel."

King was, in fact, hardly out from under fire when *Found in the Philippines* was published, copyrighted 1899. It was almost a diary, telling of experiences at Camp Merritt, California, the long voyage to Hawaii and the Philippines, the first sounding of "To Arms" at Manila, the fight with the insurgents, and even the hospitals of the island capital. Surely no novel was ever more contemporary. It seems to have been popular, and many copies were printed in several editions.

But if the novel brought added fame, it did not bring fortune. A series of disasters overtook General King's publishers, the most serious for him being the failure of F. Tennyson Neely, whose notes King had discounted. His first earnings were devoted to bringing his family back from Europe and reestablishing his home in Milwaukee.

In 1900 there appeared *Ray's Daughter: A Story of Manila*, in
132 which old friends from *The Colonel's Daughter* appeared against

the background of the Philippine Insurrection. Here again is the voyage of the *Arizona*, the battle of Santa Ana, and the burning of Guadalupe Church.

But the United States was recovering from its little adventure in two hemispheres. The Philippine Insurrection was dragging to a conclusion in a welter of guerrilla operations, and the public was ready to forget it. King had written *Between the Lines* and *A War-Time Wooing* just as interest in the Civil War was reviving after a period when the nation wanted to forget that conflict. Now he found that publishers and public were not interested in a war just past, and in this case there never was much of a revival of interest. Somehow the United States has always wanted to forget its quixotism of 1898 and 1899.

Nevertheless General Charles King, as he now signed himself, continued to write stories, for he was in desperate need of money and had little else to fall back on. For the next few years he seemed to be floundering in literature. He tried all his old subjects again and sometimes was surprisingly successful with them. He tried one publisher after another, and some were able to sell his books in considerable quantities. *The Way of the West* and *In Spite of Foes; or, Ten Years' Trial* were 1901 productions, though *In Spite of Foes* evidently was written as a war by-product, since it first appeared in *Street and Smith* magazine in 1899 and 1900. Another 1901 book opened a new field, the western campaigns of the Civil War. *Norman Holt: A Story of the Army of the Cumberland*, was published by G. W. Dillingham Company of New York.

A collection of short stories, mostly concerning the Philippines, appeared under the title *A Conquering Corps Badge* in 1902 from L. A. Rhoades and Company of Milwaukee, a publishing venture organized by General King's private secretary. Besides the stories, it contained reminiscent accounts titled "The Manila Wire" and "The Fate of Guadalupe," and also a sketch of King's career by Forrest Crissey, reprinted from *Ainslee's Magazine*.

The Iron Brigade returned to the scenes of the successful *Between the Lines* and very nearly equaled that success. It told once more of General Rufus King's stand at Gainesville, and followed the Iron Brigade through the rest of its service in the Civil War with several battle descriptions written in King's best style. Rufus F. Zogbaum, the artist of *A War-Time Wooing*, added illustrations.

Another artist's name carried the two books of 1903 to a large sale; they are still in demand because they were illustrated by Frederic Remington. *A Daughter of the Sioux* returned to the old Indian frontier with Ray's troop, now stationed at the fictitious Fort Frayne and again on the trail of warring Indians. This book, published in March, was followed in September by *An Apache Princess*, which told once more of Sunset Pass and Crook's campaigns in Arizona. But the glamour of these repeated settings of white paper and printer's ink was fading. One can hardly imagine this current pair of Indian heroines in *The Colonel's Daughter* or *Marion's Faith*. The Remington pictures helped, supplemented by a number by Edwin Willard Deming, long a successful artist of Indian subjects.

It is odd that as late as 1904 *A Knight of Columbia* could be subtitled *A Story of the War* and leave no doubt which war was meant. The scenes at Columbia College are the only new contribution, and again there appeared the early days of the Civil War and an impossibly romantic plot. In this tale readers particularly applauded the vivid account of "the wreck of the right wing" on the "ominous day" at Chancellorsville.

In a second book of 1904, *Comrades in Arms*, another *Tale of Two Hemispheres*, King introduced the imaginary "Fort Minneconjou" in the days just preceding the Spanish-American War. Although the plot skipped to some stirring fights in the Philippines, for the most part this was a story of garrison life in a new era and reflected King's most recent contacts with the army.

There were still signs of King's publishing flourish in one of the books of 1905. *A Broken Sword* interwove an impossible plot with the campaigns of the Army of the Potomac. The saving feature, as with so many of his current books, was a battle, here a rather interesting description of the charge of the Fifth Cavalry, long before King's acquaintance with it, in the Peninsula campaign.

The year 1905 also brought *The Medal of Honor: A Story of Peace and War*. This story covered a wide range of King's autobiography, including his instructorship at West Point, his campaigns in Arizona, his professorship at the University of Wisconsin, and a few added national guard experiences. Disregarding the shallow plot, *The Medal of Honor* proved quite readable and was illustrated, as was *Comrades in Arms*, by George Gibbs and E. W. Deming.

Completing the 1905 triple play, General King opened a new battle, this time against Prohibition. *A Soldier's Trial* was subtitled *An Episode of the Canteen Crusade*, one of those nearly forgotten campaigns in the long war leading to the enactment of the Eighteenth Amendment to the Constitution. It took courage in 1905 to beard the reformers on their chosen ground, for the Prohibitionists early tried their noble experiment on the army. The army's voting power was negligible, so success came easily. The post exchange, properly known then as the post canteen, existed on almost every military reservation. Before Congress enacted this reform measure, light wines and beer had customarily been served to soldiers at these combination general stores and enlisted men's clubs. King's thesis correctly noted that banning lighter alcoholic stimulants at the post, where consumption could be observed and controlled by officers, drove the enlisted men off the reservations to low dives and gin mills. The story bore the endorsement of Brigadier General Frederick Dent Grant, who contributed a foreword noting, "It is distressing that the prosperity of the keeper of vile resorts is due to the activity of good and worthy though misguided citizens, who have succeeded in abolishing the canteen in the army."

The further adventures of the hero of *A Soldier's Trial* are told in *Captured: The Story of Sandy Ray*, published in 1906 by R. F. Fenno and Company. The story featured contemporary service in the Philippines, where there were still occasional brushes with hostile Filipinos. *Tonio, Son of the Sierras*, the second book of 1906, presented what some critics thought was the best Indian character King ever contributed, and a much more favorable view of Apaches than would be expected from an army officer who had suffered so much at their hands.

In 1907 came *The Rock of Chickamauga*, a fictional biography of Major General George M. Thomas. King's only other work in 1907 was in an adventure series published by Harper and Brothers. Appropriately titled *Adventures of Uncle Sam's Soldiers*, the book carried short stories by King, John Habberton, Captain Charles A. Curtis, Lieutenant Charles D. Rhodes, and others.

Frederic Remington was again called upon for an illustration for *To The Front*, Harper's 1908 sequel to *Cadet Days*. The heroes of the earlier West Point story were here shown taking part in the Sioux troubles of 1890. The last of King's novels appeared in 1909, and it returned to the western plains for another "garrison tangle" such as had often brought him success before. *Lanier of the Cavalry; or, A Week's Arrest* was King's final army romance.

There remained to come from the general's pen one last book,

and this was one of his best. The J. B. Lippincott Company had
started publishing a series of "true" biographies and histories.
The True George Washington by Paul Leicester Ford was out-
standing in this list, and the same must be said for *The True
Ulysses S. Grant* by Charles King, which appeared in 1914.

In contrast to his customary speedy production of novels, King
devoted five years to researching, collecting, and writing this
biography of Grant. He had formidable equipment to work with.
He had personally known Grant and many of his contemporaries,
and for half a century he had read and heard about the great Civil
War commander turned president. But General King's most valuable faculty for this task was his thorough knowledge of the very
army life that pervaded Grant's history.

King knew something of the midwestern life Grant was born
into, and he made it a point to collect traditions and reminiscences
of his subject's boyhood. King followed Grant at West Point
closely enough to have had some of the same instructors, and he
well appreciated the effect the rigid rules of the Military Academy
had on one with so little sympathy for them. King was careful to
point out that Grant was by no means the failure at West Point
that was sometimes pictured, and he supported his contention
with a careful analysis of the records.

On the western frontier as well, King followed in Grant's
footsteps closely enough to find some of the same bleak garrison
conditions that brought about Grant's resignation. Although some
biographers professed it, there was no mystery about Grant's
appointment as brigadier general shortly after the beginning of
the Civil War—King had seen this in his father's history and very
recently in his own. Moreover, few outsiders could understand
Grant's regular army reputation as did King, who had lived in its
atmosphere all his life.

In the decades since 1914 better Grant biographies have appeared, but invariably King's contribution is recognized. King
told a soldier's story, using details that explained the actions and
characteristics of the leader and his subordinates while paying
considerable attention to what went on behind the scenes. There
was no attempt to "whitewash," a term King would not even have
known.

In retrospect, one of the most remarkable aspects of General
King's contribution to American literature is the sheer quantity
that came from his versatile pen. Because of many oddities in

publication, an amazing array of summary calculations are possible. Eliminating variant titles and counting all those separately issued among eight double titles, one tally is sixty-three books. This includes four titles where he appears as "editor" and two more where he is listed as author with others. His contribution to these was no larger than to some three dozen other books in which his work appears but where he does not collect a byline. He was the author of five nonfiction books and two collections of short stories. The number of novels, counting separately all double titles and including two serials never published in book form, was fifty-two.

Besides all this, General King once reported that he had written 250 short stories. This is quite possible and may even be an understatement, but no one has yet attempted a catalog. His contributions to the *United Service* magazine alone exceeded 75, and *Lippincott's*, *Harper's*, *Cosmopolitan*, *Ainslee's*, the *Cavalry Journal*, and the *Army and Navy Journal* are among others that published his stories again and again.

Charles King's contribution was large, and it was not unimportant, though little space is given to his name in histories of American literature. One study that does recognize him, and not too ungenerously, is *The Prairie and the Making of Middle America*, by Dorothy Anne Dondore. Dondore specifically mentions *The Colonel's Daughter* and *Campaigning with Crook* and correctly points out that King was about the only contemporary writer of fiction to accurately depict soldiers in the advancement of the frontier.[1]

Despite the extravagance of his plots, perhaps more the fault of the era than a peculiarity of the author, he does give a very real portrayal of life in the garrison and in the field. Although his heroes and heroines may be unduly pure and his villains unnaturally evil, he does not exaggerate the blood and disaster of his time. It is true that in most of his books Indians appear more as a story-line enemy than as real characters, but he was generally fair and in some cases romantic in the Cooper tradition. His two attempts to depict Indian heroines, *An Apache Princess* and *A Daughter of the Sioux*, are not entirely convincing. *Tonio, Son of the Sierras* is much more idealized, yet it shows surprising appreciation of the Apache mind-set.

It is noteworthy that King wrote entirely on American themes at a time when many of his contemporaries turned to Europe for subjects of literature and romance. This was the period of *When Knighthood Was in Flower*, *The Prisoner of Zenda*, and *Graustark*, but King's residence abroad brought him no substitute for the American frontier.

The influence of Charles King upon his own time was great, a fact appreciated then as well as now. He did much to bring about the popularity of stories with a western theme and also tales of military-historical romance, though he pioneered in neither field. But he was the first to celebrate the regular army in a period when it was sadly in need of recognition. As Brigadier General William Carey Brown put it, "Civilians as a whole knew little of the army and cared less. King's stories, mostly fiction, written in an attractive way, served to educate the public."[2]

Colonel John H. Parker, who commanded Gatling guns at Santiago and developed machine-gun tactics in the United States Army, recalled a visit by King to West Point in a letter he wrote to King many years later. "We cadets all knew the celebrated Captain Charles King, and we all devoured your charming army stories, as far as you had then given them to the public," he wrote. "All ignorant of army life, as I then was, and not even acquainted on the post at West Point, my first impressions of the army were derived from your tales of the Old Army. I hope we who are now trying to build up the new army, may preserve at least some of the splendid traditions so gracefully chronicled in your stories."[3]

Major General James G. Harbord, who ably commanded the Second Division and later the Services of Supply in France during World War I, once wrote of King's novels, "I read them at the impressionistic age where they had very much to do with my desire to enter the military service. Later on, when I found myself a second lieutenant in the 5th Cavalry, where the traditions of Charlie King were very strong, I think I was the happiest youngster that ever wore the uniform."[4]

The Colonel's Daughter is listed by another contemporary, Frank C. Lockwood, as among "basic and fascinating books that everyone should read who is interested in Arizona history,"[5] and it was the Colonel's Daughter series that most endeared him to the readers of his own day. Its characters were very realistic, based as so many were on actual people in or associated with the Fifth Cavalry. "Jack Truscott," for instance, was founded on George Oscar Eaton, whose actual adventures in the West have been told. "Captain Canker" is identified in his less villainous aspects as John Morrison Hamilton, brevetted captain in the Civil War and major in an Apache campaign and killed as lieutenant colonel of the Ninth U.S. Cavalry in the charge up San Juan Hill in the War with Spain. "Billy Ray," who figures largely in *The Colonel's Daughter* and is the hero of *Marion's Faith*, was one of King's most ubiquitous characters, giving his name to *Ray's Recruit* and *Ray's Daughter*. The hero of *Captured: The Story of Sandy Ray*, who also appears in *A Soldier's Trial*, is the son of Billy Ray. Arthur Tracy Lee of the West Point class of 1867 may be the original of this character, though General Samuel S. Sumner, a long-living officer of the Fifth Cavalry during the period of King's service, believed that Billy Ray was in fact William Preble Hall, the regimental quartermaster who kept the wagon train so close on the heels of the cavalry during the lightning march to Buffalo Bill's exploit on Warbonnet Creek in 1876.

Hall's exploits certainly suggest King's dashing hero, for Hall won the Medal of Honor for gallantry in action near White River, Colorado, on October 20, 1879. The citation suggests an incident King used in *Captain Blake*. It reads, "This officer, then a first lieutenant of the Fifth United States Cavalry in command of a reconnoitering party of three men and while going to the rescue of a brother officer who had been attacked by Indians, was himself attacked by about thirty-five warriors; during the engagement he several times exposed himself in order to draw the fire of his assailants and locate their position so his small party could reply with effect; Lieutenant W. B. Weir, ordnance department, and a scout who accompanied him were both killed by the Indians at this time." Hall became adjutant general of the army in 1904.

Hall's adventures may have been borrowed for both "Billy Ray" and "Gerald Blake," but Blake is believed to have been founded more directly on the career of Alfred Boyce Bache of Pennsylvania, who was regimental commissary of subsistence during King's time in the Fifth Cavalry. Bache was not a West Pointer, being appointed to the regiment in 1867. He died in service on November 12, 1876. Another officer undoubtedly in King's mind when he depicted his fictional characters was Captain Charles H. Rockwell, to whose memory he dedicated the story of Captain Blake.

"Ned Billings," who appears so frequently in the stories, is a character whose identity in real life is not questioned. Billings is

Charles King himself, and whimsically, his references to that character are not always complimentary. King also refers to himself as "Mr. X" or "Lieutenant X," but he seldom writes in the first person. "Sergeant O'Grady" in "The Worst Man in the Troop," one of the stories in *Starlight Ranch*, is Sergeant Bernard Taylor, and the story is an almost autobiographical account of the fight at Sunset Pass in which King was wounded. Lucille Rhoades, General King's secretary, typed herself into the character of "Jenny Wallen" of *A Tame Surrender*. "Colonel Atherton," a recurring figure, exhibits some of the characteristics of Lieutenant Colonel Eugene A. Carr. "The colonel's daughter" herself is variously identified, but perhaps she was Caroline F. Little, who contributed "The Colonel's Daughter's Story" to the collection *The Colonel's Christmas Dinner*.

In reality those characters whose prototypes can be identified are very few; many more are merely types. This was inevitable in King's method, for few writers have thrown such vast collections of names at their readers. King, in fact, created an entire fictional regiment. In *The Colonel's Daughter*, the names of 84 persons are counted, ranging in importance from "Colonel Pelham of the –th Cavalry" to "the widow of the late Private Moriarty," and this in a book of 440 pages. *Marion's Faith* develops 62 characters, largely the same persons, and *Captain Blake*, of about the same length as the other two, has 103. The entire officer strength of a cavalry regiment could well be kept within those figures, since the authorized total was only 56 at that time. King's fictional regiment was usually designated the "–th Cavalry," or sometimes correctly called the Fifth Cavalry, but in the "Fort Frayne" stories he gives premature publicity to the Eleventh Cavalry and the Twelfth Cavalry, units that date to 1901.

His readers soon grew to recognize the characters of Truscott, Ray, and Blake, and also Stannard, Turner, Raymond, Wilkins, Buckets, Gregg, Riggs, and their wives. But in the end these were stories of their time, and perhaps it is not surprising that they should be largely forgotten now. When *The True Ulysses S. Grant* appeared in 1914, King was seventy years old. His publishers kept many of his books in print as late as 1928, and a couple have reappeared since then. But the Indian Wars were long over, and the nation's literary tastes had changed. King's luster as the army novelist had dimmed.

A Soldier's Trial

Charles King's discharge as brigadier general of volunteers in 1899 put him outside the military service once again. He was still a retired captain of cavalry in the regular army, and for a time he was acting superintendent of the Michigan Military Academy at Orchard Lake. But in the early years of the twentieth century, especially during the period when Elihu Root was secretary of war, an attempt was made to reorganize America's national defense on a broader plane based on the well-nigh forgotten manuscript of King's old friend General Emory Upton. His *Military Policy* was the guide. As part of this movement, the state militias were federally recognized as the national guard and were given increasing aid from Washington. Among other provisions of the Dick Act of 1904 was one permitting retired regular officers to be recalled to active duty as instructors of the national guard. The state of Wisconsin lost no time recalling King under this provision. The new laws also recognized his volunteer commission as brigadier general, though as instructor he was still a retired captain.

General King had become the tradition and inspiration of the Wisconsin National Guard. Almost no outsider called upon to inspect the guard or to comment on its training failed to give a large share of credit for its high standing to General King, and certainly he had been very busy in its behalf since 1880. Perhaps most significant was a War Department report of 1914 that stated, "The Organized Militia of the State of Wisconsin may be taken as a model in training, equipment, and business administration."[1] A few years later, when war was declared against Germany, Wisconsin's troops were immediately considered among the national guard forces fit to take the field, whereas only 40,000 out of a total national guard of 120,000 were so regarded. Wisconsin and Michigan formed the Thirty-second Division in World War I ranked as one of the best shock divisions in France. Previously Wisconsin *141* had contributed a machine-gun battalion to another in the same class, the Forty-second Division, known as the "Rainbow."

The Thirty-second Division, which won from the French the nickname "Les Terribles," recognized a large debt due General King for its training before the war. "The word Les Terribles is the crowning glory to the successful campaign waged by him for nearly forty years," said Major Byron Beveridge on one occasion.

> Time and again we remarked that our success was due to the A B C of the military game which was pounded into us in Wisconsin—the salute, discipline, close order drill and shooting. We could see on the front line the benefits of our home armory and camp instructions. In Alsace, at Fismes, around Juvigny, and through the Argonne we could see the vision of the man who played such an important part in making Wisconsin's share of the 32nd what it was. Too old to take an active part himself, his work was felt as that of no other man's in the state.[2]

Similar tributes were paid by Major General William G. Hann, division commander, and Brigadier General Charles R. Boardman, who commanded the Sixty-fourth Brigade.

Meanwhile General King, physically disqualified for service in Europe, was still available for active duty on the home front, and for that he was credited with taking part in his fifth war.

If there was one place where a cool head and sound judgment was needed at the beginning of this war between the United States and Germany, it was in Milwaukee. "The War Department had been led to believe that conspiracy, sedition, treason, and heaven knows what all lay dormant in our law-abiding old city, and that every man of German birth or name was deservedly an object of suspicion," wrote General King.[3] Major General Thomas H. Barry, in command at Chicago, asked King to investigate reports that German sympathizers were preparing to resist the registration for selective service—to "burn elevators, armories, manufacturing plants, blow up railway bridges, and play the mischief generally."[4] All this proved unfounded, but there came, day and night, a perfect deluge of German spy rumors. Even the local committee of safety was stampeded by these reports and petitioned that a regiment of the national guard be called out. A staff officer from Washington came to ask if it was desirable that a regiment from some southern state be ordered to the scene of threatened uprising in Milwaukee. To these appeals King was deaf, and General Barry refused to act until King could be convinced that there was danger.

But even General Barry became apprehensive when registration day approached, and he received reports that a long-extinct organization, the Sons of Herman, had chosen that day to rise and take over Milwaukee. He ordered King to report the first sign of disorder, though even police officers were confident there would be no trouble. All day long King waited for the outbreak. At 8:30 P.M. he had received all reports from the police districts and then sent General Barry the following characteristic telegram: "Registration complete and the only disorder from start to finish a fisticuff between two young American citizens, of possible German descent, over the question of which had the right to register first."[5] That, he says, was about the "gladdest" hour of his official career.

With the departure of the Thirty-second Division, which King followed to the docks in New York, he was given a new problem, organizing a state guard to replace the division for domestic service. "At 74 years of age I am still going nightly from armory to armory, playing the part of the drill sergeant with the new guard and thanking God I have the vim to do it," he wrote to a friend in France.[6] And he made many speeches throughout the state in support of various war campaigns. Early in the century he had gone to the Pacific coast on a lecture tour, his subject being "With the Volunteers at Manila." Now he was a war propagandist. It remained for him to welcome back the Thirty-second Division in an address that was later printed as a pamphlet under the title *Badger and Wolverine.*

King was advanced to major on the retired list May 14, 1918, and attained the rank of lieutenant colonel January 14, 1922. After the war there was the large problem of reorganizing the Wisconsin National Guard, and to this General King devoted his efforts. Unfortunately there was an accident that markedly hampered his activities.

There are few men in the world who have been both wounded by an Indian arrow and run down by an automobile. It epitomizes the history of the United States. The first appears romantic, the second prosaic. But to General King an automobile accident was an event worthy of detailed record, and he left in his *Memories* a pathetically complete account of injuries he received at the busy corner of Oneida and Jefferson streets in Milwaukee on the evening of October 26, 1919. He suffered a double fracture of his right leg and an injured back, then he had the further misfortune to be neglected at the hospital because a bedside call button would not operate. He was a year or more in recovering, and he suffered ill effects from this accident for the rest of his life.[7]

But despite this he rarely missed a summer camp of the Wisconsin National Guard, nor did he spend much idle time while in camp. He was a marvel to his associates, who wondered whether he ever slept. There were times when he was present at every formation from reveille to retreat and was then seen visiting each guard relief during the night.

In 1921 there came rumors of a plan to end the practice of detailing retired officers to national guard instruction. General King was much concerned by this, and so were his associates in the Wisconsin guard. Adjutant General Orlando Holway wrote from Madison to the chief of the Militia Bureau in Washington that "it is peculiarly important both to the United States and to this State that Major King be continued in his present detail. The Governor very earnestly requests that he be so continued." Holway continued:

> There are today in the State far more than fifty thousand members of the Guard, both former and present, who have during their services come under Major King's teaching and influence. They have come and still come to him for advice and assistance, and feel free to come because of long and tried association. His counsel and assistance, always in aid of better discipline and greater loyalty, have the greater authority and effect through his official status as an officer of the Regular Army, detailed for duty in Wisconsin. It is not necessary to add that his influence is not confined merely to present and former Guardsmen, but is widespread in practically every community of the State. By long, faithful and able performance of his assigned duties, he has acquired such standing with the Guard and the people of the State as none other can possibly equal without like service.[8]

Human faith and intervention unwound the War Department's red tape. Major General George C. Richards of the Militia Bureau promptly replied, "So far as this Bureau is concerned there is no intention to have Major King relieved from his present duties, no matter what policy may be adopted with respect to retired officers in general." And Major General James G. Harbord, who received a personal appeal from the acting inspector, General Eli A. Helmick, said that orders affecting retired officers in this connection would not be applied. "General King has ceased to be an officer, he is an institution," he noted. And to make good his definition of King's status, Harbord issued the following order: "The Chief of Staff directs that no action looking to the relief of General Charles King from duty with the National Guard of Wisconsin ever be taken without personal action of himself or the Deputy Chief of Staff." The chief of staff then was General John J. Pershing.

Whatever faults inspectors may have found as they examined the Wisconsin National Guard, they seldom omitted words of praise for General King. "Brig. Gen. Charles King provides this Camp with its military inspiration," wrote one of them in 1924. His "example is a feature of the camp," said another.[9]

Equally praised was King's work at St. John's Military Academy, near Delafield, Wisconsin, where he had superintended tactical instruction since 1884. But despite his successes, the late 1920s were marked by fitful setbacks. The most crushing blow came with the death of his wife, Adelaide, on October 22, 1928. For more than a decade General King had cared for his invalid spouse. She was a constant worry, yet he felt her loss most severely, and there can be no doubt that their married life had been happy and satisfying.

King seldom mentioned his four children. One daughter, Adelaide Patton King, died in childhood. Carolyn Merritt King married Dr. Donald R. MacIntyre of Negaunee, Michigan, and bore the general two grandchildren, Anne and Dugald. Elinor Yorke King married Charles John Simeon of Providence, Rhode Island. They had one daughter, Elizabeth. The general's only son, Rufus King, graduated from the United States Naval Academy in 1908 and served in World War I. His son, a third Charles King, continued into a sixth generation the family tradition of alternating the names Rufus and Charles. None of the King children remained in Milwaukee. For the last several years of his life General King lived alone at the Hotel Carlton, and from that modest headquarters he directed his final campaigns.

Perhaps to distract his mind from grief, King plunged into new struggles. One of the most striking, and the last occasion when he won national attention, was a defense of his old friend Buffalo Bill Cody. King's friendship with Buffalo Bill began on the plains in 1871 and, strengthened by their common service in the Great Sioux War, continued throughout their lives. There were many ceremonial occasions to which both were invited, and many chance meetings. Buffalo Bill's Wild West Show was in Chicago during the time *Fort Frayne* played at the Schiller Theater. "Who would have thought, Bill, in 1876," General King remarked, "that within twenty-one years you and I would both be in the show business in Chicago."

Buffalo Bill seemed an apt subject for the "debunking" type of biography that was popular about this time. A considerable legend had grown up around Cody, much of it based on dime-novel fiction. While much of this was not generally believed, neither was it often challenged. No serious biography of Cody had ever been written, though under his own name there appeared a series of reputed autobiographies that did not always agree in details and in fact were written by various press agents. Answering to this opportunity, there appeared *The Making of Buffalo Bill: A Study in Heroics*, by Richard J. Walsh in collaboration with Milton S. Salsbury. There was much merit in Walsh's book, though it lacked somewhat in thoroughness and was prone to repeat word-of-mouth stories.

General King got the impression that an attempt was being made to cast doubt on Buffalo Bill's most famous exploit, the killing of the Indian Yellow Hair at the fight on the Warbonnet. Walsh's story of this event tended, on the whole, to credit Cody for the exploit, but it did contain one unfortunate paragraph: "Sergeant Jacob Blaut thought that he himself might have killed Yellow Hand. 'Bill and I fired at the same time,' he said, 'and I think my bullet killed him.'"[10] Every enlisted man immediately concerned in Buffalo Bill's fight with the Indian had been a member of King's company, and he declared there was no such person as Jacob Blaut among them. General King saw it as his duty to give the world a correct version of what he himself had seen, and he announced to the press his intention of making a defense of Buffalo Bill in an address to be delivered before the Order of Indian Wars.

The spectacle of this man, now nearly eighty-five years of age, daring a January blizzard to journey from Milwaukee to Washington, D.C., to defend the memory of an old friend caught the imagination of the nation's newspapers. Wide publicity was accorded his mission and his speech. The name Charles King had not been prominent for a generation, and it was as though he had risen from the grave to give his evidence on an event that had become history.

One of King's last publishing efforts was a collaboration with General W. C. Brown in preparing a map of the Big Horn and Yellowstone Expedition against the Sioux in the centennial year. Its basis was a War Department map originally prepared in 1860 by Captain William F. Raynolds of the Topographical Engineers and reissued in 1876 with additions and corrections known to that date. Undoubtedly this map was used during the Sioux War, but its greatest merit fifty years later was its preservation of place-names in use at that time. On this map King retraced the entire route of the Fifth Cavalry during the 1876 campaign, and it carried as part of its legend a partial transcription of the field diary he kept during the summer.

King's friendship with General Brown dated from 1885 when Brown was a lieutenant and instructor at the Infantry and Cavalry School at Fort Leavenworth, Kansas. Later they became well acquainted when Brown was stationed at West Point and King was a member of the Board of Visitors there. Their common interest in tactics and in the history of the Indian Wars was a bond that kept them in close contact for almost half a century.

George Eaton, the "Jack Truscott" of Camp Verde days and King's rescuer at Sunset Pass, survived until September 12, 1930. After resigning from the Fifth Cavalry in 1883 he took up residence in Montana, where he was a member of the first and second constitutional conventions of the territory and served for five years as surveyor general. He moved to New York City in 1894, where he was a member of the Mayor's Municipal Explosives Commission. During the last three years of his life he lived at Fort Myers, Florida. This friendship never flagged, and King devoted much time near the end attempting to arrange publication of some of Eaton's reminiscences of the Indian Wars.

To Milwaukee residents General King was most widely known for his annual appearances as grand marshal of the Memorial Day parade. Almost as much a feature of the parade as the general was his veteran horse, Star, whom he sometimes facetiously called "Mr. Volstead" "because he was always dry. You can't get him past a watering trough."[11] For perhaps twenty years horse and rider continued their association and grew old together. In 1929 the general wrote, "I was on duty on the 30th (Mem. Day) and found it simply 'bully' to be mounted once more on old Star, for contrary to the predictions of two or three of our horse doctors, he never slipped, never stumbled, never went amiss in any way, and actually danced all the latter half of the march where the crowds were bigger, and the band music, because of the higher buildings, was louder. It was the longest Memorial Day march we ever made together and he never went better."[12]

But setbacks continued to follow one another. The general was struck by yet another automobile, and again a leg was injured. Later a fall caused serious injury to the arm that still showed the results of his Indian wound. Yet despite this he attended the national guard camp in 1931 and again rode old Star, though with considerable difficulty because of the leg injury. Then, with the temperature at camp ranging from 102 to 106 degrees Fahrenheit, he was overcome by the heat and for a time doctors feared he would not survive. Shortly after this he was unequivocally retired from the national guard. A citation by Governor Philip F. La Follette of July 19 honored General King officially as the "Grand Old Man of the Wisconsin National Guard."

This was but one of several honors the state conferred on him in his closing years. He was commissioned major general by Governor Walter J. Kohler January 18, 1929, his first attainment of the rank so warmly recommended by General Anderson during the Philippine Insurrection. In 1929 the state of Wisconsin established the "General Charles King Medal" to be awarded to enlisted men for faithful attendance at drill. During one year 689 men qualified for the medal, which was awarded in gold, silver, and bronze classes.

King's remarkable recuperative powers were never more astonishing than in his rapid recovery from the heat prostration. Within a few weeks he was up and about again, eager for new duties. During this period he subjected himself to a thorough physical examination at Walter Reed Army Hospital in Washington. He was given a clean bill of health, and "the surgeon told me I might have ten years of life yet," he exclaimed enthusiastically. "And do you know, I believe I can use every minute of it! There are so many things I would like to do if time is given me."

One of these ambitions was to continue his autobiography. Beginning in 1921 he had contributed at the request of the *Wisconsin*

entitled "Rufus King: Soldier, Editor and Statesman," and the
others appeared as "Memories of a Busy Life" and were reprinted
as a pamphlet under this title.

Despite formal retirement, King maintained his interest in the
Wisconsin National Guard and St. John's Military Academy. And
he never neglected opportunities to enlarge general knowledge of
the Indian Wars. He had a large correspondence with students
and investigators in the fields of history he had been part of, and
most of these letters he answered by hand, though writing was
always painful to him. He also contributed introductions to a
number of books in this field.

Another enduring interest was the United States Military
Academy at West Point. There he had been cadet, instructor,
member of the Board of Visitors, and president of the Association
of Graduates, and now he was seldom absent from spring commencement exercises, sometimes being honored as the oldest
graduate attending. Nor did he hesitate to start out alone to visit
his children or to make frequent trips to Washington and Chicago.
King never had a period of feeble old age. He either was going full
tilt or was in bed. Friends of that period remember him as spring-
ing along at a full military pace, swinging his cane up and down
like a baton, and forcing a younger man almost to run to keep up.

But early in 1932 his troubles piled up again. There was another
severe attack of eczema, similar to the trouble that had caused his
retirement from the Philippines. Then there was torment from
the shattered arm and the injured leg. During the summer his
condition became pressing, and he was taken to the home of his
daughter Carolyn, the wife of Dr. Donald MacIntyre, at Negaunee, Michigan. "It is almost 12," he wrote in a fit of despair. Yet he
recovered in September and was eager to return to Milwaukee.
Later that month he resumed his residence at the Hotel Carlton.
"I am something of a phenomenon to the doctors," he rejoiced
then, but for many weeks relapse and recovery alternated in rapid
succession. At length his physical ailments subsided.

"I am still warned that I may drop down and out at any moment
on any day, but Dr. MacIntyre, who declared me dying last summer, now gives me two years before the next setback," he wrote
in October.[13] "I didn't want it, but must own that I'm glad to have
lasted so long, for the War Dept. now declares me credited with 70

years of active service completed June 30, 1932. It made me quite happy." The actual time elapsed from his appointment as a marker in the First Wisconsin is seventy-six years, but he had been retired five times, though usually for very short periods.

Another year was not to be added to his record. His last public appearance was in a parade at a reunion of Spanish-American War veterans that summer, but this time he was not riding Star. An automobile seemed to him hardly a suitable conveyance for a soldier, but he reluctantly accepted the necessity. His eighty-eighth birthday was marked on October 12. He spent the Christmas holidays at Negaunee, then he returned to Milwaukee but was confined to his room for a considerable period. He was just recovering when he tripped over a rug, fell, and fractured his shoulder.

Two days later he was discussing plans for the future with Lucille Rhoades, his nurse Leila Spade at hand, when he was seized with a chill. Within a few minutes death came, on March 17, 1933. He was buried with full military honors at Milwaukee. Governor Albert G. Schmedeman of Wisconsin, Major General Frank Parker, commanding the Sixth Corps Area, and Rear Admiral Wat T. Cluverius were among those who came to pay the last tribute.

Of the end, prophetically, King may have told it best:

Another stir and rattle down beyond the trees and then as suddenly the leaves all leap and quiver as a flashing volley shoots aloft—another—another, and the pale blue clouds come drifting slowly up the foliage, and then—last scene of all—there appears at the head of the grave one silent, statuesque, solitary form, clad in the full dress uniform of the trooper. A moment's pause until the echo of the final volley has died away in the distance and then he raises the trumpet to his lips. Soft, tremulous and low as we have heard it many a time in windy nights on the far frontier, and in mountain bivouac in the old campaigns, the first notes of "taps" float out upon the hushed and pulseless air; then louder, throbbing, wailing, well-nigh passionate, it thrills through every heart— a sobbing requiem, the trooper's one adieu to cherished comrade, then, sinking, fading, falling, it slowly dies away and all is done.[14]

NOTES

INTRODUCTION

1. The monthly Chicago Westerners program and much related material was customarily published later in the group's *Brand Book*, which Russell edited for nearly four decades. Many of these meeting/*Brand Book* appearances are cited in this Introduction. Much additional related material is found in the Bibliographical Essay.

2. Don Russell, Introduction to *Campaigning with Crook*, by Charles King (Norman: University of Oklahoma Press, 1964); Don Russell, "Captain Charles King, Chronicler of the Frontier," Chicago *Westerners Brand Book* 9 (March 1952): 1–3, 7–8; Don Russell, Foreword to *Charles King, American Army Novelist: A Bibliography from the Collection of the National Library of Australia, Canberra*, by C. E. Dornbusch (Cornwallville, N.Y.: Hope Farm Press, 1963).

3. Don Russell, "Gathering Western History through Personal Inquiry: Indian Wars Veterans," Chicago *Westerners Brand Book* 24 (June 1967): 27; Don Russell, "How I Got This Way," *Western Historical Quarterly* 4 (July 1973): 257–58; Don Russell, "A Very Personal Introduction" to *First Scalp for Custer: The Skirmish at Warbonnet Creek, Nebraska, July 17, 1876*, by Paul L. Hedren (Glendale, Calif.: Arthur H. Clark, 1980), 15–16; Charles King letter to Don Russell, March 18, 1929, Don Russell Papers, Elmhurst, Illinois.

4. Richard J. Walsh, in collaboration with Milton S. Salsbury, *The Making of Buffalo Bill: A Study in Heroics* (Indianapolis: Bobbs-Merrill, 1928); Russell, "How I Got This Way," 258; Russell, "Very Personal Introduction," 16.

5. Russell, "Gathering Western History," 37.

6. Charles King letter to Don Russell, June 30, 1930.

7. A. H. Smith, "Remarks on Receiving the John A. Neilson Portrait of Gen. Charles King, June 30, 1936," Archives Division, State Historical Society of Wisconsin, Madison; citation dated July 19, 1931, General Charles King File, Office of the Adjutant General, state of Wisconsin, Madison.

8. Charles King letter to Don Russell, October 27, 1932.

9. Nina B. Smith, *St. John's Military Academy: A Centennial History* (Delafield, Wisc.: St. John's Military Academy, [1984]), 4–8; Charles King letter to W. C. Brown, April 14, 1928, William Carey Brown Collection, University of Colorado, Boulder.

10. Charles King letter to W. C. Brown, May 29, 1931; unidentified

newspaper clipping, H. J. McGinnis, M.D., Notebooks, Waupaca, Wisconsin.

11. Charles King letter to Grace Raymond Hebard, October 11, 1929, Hebard Collection, Archives–American Heritage Center, University of Wyoming, Laramie; Charles King letter to Don Russell, April 7, 1929.

12. Charles King letters to W. C. Brown, May 23, June 14, June 27, 1926.

13. "Ghastly desert" appears in the Charles King letter to W. C. Brown, July 31, 1930. The King-Brown correspondence is rich with detail on the Warbonnet quest, as is the King-Griffith correspondence in the Robert F. Canaday Collection, Archives–American Heritage Center, University of Wyoming, Laramie. See also Hedren, *First Scalp for Custer*, 87–94. For insight on Camp's obsession with Indian Wars battlefields, see Kenneth Hammer, ed., *Custer in '76: Walter Camp's Notes on the Custer Fight* (Provo, Utah: Brigham Young University Press, 1976), 4–5, 10–25; and Jerome A. Greene, *Slim Buttes, 1876: An Episode of the Great Sioux War* (Norman: University of Oklahoma Press, 1982), 140–47. Notes on Ellison's interest in these affairs are found in Katherine Troxel, "Robert Spurrier Ellison—Collector of Western America," *Westerners New York Posse Brand Book* 2, 4 (1955): 77–78.

14. Charles King letters to W. C. Brown, February 28, May 22, 1929.

15. Charles King letter to W. C. Brown, July 13, 1928; Charles King letter to Don Russell, July 15, 1929.

16. Charles King letter to Don Russell, January 21, 1930. *Proceedings of the Annual Meeting and Dinner of the Order of the Indian Wars of the United States* (1925), 21–22, 27. The 1921 address was first published by the OIW in its annual *Proceedings* and is reprinted in Anson Mills, *My Story*, 2d ed. (Washington, D.C.: Press of Byron S. Adams, 1921), 409–27, and in John M. Carroll, ed., *The Papers of the Order of Indian Wars* (Fort Collins, Colo.: Old Army Press, 1975), 37–47. Recent uses of the 1921 address include Robert M. Utley, *Frontier Regulars: The United States Army and the Indian, 1866–1891* (New York: Macmillan, 1973), xiii–xiv; Robert M. Utley, "Good Guys and Bad: Changing Images of Soldier and Indian," *Periodical: Journal of the Council on Abandoned Military Posts* 8 (Fall 1976): 30, 32; and Paul L. Hedren, "Captain Charles King at Sunset Pass," *Journal of Arizona History* 17 (Autumn 1976): 263.

17. Charles King, "Memories of a Busy Life," *Wisconsin Magazine of History* 5 (March/June 1922) and 6 (September/December 1922). This was reprinted as a pamphlet with the same title and is cited hereafter as *Memories*. Charles King letter to Don Russell, July 25, 1929. King's "Thirty Years of Pencraft: What It Came to and What It Cost," *Lippincott's Monthly Magazine*, October–November 1910, is a related memoir detailing his affairs as a writer.

18. George O. Eaton, "Stopping an Apache Battle: An Episode of the

Indian Wars," revised and edited by Don Russell, foreword by Charles King, *Cavalry Journal* 42 (July–August 1933): 12–18.

19. Charles King and Don Russell, "My Friend, Buffalo Bill," *Cavalry Journal* 41 (September–October 1932): 17–20; Charles King and Don Russell, "My Friend, Buffalo Bill," *Winners of the West*, December 30, 1932; Russell, "Gathering Western History," 27, 30–31.

20. Russell, "How I Got This Way," 258.

21. Charles King letter to W. C. Brown, March 26, 1930.

22. Paul L. Hedren, ed., "Eben Swift's Army Service on the Plains, 1876–1879," *Annals of Wyoming* 50 (Spring 1978): 150–51; Paul L. Hedren, "Charles King," in *Soldiers West: Biographies from the Military Frontier*, ed. Paul A. Hutton (Lincoln: University of Nebraska Press, 1987), 246–47, 249; Charles King, "Thirty Years of Pencraft," 474. The pencil manuscript of *Grant* is preserved in the collections of the Milwaukee County Historical Society. Harry H. Anderson letter to Paul L. Hedren, February 12, 1974, Editor's Collection.

23. King, *Memories*, 80–81.

24. Don Russell letter to Paul L. Hedren, August 28, 1981, Editor's Collection; Charles King letter to Don Russell, June 29, 1930; Lucille Rhoades letter to Don Russell, November 9, 1933, Don Russell Papers, Elmhurst, Illinois.

25. Charles King letter to Don Russell, October 27, 1932; Death Record no. 2438, April 17, 1933, Milwaukee County Register of Deeds, interpretation by Edward J. Hagan, M.D., January 20, 1988, Williston, North Dakota, Editor's Collection.

26. Don Russell letter to Paul L. Hedren, January 6, 1976; Bill Hendrix letter to Don Russell, [March 20, 1933], Don Russell Papers, Elmhurst, Illinois.

27. In the biography Russell did not distinguish among scrapbook volumes, and he did not have access to any of King's meticulously kept diaries, believing incorrectly that they had all been destroyed by fire. Although today one scrapbook and at least one diary are privately held, most of the primary reference material Rhoades lent Russell is in the collections of the State Historical Society of Wisconsin, Madison.

28. What Russell started as he winnowed King's history from fiction, others have continued. See Harry H. Anderson, "Home and Family as Sources of Charles King's Fiction," *Historical Messenger of the Milwaukee County Historical Society* 31 (Summer 1975): 50–68; Paul L. Hedren, "Captain King's Centennial Year Look at Fort Laramie, Wyoming," *Annals of Wyoming* 48 (Spring 1976): 102–8; Oliver Knight, *Life and Manners in the Frontier Army* (Norman: University of Oklahoma Press, 1978); and Harry H. Anderson, "Fiction as History: Milwaukee Novelists Depict the Local Heritage," *Milwaukee History* 3 (Spring 1980): 2–15.

29. Don Russell letter to Paul L. Hedren, December 21, 1974; Don Russell, *One Hundred and Three Fights and Scrimmages: The Story of General Reuben F. Bernard* (Washington, D.C.: U.S. Cavalry Association, 1936). A useful biography of General Brown is George F. Brimlow's *Cavalryman out of the West: Life of General William Carey Brown* (Caldwell, Idaho: Caxton, 1944).

30. Rufus King letter to Don Russell, May 21, 1933, Don Russell Papers, Elmhurst, Illinois.

31. J. B. Lippincott Company letter to Don Russell, April 18, 1933, and Harper and Brothers letter to Don Russell, May 17, 1933, Don Russell Papers, Elmhurst, Illinois; Rufus King letter to Don Russell, December 16, 1933.

32. W. C. Brown letter to Rufus King, December 7, 1933, Don Russell Papers, Elmhurst, Illinois; Rufus King letter to Don Russell, August 1, 1934.

33. Russell, "How I Got This Way," 257.

34. Michael Harrison's "A Bibliography of Don Russell Articles, Books, Pamphlets and Other Materials in the Michael and Margaret B. Harrison Western Research Center, Fair Oaks, California. As of February 14, 1986" (typewritten) lists eighty-eight books, articles, and introductions by Russell; Don Russell, *Custer's Last; or, The Battle of the Little Big Horn in Picturesque Perspective* (Fort Worth, Tex.: Amon Carter Museum, 1968); Don Russell, *Custer's List: A Checklist of Pictures* (Fort Worth, Tex.: Amon Carter Museum, 1969); and Russell, "How I Got This Way," 258–59.

35. Don Russell letters to Paul L. Hedren, November 5, 1973, August 5, 1976, and April 29, 1985. Obituaries of Russell appeared in the *Chicago Tribune*, February 19, 1986, and the *Chicago Sun-Times*, February 20, 1986. See also Fred R. Egloff, "Across the Great Divide: Don Russell," *Buckskin Bulletin* 20 (Spring 1986): 1.

36. King and Russell, "My Friend, Buffalo Bill"; Don Russell, "The Duel on the War Bonnet," *Journal of the American Military History Foundation* 1 (Summer 1937): 55–69; Don Russell, *The Lives and Legends of Buffalo Bill* (Norman: University of Oklahoma Press, 1960), chaps. 17–18.

37. Russell, "Captain Charles King, Chronicler of the Frontier."

38. Mari Sandoz, "Capt. Charles King as Portrayer of the West," *Westerners New York Posse Brand Book* 2, 4 (1955): 84; David L. Hieb letter to Don Russell, March 15, 1956, Research Collections, Fort Laramie National Historic Site, Fort Laramie, Wyoming.

39. Art Woodward, "More on Captain Charles King—A Defense," *Westerners New York Posse Brand Book* 3, 1 (1956): 13–14. Here and elsewhere one sees the interchangeable usage of the names Yellow Hair

and Yellow Hand, a curiosity of little consequence that has carried on since 1876. Russell suggests that the Cheyenne name Hay-o-wei was mistranslated at the time as Yellow Hand. The correct translation, Yellow Hair, referred to the scalp of a white woman taken by Hay-o-wei. See Russell, *Lives and Legends*, 215.

40. Don Russell letter to David L. Hieb, April 19, 1956, and Hieb to Russell, April 23, 1956, Research Collections, Fort Laramie National Historic Site.

41. Don Russell, "Captain Charles King," *Westerners New York Posse Brand Book* 4, 2 (1957): 26, 39–40.

42. Russell, Introduction, *Campaigning with Crook*.

43. Russell, "A Very Personal Introduction."

CHAPTER 1

1. S. Augustus Mitchell, *Mitchell's School Geography* (Philadelphia: Thomas, Cowperthwait, 1847). Although not known to have been used by King, this is a typical contemporary textbook. The series of Latin texts edited by Dr. Charles Anthon and published by Harper might quite safely be assumed to have been among King's schoolbooks.

2. King's interest in fire fighting is noted in Charles King, *Memories of a Busy Life* (Madison: State Historical Society of Wisconsin, 1922), 5. This autobiographical essay first appeared in *Wisconsin Magazine of History*, 1922, and is hereafter cited as *Memories*.

3. "Charles King (Mar. 16, 1789–Sept. 27, 1867)," *Dictionary of American Biography*, vol. 5, ed. Dumas Malone (New York: Charles Scribner's Sons, 1933), 382–83. Hereafter cited as Malone, *DAB*.

4. "John Alsop King (Jan. 3, 1788–July 7, 1867)," Malone, *DAB*, 394–95.

5. "Rufus King (Mar. 24, 1755–Apr. 29, 1827)," Malone, *DAB*, 398–400; and Charles Ray King, ed., *The Life and Correspondence of Rufus King: Comprising His Letters, Private and Official, His Public Documents, and His Speeches*, 6 vols. (New York: G. P. Putnam's Sons, 1894–1900).

6. "Rufus King (Jan 26, 1814–Oct. 13, 1876)," Malone, *DAB*, 400; and General Charles King, "Rufus King: Soldier, Editor and Statesman," *Wisconsin Magazine of History* 4 (June 1921): 371–81.

7. Justin H. Smith, *The War with Mexico*, 2 vols. (New York: Macmillan, 1919), 1:197.

8. "James Gore King (May 8, 1791–Oct. 3, 1853)," Malone, *DAB*, 392–93.

9. He had incurred the wrath of Martin Van Buren. For their reconcilia-

tion see Denis Tilden Lynch, *An Epoch and a Man: Martin Van Buren and His Times* (New York: Horace Liveright, 1929), 461.

CHAPTER 2

1. Charles King, *The True Ulysses S. Grant* (Philadelphia: J. B. Lippincott, 1914), 157.

2. Charles King, *A Knight of Columbia* (New York: Hobart, 1904), 15.

3. Charles King, *The Iron Brigade* (New York: G. W. Dillingham, 1902), 235.

4. Charles King, "A Boy's Recollection of Our Great Generals," in *War Papers Read before the Commandery of the State of Wisconsin, Military Order of the Loyal Legion of the United States*, vol. 3 (Milwaukee: Burdick and Allen, 1903), 130–33.

5. *Memories*, 95–98; Charles King, "Major General Winfield S. Hancock," in *War Papers Read before the Commandery of the State of Wisconsin, Military Order of the Loyal Legion of the United States*, vol. 1 (Milwaukee: Burdick, Armitage and Allen, 1891), 294–99.

6. *Memories*, 7.

7. Original in the General Charles King Scrapbooks.

8. *Memories*, 9.

9. Charles King explored and defended his father's controversial course at Gainesville in the following writings: "Ropes on Gainesville," *United Service* 6(April 1882): 389–95; "In Vindication of General Rufus King," in *Battles and Leaders of the Civil War*, ed. Robert Johnson and Clarence Buel, 4 vols., vol. 2, *North to Antietam* (New York: Century, 1888), 495; *Famous and Decisive Battles of the World* (Philadelphia: J. C. McCurdy, 1884), 559–86; "Gainsville, 1862," *War Papers*, 3:259–83; "Rufus King: Soldier, Editor and Statesman," in *Between the Lines* (New York: Harper and Brothers, 1889); and *Iron Brigade*.

10. King, *Iron Brigade*, 218; John C. Ropes, *The Army under Pope* (New York: Charles Scribner's Sons, 1882).

11. King, "In Vindication of General Rufus King."

12. *The War of the Rebellion: A Compilation of the Official Records of the Union and Confederate Armies*, ser. 1, vol. 12, pt. 2 (Washington, D.C.: Government Printing Office, 1885), 253.

13. Ibid., 505–56; Richard B. Irwin, "The Case of Fitz John Porter," in *Battles and Leaders of the Civil War*, vol. 2, *North to Antietam*, 695–97. A recent study is Otto Eisenschiml, *The Celebrated Case of Fitz John Porter* (Indianapolis: Bobbs-Merrill, 1950).

14. "*Papers Relating to Foreign Affairs*, 1867, pt. 1, p. 708," quoted in "Rufus King (Jan. 26, 1814–Oct. 13, 1876)," Malone, *DAB*, 400.

15. King, *Iron Brigade*, 245; for Gettysburg see 295–319.

1. The quotations in these paragraphs are from the first several pages of "A West Point Parallel," in Charles King's *Noble Blood and A West Point Parallel* (New York: F. Tennyson Neely, 1896). Other sources on the "Boyd Affair" include Richard H. Savage, "Orsemus B. Boyd," in *Association of the Graduates of the United States Military Academy, Annual Reunion, June 10, 1886* (East Saginaw, Mich.: Evening News, 1886), 46–50, cited hereafter as "Boyd Obituary"; *Memories*, 11–21; and Mrs. Orsemus Bronson Boyd, *Cavalry Life in Tent and Field* (New York: J. S. Tait, 1894). In her preface Mrs. Boyd gives a long account of the "Boyd Affair." Noted also are G. I. Cervus [William James Roe, class of 1867], *Cut: A Story of West Point* (Philadelphia: J. B. Lippincott, 1886), a novel based on the Boyd affair; and personal recollections and suggestions of graduates who were cadets at West Point during the time of this episode and shortly thereafter.

2. *Memories*, 12.

3. Mrs. Boyd says eight cadets were involved in the affair. These may be accounted for as the adjutant, the four captains, the sentinel, the officer of the guard, and Casey.

4. "Boyd Obituary."

5. *Memories*, 21.

6. Ibid., 13, 15.

7. Ibid., 17–18.

8. Mrs. Boyd quotes the general's words in *Cavalry Life*, 15. The reply is as recalled by a graduate of West Point familiar with the records.

9. Mrs. Boyd, *Cavalry Life*, 16, mentions the three hundred dollars, and presumably evidence to that effect was brought before the court of inquiry.

10. Identified by officers present at the time or familiar with the case. King mentions Soule and Wright, stating that they were not deprived of their offices of cadet captain and cadet lieutenant.

11. King's statement appears in *Memories*, 19. See also General Court Martial Order No. 40, War Department, February 10, 1866. Cadet Richard C. Churchill succeeded King as adjutant.

12. "Boyd Obituary."

13. Ibid. King in *Memories*, 21, says the "villain" committed suicide, but Savage is definite. Mrs. Boyd also states that Casey was killed by one of his own men, and this is the recollection of others familiar with the case, who believe the killing was accidental. Savage says, "Of the principal actors in the outrage on Cadet Boyd, other than Casey, one blew his brains out and one poisoned himself," and Mrs. Boyd mentions two suicides, but neither gives any evidence that these suicides were connected with the episode. It seems probable that King confused the occur-

rences. Savage says Boyd was "mobbed and maltreated," but all the evidence shows that there was no outrage beyond the ignominious drumming out.

14. "Last Days as a Plebe," newspaper article in Charles King Scrapbooks.

15. *Memories*, 14.

16. The young cadets included Richard Cuyler Churchill of the class of 1866; Allyn Capron of the class of 1867, probably the son of Erastus A. Capron, killed at Churubusco in 1847, and the father of Allyn K. Capron, captain of the Rough Riders killed in Las Guasimas in 1898; and Charles Stewart Heintzelman of the class of 1867, son of Major General Samuel P. Heintzelman, notable in the Civil War. Also *Memories*, 94–95.

CHAPTER 4

1. *Memories*, 7.

2. Henry C. Warmoth, *War, Politics and Reconstruction: Stormy Days in Louisiana* (New York: Macmillan, 1930), 49; *Memories*, 22.

3. *Reports of the United States Commissioners to the Paris Universal Exposition, 1867* (Washington, D.C.: Government Printing Office, 1870), 71–76.

4. *Memories*, 23.

5. So called in several of Charles King's novels.

6. George L. Moreland, *Balldom: The Britannica of Baseball* (Youngstown, Ohio: Balldom, 1914).

7. *Memories*, 25.

8. Ibid., 23; W. C. Brown, "A Tribute to General Charles King," *Cavalry Journal* 42 (May–June 1933): 43–45. Brown's essay also appeared in the *Army and Navy Register*, March 25, 1933, and in *Winners of the West*, April 30, 1933.

9. Charles King, *Trials of a Staff-Officer* (Philadelphia: L. R. Hamersly, 1891), 61–112.

10. John A. Logan, *The Volunteer Soldier in America* (Chicago: R. S. Peale, 1887).

11. King, *Trials of a Staff-Officer*, 61–112.

CHAPTER 5

1. George F. Price, *Across the Continent with the Fifth Cavalry* (New York: Van Nostrand, 1883), 12–28, 104; Lloyd Lewis, *Sherman: Fighting Prophet* (New York: Harcourt, Brace, 1932), 166; and Eben Swift, "The Fifth Regiment of Cavalry," in *The Army of the United States*, ed. Theo.

F. Rodenbough and William L. Haskin (New York: Maynard, Jerrill, 1896), 221–31.

2. Frank C. Lockwood, *Pioneer Days in Arizona: From the Spanish Occupation to Statehood* (New York: Macmillan, 1932), 99.

3. Philip H. Sheridan, *Personal Memoirs of P. H. Sheridan, General, United States Army*, 2 vols. (New York: C. L. Webster, 1888), 2:300–301.

4. *Memories*, 99–100.

5. Ibid., 25–27; Frances Stover, "Seventy Romantic Years of Soldiering," *Milwaukee Journal*, April 9, 1933.

6. Information from Commander Rufus King, U.S.N.

7. Officially, King was General Emory's aide from November 18, 1871, to January 31, 1874.

CHAPTER 6

1. Lockwood, *Pioneer Days in Arizona*, 94.

2. Ibid., 311.

3. Charles King, "George Crook," in *War Papers*, 1:260–61.

4. Personal conversation with King.

5. "George Crook," 266–67.

6. Unidentified clippings in General King's Scrapbooks.

7. John G. Bourke, *On the Border with Crook* (New York: Charles Scribner's Sons, 1891), 208–14.

CHAPTER 7

1. *Memories*, 27–28; Don Russell, ed., "Stopping an Apache Battle," by George O. Eaton, with an introduction by Charles King, *Cavalry Journal* 42 (July–August 1935): 12–18; Charles King, "The Worst Man in the Troop," in *Starlight Ranch and Other Stories of Army Life on the Frontier* (Philadelphia: J. B. Lippincott, 1890), 201–33; Theo. F. Rodenbough, *Uncle Sam's Medal of Honor: Some of the Noble Deeds for Which the Medal Has Been Awarded Described by Those Who Have Won It, 1861–1886* (New York: G. P. Putnam's Sons, 1886), 248–65.

2. Dr. Warren E. Day letter to Thomas E. Parish, former Arizona state historian, September 30, 1913, copy supplied by Will C. Barnes of Phoenix, Arizona; a similar statement was made in 1912, copy supplied by Elizabeth Toohey, Arizona state historian. By the time of the letter King was widely known as "Captain."

3. Charles King, *Campaigning with Crook and Stories of Army Life* (New York: Harper and Brothers, 1890), 134.

4. Eaton's exploits are told in Russell, "Stopping an Apache Battle," in

manuscript accounts provided the author before his death, and in S. E. Tillman, "George Oscar Eaton," in *Sixty-fourth Annual Report of the Association of Graduates of the United States Military Academy at West Point, New York, June 12, 1933* (Newburgh, N.Y.: Moore, 1933), 81–87.

CHAPTER 8

1. *Annual Report of the Secretary of War* [1875] (Washington, D.C.: Government Printing Office, 1875).

2. King, *Famous and Decisive Battles of the World*, 723. King compares them to the Cossacks. Patrick E. Byrne, in *Soldiers of the Plains* (New York: Minton, Balch, 1926), comes to the same conclusion, citing King in a different quotation to the same effect. Bourke, in *On the Border with Crook*, 338, calls them the "finest light cavalry in the world." See also Arthur L. Wagner, *The Service of Security and Information* (Washington, D.C.: J. J. Chapman, 1893).

3. The bibliography on Custer in the Sioux War of 1876 is very large, and no attempt is made to represent all the sources consulted.

4. Quoted in King, *Campaigning with Crook*, 166–67.

5. Bourke, *On the Border with Crook*, p. 337.

6. His story of the Rosebud fight is told by Frank B. Linderman in *American: The Life Story of a Great Indian* (New York: John Day, 1930).

7. Price, *Across the Continent with the Fifth Cavalry*, 585.

8. These are King's figures after a careful study of the reports and terrain.

9. Warbonnet Creek and Hat Creek are variant translations of the same Indian word, but in the course of time Hat became applied to the lower stream and Warbonnet to the upper fork. The "Record of Events" sections of the Fifth Cavalry company returns for the most part locate the fight on Indian Creek, another branch, although Company I uses "War Bonnet." The site of the battle was identified in the early 1930s by a group that included General King, Brigadier General W. C. Brown, Chris Madsen, and Al Rundquist, who drafted a map of the battlefield. The site is on Hat Creek within the present limits of Montrose, Nebraska, and is marked by two small monuments.

10. *Daily Oklahoman*, November 4, 1934; reprinted in *Winners of the West*, November 30 and December 30, 1934, and in the *Farmer-Stockman*, June 1, 1941.

11. White's first name is given as Jonathan on his headstone at the Slim Buttes battlefield, where he was killed. King calls him James, and he is referred to as Charley and Frank in other accounts. He was devoted to Cody and copied him in every way possible, so he was jokingly called "Buffalo Chips." He accepted the nickname as a compliment.

12. King says two companies of infantry, but only one can be verified.

13. The couriers were identified by Frederick Post, a former sergeant in their company, in a letter to King dated May 2, 1929.

14. The direct quotations are from King's *Campaigning with Crook*. Essentially they agree with those given in the *New York Herald* account of July 23, 1876, which was also written by King only days after the episode.

15. Many years later Wilkinson expressed the opinion that he, not Cody, had shot Yellow Hair. King stated that this was the only shot Wilkinson fired in the action and that it was a miss. Wilkinson himself later agreed with the version of the incident given here.

16. Because of the Warbonnet march, Merritt arrived at Fort Fetterman about a week later than expected, and quite naturally General Crook was not pleased. However, he appears to have taken no action in the matter. Muster Roll Record of Events sections of the Fifth Cavalry tell the story, with some variations. Company A reported, "Early on the morning of July 17, a party of seven Indians was discovered trying to cut off two couriers with dispatches for the command. The Regimental Commander immediately dispatched a party in pursuit which succeeded in killing one Indian." Company I's record reads: "Returned 73 miles by Sage Creek to War Bonnet Creek to assist in preventing certain Cheyenne Indians from leaving Red Cloud Agency, which Indians, numbering several hundred, were turned back July 17, two or three of them being killed." Most of the other returns mention only one Indian killed. Company B records, "one (1) Indian and pony killed." Indian sources agree that Hay-o-wei was the only casualty. A diary kept by James B. Frew, private of Company D, published in part in *Winners of the West*, April 30, 1936, states: "July 17, 1876. Indians reported by the pickets. Command ordered to secrete in the ravines, but two couriers arriving from the agency being in danger Cody fired on them, killing the chief, Yellow Hand. The rest tried to rescue him but we charged, killing six. Followed them into the agency 40 miles." See also Price, *Across the Continent with the Fifth Cavalry*, 158.

17. Cody's first account, possibly the only one he himself wrote, is contained in a letter to his wife, dated Red Cloud Agency, July 18, 1876. It reads: "We have come in here for rations. We have had a fight. I killed Yellow Hand a Cheyenne Chief in a single-handed fight. You will no doubt hear of it through the paper. I am going as soon as I can reach Fort Laramie the place we are heading for now [to] send the war bonnet, shield, bridle whip, arms and his scalp to Kerngood to put up in his window. I will write Kerngood to bring it up to the house so you can show it to the neighbors. We are now ordered to join General Crook and will be there in two weeks. Write me at once to Fort Fetterman, Wyoming. My health is not very good. I have worked myself to death. Although I have

shot at lots of Indians I have only one scalp I can call my one [own], that fellow I fought single handed in sight of our command and the cheers that went up when he fell was deafening." This letter was printed in the *Baltimore Sun* on December 21, 1936, with the statement that it was in the possession of Mrs. Harry C. Schloss of Baltimore, Maryland, daughter of the Moses Kerngood referred to in the letter. In 1876 Kerngood owned a clothing store in Rochester, New York. Courtney Riley Cooper, who wrote *Last of the Great Scouts* in collaboration with Helen Cody Wetmore, Cody's sister, says she told him about opening the box referred to and fainting when she saw the scalp.

On his arrival at Fort Laramie on July 21, Cody found a wire from James Gordon Bennett, editor of the *New York Herald*, asking for an account of the fight. Cody, in turn, asked King to write this for him, and King composed what he later referred to as "a brief telegraphic story, say one-eighth of a column." He read it over to Cody, who suggested no changes, though King recalled the scout's remarking, "It's fine, only . . . ," and then saying no more. King did not read the printed account in the *New York Herald* of July 23, 1876, until 1929, and then he denied that it was as he had written it, since it had been expanded to nearly a column, with some inaccurate additions—for example, it credited Wilkinson with killing an Indian and used such language as "Yellow Hand, a young Cheyenne brave, came foremost, singling out Bill as a foeman worthy of his steel. Cody coolly knelt, and taking deliberate aim, sent his bullet through the Chief's leg and into his horse's head." Charles King letter to Don Russell, March 20, 1929.

From this modest beginning, Cody's press agents expanded the story into a thrilling yarn of a challenge to single combat between the lines of opposing armies. One of the most elaborate and apocryphal of these is quoted in Richard J. Walsh, *The Making of Buffalo Bill: A Study in Heroics* (Indianapolis: Bobbs-Merrill, 1928), 190–93. *The Life of Hon. William F. Cody Known as Buffalo Bill, the Famous Hunter, Scout and Guide: An Autobiography* (Hartford, Conn.: Frank E. Bliss, 1879) is the least exaggerated of Cody's published accounts, which grew with the years.

King's account was first written in 1879 for the *Milwaukee Sentinel* and was reprinted as *Campaigning with Crook* (Milwaukee: Sentinel, 1880). His final conclusions are recounted in an article, "My Friend, Buffalo Bill," by General Charles King as told to Don Russell, *Cavalry Journal* 41(September–October 1932): 17–20.

This chapter revises my account "The Duel on the War Bonnet," *Journal of the American Military History Foundation* 1 (Summer 1937): 55–69. After that article was written, valuable commentary on King's account came from Chris Madsen (see note 9 above), who called attention to a number of incongruous details in King's story, some of which were corrected in the *Cavalry Journal* article and others in this chapter, though most of them were minor.

Meticulous detail has appeared necessary because of a curious effort to discredit the entire story, not entirely surprising, considering the extravagances of Buffalo Bill's press agents. However, there seems to be abundant contemporary evidence to substantiate the principal facts. Proof seems overwhelming that Cody killed an Indian on July 17, 1876.

CHAPTER 9

1. This chapter is based largely on King's *Campaigning with Crook*. See also W. C. Brown and Charles King, *Map Showing Many Battlefields of the Indian Wars and Trail of the Big Horn and Yellowstone Expedition of 1876* (Denver: Clason Map Company, 1930); Price, *Across the Continent with the Fifth Cavalry*; Bourke, *On the Border with Crook*; and John F. Finerty, *War-Path and Bivouac; or, The Conquest of the Sioux* (Chicago: Donahue Brothers, 1890).

2. Finerty, *War-Path and Bivouac*, 246.

3. King, *Campaigning with Crook*, 113. Much misinformation has been printed about Frank Grouard, often spelled Gruard. He usually is called Hawaiian, and sometimes a renegade Sioux. According to T. J. Gatchell, noted student of the West living in Sheridan, Wyoming, who knew Grouard well and collected his family history, Frank was born September 20, 1850, on Anaa Island, in the Tuamotu Archipelago of French Polynesia, the son of Benjamin F. Grouard, who had served in the United States Navy and later became a missionary, and the daughter of the high chief of Anaa. The family came to California in 1852 and Frank was put in school, but he soon joined a freighting outfit going to Montana. While carrying mail between Fort Ellis and Fort Hall about 1869, he was captured by the Sioux and saved from death by the intervention of Sitting Bull. After living with the Sioux for several years he quarreled with Sitting Bull, escaped, and eventually became a scout for General Crook, who valued him highly. See the Chicago *Westerners Brand Book* 6 (December 1949).

John Wallace Crawford, known variously as "Captain Jack" and the "poet scout," was born in county Donegal, Ireland, on March 4, 1847, and died in Brooklyn on February 28, 1917. During the Civil War he served in the Forty-eighth Pennsylvania Volunteers. He was a scout in the West, succeeding Cody as chief of scouts with Crook's 1876 expedition. His verse includes *The Poet Scout* (San Francisco: H. Keller, 1879; rev. ed. 1886); *Camp Fire Sparks* (Chicago: C. H. Kerr, 1893); *Lariattes; A Book of Poems and Favorite Recitations* (Sigourney, Iowa: W. A. Bell, 1904); and *The Broncho Book: Being Buck-Jumps in Verse* (East Aurora, N.Y.: Roycrofters, 1908).

4. General Charles King, Address delivered at the annual meeting of the Order of Indian Wars of the United States, February 26, 1921, MS, p. 30.

5. Ibid., 31.

6. Finerty, *War-Path and Bivouac*, 253.

7. King, *Campaigning with Crook*, 122.

8. King, "Address," 32.

9. King, *Campaigning with Crook*, 137.

10. Finerty, *War-Path and Bivouac*, 266.

11. Bourke, *On the Border with Crook*, 379.

12. King, *Campaigning with Crook*, 140.

13. Charles King, "Van," in *Starlight Ranch and Other Stories of Army Life on the Frontier*, 252.

14. King, *Campaigning with Crook*, 156.

CHAPTER 10

1. Roy F. Lynd, "Fort D. A. Russell," *Recruiting News* [1924].

2. King, *Trials of a Staff-Officer*, 180–81.

3. Swift, "Fifth Regiment of Cavalry."

4. King, *Trials of a Staff-Officer*, 46–47.

5. Ibid., 50–51.

6. Ibid., 51.

7. Ibid., 53–54.

8. Ibid., 6–7.

9. These incidents were used by Charles King in *Foes in Ambush* (Philadelphia: J. B. Lippincott, 1893).

10. *Memories*, 29.

11. "Copies of Orders, Letters, Citations, Etc." (privately printed by General Charles King, ca. 1925).

CHAPTER 11

1. Charles King letter to Don Russell, April 27, 1929.

2. Interview in a Chicago newspaper, 1897, clipping not further identified, General Charles King Scrapbooks.

3. The preface is dated November 21, 1882, and copies were available for Christmas 1882. In the publication of General King's works copyright dates are used where dates of first publication, usually shown on the title page, are not more definitely known.

4. "Some Tellers of Stories," *Boston Transcript*, January 5, 1895.

5. Frank L. Dyer and Thomas C. Martin, with the collaboration of William H. Meadowcraft, *Edison: His Life and Inventions*, 2 vols. (New

York: Harper and Brothers, 1929), 1:216, quoting an article by Edison in an 1878 issue of *North American Review*.

6. Ibid., 1:218, 222.

7. Stover, "Seventy Romantic Years of Soldiering," April 23, 1933.

8. Ibid.

9. "A boy yarn told long ago into the phonograph—my introduction to that useful instrument," King's inscription on a copy for Frank M. Weinhold; and interview with Lucille Rhoades, n.d.

10. The Steele-Wild affair of 1890, a much sensationalized and drawn-out court case involving a shiftless enlisted soldier, Dell P. Wild, and a no-nonsense first lieutenant, Matthew F. Steele, was the background for this novel.

11. Inscription in Frank Weinhold's Charles King book collection.

CHAPTER 12

1. General King's scrapbooks contain a full newspaper account of the production of *Fort Frayne*.

2. *Peck's Sun*, February 2, 1895.

3. Interviews appearing in Marinette, Wisconsin, newspapers. Collected in the King Scrapbooks.

CHAPTER 13

1. *Memories*, 30–41. King's experiences at the University of Wisconsin are told in detail in this work. King used them fictionally, with imaginative additions, in *The Medal of Honor* (New York: Hobart, 1905).

2. King, "The Telephone as an Adjunct to the National Guard," in *Trials of a Staff-Officer*, 113–51.

3. Copies from original telegrams in the King Scrapbooks. King kept a particularly complete scrapbook for 1898–99, which contains many original field orders, reports, letters, and maps.

4. Original bill in King Scrapbooks. The incident is used fictionally in King's *Ray's Daughter* (Philadelphia: J. B. Lippincott, 1901).

5. Frederick Funston, *Memories of Two Wars* (New York: Charles Scribner's Sons, 1911), 159–60.

6. *Chicago Tribune*, April 1, 1933.

7. Roosevelt's original letter is in the King Scrapbooks.

CHAPTER 14

1. Walter Millis's *The Martial Spirit: A Study of Our War with Spain* (Boston: Houghton Mifflin, 1931), gives a realistic view of the nego-

tiations with Aguinaldo, as it does of the entire Spanish-American War.

2. *Memories*, 68.

3. Original in the King Scrapbooks.

4. *Annual Report of the Major-General Commanding the Army, 1899*, in three parts (Washington, D.C.: Government Printing Office, 1899). Part 2 gives full reports of the outbreak of the insurrection and of the battles around Manila. Hereafter cited as *Report, 1899*.

5. Originals of these reports are in the King Scrapbooks. See also *Memories*, 71–73.

6. *Memories*, 68–74; *Report, 1899*, particularly reports of General Otis, 98, General Anderson, 373, and General King, 376, for details of the lines and battle.

7. *Report, 1899*, 376.

8. Ibid., 373.

9. Ibid., 98. The unique plural form is that used in the official reports.

10. Ibid., 419 for Company A, Battalion of Engineers; 382 for First California.

11. One of these photographs is reproduced in King's *A Conquering Corps Badge*, opposite p. 304. The original is among King's papers. See also *Report, 1899*, 409.

12. Senator Albert J. Beveridge of Indiana in *Saturday Evening Post*, March 5, 1900.

13. Ibid.

14. Unidentified article dated March 20, 1899, in King Scrapbooks.

15. Carbon copies of the original recommendations by Otis and Anderson are in King's correspondence file and are reprinted in *Memories* and in "Copies of Orders, Letters, Citations, Etc."

16. Original in the King Scrapbooks.

17. In addition to sources previously cited, a story "The Fate of Guadalupe," in King's *Conquering Corps Badge*, 254–59, gives details of the fighting at that point.

18. Original letter in the King Scrapbooks.

19. *Report, 1899*, 390.

20. Interview on his return to Milwaukee, probably in the *Milwaukee Sentinel*, in King Scrapbooks.

21. Original letter in the Scrapbooks. The correspondence indicates King turned over command to Colonel Smith after February 19 (suggested by General Anderson, February 15) and that Wheaton assumed command before February 27. King resumed command by order of March 11.

22. *Memories*, 80.

23. *Report, 1899*, Lawton's report, 30–75.

24. Ibid., 35.

25. Ibid., 44.

26. *San Francisco Examiner*, June 2, 1899.

27. *Memories*, 107.

28. Original letters in King's correspondence file, copied in *Memories*, 83.

29. Ibid.

30. Andrew Marker in the *Boise News*, reprinted in the *Spokane Spokesman-Review*, October 27, 1901.

31. Original telegram from adjutant general's office and original order in King Scrapbooks.

CHAPTER 15

1. Dorothy Anne Dondore, *The Prairie and the Making of Middle America: Four Centuries of Description* (Cedar Rapids, Iowa: Torch Press, 1926), 346.

2. General W. C. Brown letter to Don Russell, April 25, 1933.

3. Colonel John H. Parker letter to General King, December 9, 1922.

4. General J. C. Harbord letter to W. C. Brown, April 10, 1933.

5. Lockwood, *Pioneer Days in Arizona*, 351–52.

CHAPTER 16

1. "Copies of Orders, Letters, Citations, Etc."

2. Ibid.

3. *Memories*, 109.

4. Ibid., 109–10.

5. Ibid., 112.

6. "Copies of Orders, Letters, Citations, Etc."

7. *Memories*, 86–87.

8. "Copies of Orders, Letters, Citations, Etc."

9. Ibid.

10. Walsh, *Making of Buffalo Bill*, 192.

11. *Milwaukee Journal*, March 19, 1933.

12. General King letter to Don Russell, June 1, 1929.

13. Ibid., October 27, 1932.

14. Charles King, "Sheridan," *Cavalry Journal* 1 (November 1888): 14.

In the many years since Don Russell finished his biography of General Charles King, other writers and historians have explored aspects of King's military and literary careers. I cited many of these newer essays in my introduction, and I refer readers to those notes. Other related scholarship is explored here. All these more recent studies complement Russell's work remarkably well, particularly since he never intended to document the general's seventy-year military career minutely, and a full literary assessment could come only after the passage of time.

Harry H. Anderson, executive director of the Milwaukee County Historical Society and foremost among recent King scholars, often uses his hometown advantage to carry King scholarship into new realms. In his *The MacArthurs of Milwaukee* (Milwaukee: Milwaukee County Historical Society, 1979), for instance, he explored the long-standing friendship between the MacArthur and King families. They shared not only the "King's Corner" neighborhood, but also parallel and illustrious military histories and considerable social prominence in their city.

In three essays, "Buffalo Bill and General Charles King," Chicago *Westerners Brand Book* 36 (March–April 1979), "General Charles King and Buffalo Bill's Silent Western Movies," *Historical Messenger of the Milwaukee County Historical Society* 22 (September 1966), and "The Friendship of Buffalo Bill and Charles King," *Milwaukee History* 9 (Winter 1986), Anderson constructed a framework for understanding the spirited Cody-King relationship that is quite unlike anything Don Russell presented in his biography of either Cody or King.

In "Charles King's *Campaigning with Crook*," Chicago *Westerners Brand Book* 32 (January 1976), and *Indian Campaigns: Sketches of Cavalry Service in Arizona and on the Northern Plains* (Fort Collins, Colo.: Old Army Press, 1984), Anderson gives new insight to King's participation in the Apache War and the Great Sioux War. The former presents some very personal and frank letters King wrote to his family from the northern plains in 1876, and the latter consists of sketches King wrote for the *Milwaukee Sentinel*, though these were not previously collected, as many others were in 1880 for *Campaigning with Crook*. In addition to the intrinsic value of these primary documents, Anderson's insightful annotations make these works doubly valuable.

Three times I have written on specific aspects of King's military career, and each essay provides a perspective that adds to Russell's work. My "Captain Charles King at Sunset Pass," *Journal of Arizona History* 17 (Autumn 1976), and a subsequent biographical sketch, "Charles King," in *Soldiers West: Biographies from the Military Frontier,* ed. Paul A. Hutton (Lincoln: University of Nebraska Press, 1987), make the first scholarly use of King's Appointments, Commissions, and Personal File, originally maintained by the army's adjutant general's office in Washington, D.C. The ACP File, as these papers are commonly known, contains all King's official orders and much personal correspondence. My book *First Scalp for Custer: The Skirmish at Warbonnet Creek, Nebraska, July 17, 1876* (Glendale, Calif.: Arthur H. Clark, 1980) is the most recent telling of the dramatic King–Cody–Yellow Hair episode, and I drew heavily on regimental and military post records for this interpretation.

Another particularly noteworthy essay having King as a central figure is Jerry M. Cooper's "The Wisconsin National Guard in the Milwaukee Riots of 1886," *Wisconsin Magazine of History* 55 (Autumn 1971). Russell gave limited attention to this critical episode of the national guard versus labor.

Additional recent scholarship has greatly enhanced our understanding of King's stature as a literary figure and as a historian of the army and the Indian frontier. In his 1962 Ph.D. dissertation titled "The Novels of Charles King, 1844–1933" (New York University, 1962), Wilfred C. Burton focused on the literary constructs of personalities, plot structures, and character development, along with the themes recurrent in King's works and other romantic novels of that period. Although Burton dismissed much in King's fiction, he realized, as Russell did, that King's attention to military detail had an overriding value. Hazel M. Flock drew a similar conclusion in her monograph *Frontier Army Life Revealed by Charles King, 1844–1933,* Fort Hays Studies, Literature Series 3 (Hays: Fort Hays Kansas State College, 1964). So did Oliver Knight in his book *Life and Manners in the Frontier Army* (Norman: University of Oklahoma Press, 1978), a study based almost exclusively on the social order found in King's western novels.

One other essay takes a somewhat different literary tack. In "Captain Charles King, U.S.A.," *Midwest Quarterly* 3 (Autumn 1961), Samuel J. Sackett poses but never adequately answers the question how a writer as internationally popular as Charles King could fade so quickly into obscurity. In his search for an overriding literary attribute, Sackett dismisses the values of background and color, the very qualities Russell, Knight, and others praised so highly.

The first formal bibliography of King's writings was prepared by Russell for the biography and was revised in 1952 for the Chicago Westerners. Subsequently Charles E. Dornbusch's *Charles King, American*

Army Novelist: A Bibliography from the Collection of the National Library of Australia, Canberra (Cornwallville, N.Y.: Hope Farm Press, 1963), particularly focused on first editions, but he listed nearly one hundred other printing variations. Twenty-five years later Dornbusch remains a standard reference to King's books, but is soon to be replaced by a comprehensive bibliography now in production by Louis A. Hieb, son of Russell's Fort Laramie friend David Hieb. This new bibliography, in final draft and tentatively titled *Captain Charles King: A Descriptive and Analytic Bibliography*, corrects Dornbusch's identification of first editions and recognizes, all told, nearly five hundred distinct American printing variations of King's books.

In a 1973 article, "Some Footnotes to Charles King's 'Campaigning with Crook,'" *Historical Messenger of the Milwaukee County Historical Society* 29 (Spring 1973), Harry Anderson discusses the somewhat tortured printing history of King's greatest book. In five or six different editions over a century, *Campaigning* has rarely been out of print, yet its passing from a now scarce paper-wrapped edition to one jeopardized by a well-publicized libel suit, to the current printings makes for a melodramatic tale typical of Charles King. In *King on Custer: An Annotated Bibliography* (College Station, Tex.: Brazos Corral of the Westerners, 1982), I compiled a thirty-item list of King's writings on that reckless Indian fighter and the 1876 Battle of the Little Bighorn. I also prepared the researcher's guide *Campaigning with Crook Index* (Brigham City, Utah: Regimental Press, 1981) for the earliest but most commonly used editions of *Campaigning*.

Unquestionably the greatest single source of recent King material has been the pages of Don Russell's own Chicago *Westerners Brand Book*. I noted many related items in the Introduction, and I add the following to complete the Chicago *Brand Book* Charles King bibliography. Elmo Scott Watson and Don Russell, "The Battle of the Washita; or, Custer's Massacre?" 5 (November 1948); Herbert O. Brayer, "Westerners Select the Big Ten," 12 (September 1955); Don Russell, "Campfire Comment," 16 (June 1959); James T. King, "The Military Frontier—What Was It?" 21 (February 1965); Don Russell, ed., "Charles King on General Crook and the Apache Problem," 22 (October 1965); Don Russell, "Magazines," 22 (January 1966); Don Russell, "Chapter Notes," 23 (July 1966); John S. DuMont, "A Debate of Authors on the Custer Fight, I," 30 (July 1973); Don Russell, "Chapter Notes," 30 (July 1973); John S. DuMont, "A Debate of Authors on the Custer Fight, II," 30 (August 1973); and Don Russell, "Campfire Comment," 32 (January 1976). Of the thousands of book reviews Russell wrote, the following in the Chicago *Brand Book* refer to Charles King: *Fifty Years on the Old Frontier as Cowboy, Hunter, Guide, Scout, and Ranchman*, by James H. Cook, 14 (April 1957); *Charles King, American Army Novelist*, by C. E. Dornbusch, 20

(December 1963); *Custer's Last Battle,* by Charles King, 32 (May–June 1975); *Life and Manners in the Frontier Army,* by Oliver Knight, 34 (January–February 1978); *This Was Klondike Fever,* by Harold M. Stumer, 37 (March–April 1980); *First Scalp for Custer: The Skirmish at Warbonnet Creek, Nebraska, July 17, 1876,* by Paul L. Hedren, 38 (November–December 1981); *Cavalry Life in Tent and Field,* by Mrs. Orsemus Bronson Boyd, 39 (July–August 1982); and *Campaigning with Crook,* by Charles King, 40 (March–April 1983–85). Harry H. Anderson reviewed the initial 1964 edition of *Campaigning with Crook* 21 (May 1964), which bore Don Russell's introduction.

BIBLIOGRAPHY OF

CHARLES KING'S BOOKS

Listed here are the first editions of King's books. The contents were occasionally revised, combined, or separated, and the titles sometimes changed in later editions. Nearly all were reprinted.

Adventures of Uncle Sam's Soldiers. With John Habberton, Charles A. Curtis, Charles D. Rhodes, and others. New York and London: Harper and Brothers, 1907.

An Apache Princess: A Tale of the Indian Frontier. New York: Hobart, 1903.

An Army Portia. Philadelphia: J. B. Lippincott, ca. 1890.

An Army Wife. New York: F. Tennyson Neely, 1896.

Between the Lines: A Story of the War. New York: Harper and Brothers, 1889.

Boy's Book of the Army. With John Habberton, Charles A. Curtis, Charles D. Rhodes, and others. New York and London: Harper and Brothers, ca. 1907.

A Broken Sword: A Tale of the Civil War. New York: Hobart, 1905.

By Land and Sea. (Edited.) Philadelphia: L. R. Hamersly, 1891.

Cadet Days: A Story of West Point. New York: Harper and Brothers, 1894.

Campaigning with Crook: The Fifth Cavalry in the Sioux War of 1876. Milwaukee: Sentinel, 1880.

Campaigning with Crook and Stories of Army Life. New York: Harper and Brothers, 1890.

Captain Blake. Philadelphia: J. B. Lippincott, 1891.

Captain Close and Sergeant Croesus: Two Novels. Philadelphia: J. B. Lippincott, 1895.

Captain Dreams and Other Stories. (Edited.) Philadelphia: J. B. Lippincott, 1895.

Captured: The Story of Sandy Ray. New York: R. F. Fenno, ca. 1906.

The Colonel's Christmas Dinner. (Edited.) Philadelphia: L. R. Hamersly, 1890.

The Colonel's Christmas Dinner and By Land and Sea. (Edited.) Philadelphia: J. B. Lippincott, 1892.

The Colonel's Christmas Dinner and Other Stories. (Edited.) Philadelphia: J. B. Lippincott, 1893.

174

Biblio-
graphy
of
Charles
King's
Books

The Colonel's Daughter; or, Winning His Spurs. Philadelphia: J. B. Lippincott, 1883.

Comrades in Arms: A Tale of Two Hemispheres. New York: Hobart, 1904.

A Conquering Corps Badge and Other Stories of the Philippines. Milwaukee: L. A. Rhoades, 1902.

A Daughter of the Sioux: A Tale of the Indian Frontier. New York: Hobart, 1903.

The Deserter. Philadelphia: J. B. Lippincott, ca. 1887.

The Deserter and From the Ranks: Two Novels. Philadelphia: J. B. Lippincott, 1888.

Dunraven Ranch. Philadelphia: J. B. Lippincott, ca. 1888.

Famous and Decisive Battles of the World; or, History from the Battle-field. Philadelphia and St. Louis: J. C. McCurdy, 1884.

Foes in Ambush. Philadelphia: J. B. Lippincott, 1893.

Fort Frayne. London and New York: F. Tennyson Neely, ca. 1895.

Found in the Philippines: The Story of a Woman's Letters. London, New York, and Chicago: F. Tennyson Neely, ca. 1899.

From Marathon to Santiago: Famous and Decisive Battles of the World. London, New York, and Chicago: F. Tennyson Neely, ca. 1899.

From School to Battle-field: A Story of the War Days. Philadelphia: J. B. Lippincott, 1899.

From the Ranks: A Novel. Philadelphia: J. B. Lippincott, ca. 1887.

A Garrison Tangle. New York: F. Tennyson Neely, 1896.

The General's Double: A Story of the Army of the Potomac. Philadelphia: J. B. Lippincott, 1898.

Great Battles of History. Vol. 1. *From Marathon, B.C. 490 to Auerstadt, A.D. 1806*. Philadelphia: P. W. Ziegler, ca. 1905.

Great Battles of History. Vol. 2. *From Waterloo, A.D. 1815 to Port Arthur and Mukden, 1905*. Philadelphia: P. W. Ziegler, ca. 1905.

Indian Campaigns: Sketches of Cavalry Service in Arizona and on the Northern Plains. Edited by Harry H. Anderson. Fort Collins, Colo.: Old Army Press, 1984.

An Initial Experience and Other Stories. (Edited.) Philadelphia: J. B. Lippincott, 1894.

In Spite of Foes: or, Ten Years' Trial. Philadelphia and London: J. B. Lippincott, 1901.

The Iron Brigade: A Story of the Army of the Potomac. New York: G. W. Dillingham, ca.1902.

Kitty's Conquest. Philadelphia: J. B. Lippincott, 1884.

A Knight of Columbia: A Story of the War. New York: Hobart, 1904.

Lanier of the Cavalry; or, A Week's Arrest. Philadelphia and London: J. B. Lippincott, 1909.

175
Biblio-
graphy
of
Charles
King's
Books

"*Laramie*"; or, *The Queen of Bedlam: A Story of the Sioux War of 1876*. Philadelphia: J. B. Lippincott, 1889.

Marion's Faith: A Sequel to The Colonel's Daughter. Philadelphia: J. B. Lippincott, 1886.

The Medal of Honor: A Story of Peace and War. New York: Hobart, 1905.

Memories of a Busy Life. Madison: Wisconsin Historical Society, ca. 1922.

Noble Blood: A Prussian Cadet Story, Translated from the German of Ernst Von Wildenbruch of the German Army by Charles King, U.S. Army, and Anne Williston Ward, and A West Point Parallel: An American Cadet Story. New York: F. Tennyson Neely, 1896.

Norman Holt: A Story of the Army of the Cumberland. New York: G. W. Dillingham, ca. 1901.

Rancho del Muerto, by Capt. Charles King, and Other Stories from Outing. New York and London: Outing, ca. 1895.

Ray's Daughter: A Story of Manila. Philadelphia: J. B. Lippincott, ca. 1900.

Ray's Recruit. Philadelphia: J. B. Lippincott, 1898.

Ray's Recruit and A Tame Surrender: A Story of the Chicago Strike. Philadelphia: J. B. Lippincott, 1900.

The Rock of Chickamauga. New York: G. W. Dillingham, ca. 1907.

A Soldier's Secret: A Story of the Sioux War of 1890 and An Army Portia: Two Novels. Philadelphia: J. B. Lippincott, 1893.

A Soldier's Trial: An Episode of the Canteen Crusade. New York: Hobart, 1905.

Starlight Ranch and Other Stories of Army Life on the Frontier. Philadelphia: J. B. Lippincott, 1890.

The Story of Fort Frayne. Chicago and New York: F. Tennyson Neely, ca. 1895.

Sunset Pass; or, Running the Gauntlet through Apache Land. New York: John W. Lovell, ca. 1890.

A Tame Surrender: A Story of the Chicago Strike. Philadelphia: J. B. Lippincott, 1896.

Tonio, Son of the Sierras: A Story of the Apache War. New York: G. W. Dillingham, ca. 1906.

To the Front: A Sequel to Cadet Days. New York and London: Harper and Brothers, 1908.

Trials of a Staff-Officer. Philadelphia: L. R. Hamersly, 1891.

A Trooper Galahad. Philadelphia: J. B. Lippincott, 1899.

Trooper Ross and Signal Butte. Philadelphia: J. B. Lippincott, 1896.

The True Ulysses S. Grant. Philadelphia and London: J. B. Lippincott, 1914.

Trumpeter Fred: A Story of the Plains. New York and Chicago: F. Tennyson Neely, 1896.

176

Biblio-
graphy
of
Charles
King's
Books

Trumpeter Fred and Noble Blood. New York: R. F. Fenno, ca. 1901.

Two Soldiers. Philadelphia: J. B. Lippincott, ca. 1890.

Two Soldiers and Dunraven Ranch: Two Novels. Philadelphia: J. B. Lippincott, 1891.

Under Fire. Philadelphia: J. B. Lippincott, 1895.

Waring's Peril. Philadelphia: J. B. Lippincott, 1894.

Warrior Gap: A Story of the Sioux Outbreak of '68. London and New York: F. Tennyson Neely, ca. 1897.

A War-Time Wooing: A Story. New York: Harper and Brothers, 1888.

The Way of the West. Chicago and New York: Rand, McNally, ca. 1902.

A Wounded Name. London and New York: F. Tennyson Neely, ca. 1898.

INDEX